GLOBALONEY 2.0

GLOBALIZATION

Series Editors
Manfred B. Steger
*Royal Melbourne Institute of Technology
and University of Hawai'i–Mānoa*
and
Terrell Carver
University of Bristol

"Globalization" has become the buzzword of our time. But what does it mean? Rather than forcing a complicated social phenomenon into a single analytical framework, this series seeks to present globalization as a multidimensional process constituted by complex, often contradictory interactions of global, regional, and local aspects of social life. Since conventional disciplinary borders and lines of demarcation are losing their old rationales in a globalizing world, authors in this series apply an interdisciplinary framework to the study of globalization. In short, the main purpose and objective of this series is to support subject-specific inquiries into the dynamics and effects of contemporary globalization and its varying impacts across, between, and within societies.

Supported by the Globalization Research Center at the University of Hawai'i, Mānoa

GLOBALONEY 2.0

THE CRASH OF 2008 AND THE FUTURE OF GLOBALIZATION

MICHAEL VESETH

ROWMAN & LITTLEFIELD PUBLISHERS, INC.
Lanham • Boulder • New York • Toronto • Plymouth, UK

Published by Rowman & Littlefield Publishers, Inc.
A wholly owned subsidiary of The Rowman & Littlefield Publishing Group, Inc.
4501 Forbes Boulevard, Suite 200, Lanham, Maryland 20706
http://www.rowmanlittlefield.com

Estover Road, Plymouth PL6 7PY, United Kingdom

British Library Cataloguing in Publication Information Available

Library of Congress Cataloging-in-Publication Data

Veseth, Michael.
  Globaloney 2.0 : the crash of 2008 and the future of globalization / Michael Veseth. — 2nd ed
      p. cm. — (Globalization)
  Includes bibliographical references and index.
  ISBN 978-0-7425-6745-0 (cloth : alk. paper) — ISBN 978-0-7425-6746-7
(pbk. : alk. paper) — ISBN 978-0-7425-6747-4
  1. Globalization. 2. Globalization—Economic aspects. 3. Financial crises. I. Title.
JZ1318.V468 2010
  303.48'2—dc22

                                                                          2009043128

♾️™ The paper used in this publication meets the minimum requirements of American National Standard for Information Sciences—Permanence of Paper for Printed Library Materials, ANSI/NISO Z39.48-1992.

Printed in the United States of America

CONTENTS

ACKNOWLEDGMENTS

I have run up more than the usual number of intellectual debts in the process of writing this book. I'd like to acknowledge my creditors in partial repayment of their generosity without in any way implicating them for the mistakes that remain.

Thanks, first of all, to everyone who helped me with the first edition of this book, whose names I named there. More thanks to everyone to attended my talks and asked tough questions during the Globaloney World Tour stops in Seattle, Tacoma, Olympia, Portland, Berkeley, San Francisco, Santa Monica, San Diego, Los Angeles, Washington, D.C., Bologna, and Prague.

Special thanks go out to my colleagues, students, and former students at the University of Puget Sound who have stimulated my thinking and challenged my logic for many years. Thanks as well to Jim, Matt, Scott, Colleen, Wendy, Kirsten, and my international students at the American Institute on Political and Economic Systems in Prague.

I appreciate the expertise and support of the professionals at Rowman & Littlefield who guided and encouraged me at each stage of this book's development. Special thanks to editorial director Susan McEachern, senior production editor Jehanne Schweitzer, and copyeditor Julia Voelker.

Finally, thanks to Sue Veseth for helping me recognize globaloney in the first place and for putting up with my compulsive interest in finding out where things come from and why.

INTRODUCTION

Economists tell stories—that's what we do. Microeconomists tell stories about specific things like corn prices. Macroeconomists tell stories about larger things like interest rates. I am a global economist, so I tell the biggest stories of all.

Because it is our business to tell stories, we economists particularly appreciate how powerful stories can be. People tell themselves that their views of complicated issues are based upon sound arguments and detailed data analysis, but economists know that we are all really suckers for a good story. It is common knowledge within the profession that, when it comes to persuading an audience, all the charts, graphs, and econometric evidence in the world are worth less than a single well-told anecdote.

Some stories stick close the facts. Others are exaggerated or over-blown—the slang term for these stories is *baloney*. I call exaggerated stories about globalization *globaloney*.

Stories are powerful—and useful, too, when they help us under-stand complex problems and make sound decisions. But stories can be dangerous; they can distort as well as enlighten. This is a book about how dangerous stories helped create the global economic crisis—and why we need to have better stories if we want the next wave of global-ization to avoid the same mistakes. The stories I'm concerned with in this book created three globalization myths, which I think of as three types of globaloney.

Financial Globaloney. The first myth is that globalization is "safe as houses"—a stable, certain economic platform. The British use the phrase "safe as houses" to describe something that is a sure thing, which is ironic given the role that "safe" investments in housing played in the financial crisis. Why did people believe that global financial mar-kets were safe as houses (when they obviously were not)? Because of the stories that were told and the images that were used.

Golden Arches Globaloney. The second myth is that globalization is really Americanization and that it sucks in the diverse cultures and in-stitutions of the world and replaces them with simplified, homogenized American imitations, much as the McDonald's restaurant chain with its distinctive Golden Arches logo has apparently sucked in the world's great cuisines and replaced them with juicy Big Macs and salty golden fries. Why is Golden Arches Globaloney so powerful? Because McDon-ald's itself is so seemingly ubiquitous and its iconic image so strong. It makes a convincing story, even if it isn't completely true.

Grassroots Globaloney. I call the third myth "grassroots globaloney" because it is the story that globalization is a top-down phenomenon that individuals are fundamentally powerless to shape, transform, or resist. Globalization is the only game in town—there is no alterna-tive—and so the people down at the grass roots better get used to it!

THE GLOBALONEY SANDWICH

All three types of globaloney contain a kernel of truth (or else they would be instantly recognized as "baloney"). These arguments contain insufficient evidence to back up their extravagant claims, in my view, but more than enough memorable facts to be crafted into a persuasive story. Taken together as a sort of triple-stack globaloney sandwich, however, they become a particular idea of what globalization is and how it works that has proved to be exceptionally dangerous.

Grassroots Globaloney stories characterize globalization as an irresistible force. Individuals, communities, and nation-states are essentially powerless to shape or resist globalization. So the only thing to do is to embrace it. This story exists in many forms, but perhaps the most famous versions were created by *New York Times* columnist Thomas Friedman in his best-selling books *The Lexus and the Olive Tree* (2000) and *The World is Flat* (2006).

Now add *Golden Arches Globaloney* to the mix. These stories, which focus on the homogenizing and Americanizing power of globalization, undermine the idea of global diversity. Irresistible global forces (*Grassroots Globaloney*) replace diverse cultures and political economy institutions with a simplified, rationalized, commercialized form that shouts "Made in USA" even if it is actually produced in Mexico or China, Latvia or Mauritius. The most powerful statement of this story remains Benjamin Barber's classic *Jihad vs. McWorld* (1996).

Globalization, it seems, creates a world that is like a vast American strip mall. It is simple, cheap, impossible to resist—and completely safe. Safe as houses, as the British say, because it is built on a rock-solid foundation of global financial markets. Well, you can see the problem right away when you connect the dots in this way.

The world economic crisis has revealed globalization's Achilles' heel: the fundamental instability of global financial markets and the unsettled foundation of economic globalization generally. This realization is a necessary first step toward recasting our understanding of globalization so that we can avoid a repeat of the global collapse, but it alone is not enough. We must rethink the rest of globalization's myths—take the globaloney sandwich apart—if we want to move beyond boom and bust to a sustainable global future.

It seems ridiculous to say that feasible, sustainable globalization depends upon the stories we tell about it, but it is true. I've learned this lesson the hard way, through twenty years of research.

FROM *MOUNTAINS OF DEBT* TO *GLOBALONEY 2.0*

I was walking through the market in Florence, looking for the entrance to Medici Chapel, when I was struck by the question: How did the Florentines of the Renaissance pay for all this? That question became a book, *Mountains of Debt* (1990), that probed the economic histories of Renaissance Florence and Victorian Britain to try to understand how rich, sophisticated economic centers end up straining under, well, mountains of debt and how they recover from this condition, if they do. My method was historical but my goal was purely practical—I wanted to understand the mountains of debt we had accumulated in the United States and to have a better idea of how we might best respond to them.

Mountains of Debt was a minor sensation when it was published, but interest declined as the U.S. budget deficit shrank and then briefly turned to surplus. *Mountains of Debt* went out of print. Then George W. Bush was elected president, big deficits returned, and Oxford University Press put *Mountains of Debt* back on its list.

Mountains of Debt taught me that finance really matters. Financial markets are not abstract theoretical creations, they reflect the societies in which they are embedded and shape them, too. As the 1990s unfolded and truly global financial markets emerged, my interests naturally shifted in this direction. My next book, *Selling Globalization: The Myth of the Global Economy* (1998) started out as an application of chaos theory to international finance and ended up as a critical examination of the methods and motives of the neoliberal pro-globalization movement.

Selling Globalization was initially a book about financial bubbles, speculative attacks, and chaos theory. It argued that the fundamental instability of global financial markets makes it impossible for globalization to be as complete, as powerful, and as encompassing as some people seem to think. Globalization is built on a foundation of global finance, but this foundation is inherently unstable. The more global the finance structure becomes, the less stable it is. It cannot possibly support the elaborate global structures that some people hope for and other people fear.

It was a sound argument, but I had a hard time getting people to take it seriously at first because, in the boom years of the late 1990s, it just didn't fit the way that most people had been conditioned to see the grand design of globalization. How could I get people to take the idea of *fragile* globalization seriously when the stories they were told conditioned them to see it as an unstoppable universal force?

I decided to try to undermine the conventional wisdom about globalization's grand design through close analysis of its details. I put together four brief case studies of "global" corporations and then looked closely to see if the details of their businesses were consistent with the most common metaphors and images of economic globalization. In other words, I asked, do the facts fit the stories?

One of the companies I selected—Nike—fit the standard globalization/multinational corporation story very well. But Nike turned out to be the noteworthy exception, not the representative case. The other three firms I studied—Boeing, Microsoft, and the Frank Russell Company,[1] a global investment advisor widely known for its Russell stock market indices—all were very different indeed, and the details of the differences revealed a lot. For most global firms, I concluded, the fact that they are global is a secondary attribute. The most important factors are specific to their particular businesses or industries.

These case studies attracted a lot of interest not because they were so good but mainly because they were so rare—hardly anyone was looking to see if the facts of globalization fit the popular stories and images. The stories that were told about globalization were seldom questioned, much less tested, because the rhetoric of globalization is so convincing, the simple images used to reinforce the rhetoric are so compelling, and the interests of the "sellers" so strong. *Selling Globalization* argued that some of the pro-globalization rhetoric was used to sell the idea of globalization in order to advance a particular set of economic, political, and intellectual interests.

My next project was an edited volume, *The New York Times Twentieth Century in Review: The Rise of the Global Economy*. I was given a century's worth of everything in *The New York Times* and asked to tell the story of globalization. The story I told was based on Karl Polanyi's theory of the double movement. Markets are active and dynamic—they initiate disruptive change (the first movement). Society responds to these changes (the second movement—a backlash), trying to protect itself from the forces of creative destruction. I told the story of "the rise of the global economy" (the title I was given) as a push-me pull-you tale of globalization and its discontents. It wasn't so much the rise of the global economy, I explained, but its rise early in the twentieth century, followed by collapse in the 1930s. Then rise again in the postwar years followed by . . . another collapse? The story of the 1999 antiglobalization riots at the WTO meetings in Seattle put that last question mark in boldface.

The first edition of *Globaloney* came next. My goal this time, I wrote in the Introduction,

> is not to persuade you that global financial markets are an unstable foundation for global capitalism—hopefully my previous book and the continuing series of international financial crises have already done that. Now I want to persuade readers that they might be misunderstanding the very nature of globalization because they have accepted a distorted "big picture" that is fundamentally different from the facts. And I want them to consider that this might be a very serious problem.[2]

I was right about the bogus stories that were told about globalization and about how dangerous they can be. But I was clearly wrong about financial instability. I thought that twenty years of financial crises would teach the world that globalization's financial foundation is dangerously cracked. Boy, was I wrong about that!

Which is why I've written this book, *Globaloney 2.0*, a major revision of the 2005 volume, which both updates it to include analysis of the impact of the economic crisis on globalization and, more important, brings the critical issues of unstable global finance back in. Because it's pretty clear that we didn't learn as much from the history of financial crises as I thought. We can't afford to make the same mistakes again.

HOW *GLOBALONEY 2.0* IS ORGANIZED

The book begins with a discussion of the difference between globalization, a complex and multidimensional process, and *globaloney*, its simplified, highly processed, popularized substitute. I argue that a lot of what we mistake for facts about globalization is really the result of the clever application of standard rhetorical forms. Adam Smith, the father of economics, was also a great storyteller, a master of rhetoric (he even lectured on it). Smith wasn't the father of globaloney, but he was perhaps its most successful early practitioner. In a real sense, I think Adam Smith taught today's globalonists their trade. So, as I say in chapter 1, you can blame it all on Adam Smith. Readers of the first edition will recognize many of the key points presented here.

The discussion of "Financial Globaloney: Safe as Houses" and "The Crash of 2008 and the Global Market Myth" in chapters 2 and 3 is new material, especially prepared for the second edition. Chapter 2 examines the financial underpinnings of globalization and explains both why it is an unstable foundation upon which to build a complex world economic system and why so many smart people thought it would work. Chapter 3 puts the current economic meltdown in the context of the financial crises of the recent past to see what role Financial Globaloney played in the Crash of 2008 and its aftermath.

Chapter 4 examines Golden Arches Globaloney, drawing heavily upon ideas I developed in the first edition of this book. Globalization is so closely associated with American hamburgers that the entire complex process of economic and social change is often characterized simply as McDonaldization, a process that destroys local cultures and traditions, replacing them with the fat-filled empty calories of American consumer capitalism. Thomas Friedman, in his book about globalization, *The Lexus and the Olive Tree*, cannot seem to resist having "Golden Arches" moments that define globalization wherever he goes.

Although it is tempting to see the spread of fast food as the essence of globalization, it is also wrong to do so. Even the McDonald's story is more complicated than is commonly appreciated; it is *both* a story of global business *and* the story of the vitality of local culture, as we will learn as we search for the truth about the McAloo Tikki Burger.

I use chapter 5, "The Only Game in Town," as a link between Golden Arches Globaloney, the idea that globalization really is homogenized American cheese, and Grassroots Globaloney, the "resistance is futile" argument discussed earlier. Drawing upon material developed for the first edition, I use global sports as a metaphor for globalization generally. Sports are big business, of course, but they also reflect deep cultural norms and values, so they are a good test-bed for globalization theories. The point I make here is that there is no "only game in town," as the globaloney storytellers would have us believe. If resistance is futile in the face of global markets, then how can we explain the inconvenient truth that America remains just about the last culture to embrace the most commercialized (and therefore, I suppose, the most Americanized) global sport: soccer?

What does globalization look like to the people who don't live in McWorld, who are too poor to buy a Big Mac, who live in the countries that cannot even attract a McDonald's in the first place? How does it change their lives down at the grassroots level? Does it give them hope and opportunity, or does it crush them and their cultural heritage?

The conventional wisdom, which I call Grassroots Globaloney, is that globalization is like the Borg Collective in the *Star Trek: The Next Generation* series and movies: Resistance is futile; you will be assimilated (and homogenized and dehumanized). Because I am suspicious of simple, deterministic conclusions, I suspect that resistance is possible and that even the poorest people in the world have at least some ability to shape globalization to suit their needs. I explore these ideas in chapters 6 and 7 through case studies of global trade in used clothing (the rag trade) and the Slow Food movement, a global network that uses the methods of McWorld to offer an alternative to it.

The rag trade shows us how people, even very poor and seemingly powerless groups, can shape globalization to suit their needs. The Slow Food movement shows us how the tools and techniques of globalization may be used to oppose globalization or correct some of its negative consequences.

Taken together, these case studies make an argument for a more complex idea of globalization and suggest the types of local, regional, national, international, and global patterns we need to visualize if we are going to try to understand globalization in a meaningful way.

Globaloney continues with an exercise in creative destruction, where I try to uncover some deeper truths about globaloney and globalization. Chapter 8, "Globalization and the French Exception," presents my own theory of why the French hate globalization. Like all great global narratives, my theory contains a lot of globaloney (but it is high-quality globaloney, I assure you). I then subject my own theory to critical analysis, an exercise that raises doubts about the premise—the notion that the French really do hate globalization—as much as the theory and sets the stage for my attempt to draw a conclusion about the future of globalization and the importance of stories.

The book concludes with an examination of "The Future of Globalization (and Globaloney)." Globalization will return once the current crisis has passed—but in what form? Feasible and sustainable globalization is possible, I argue, but not if we keep believing the same stories and accepting the same globaloney. Using maps drawn by Robert Mundell and Dani Rodrik, I try to track down the useful future of globalization—and consider the stories that we need to learn to tell if we are to find it.

If we want a better global future, we need to tell better stories. Because stories matter—that's why economists tell them. And that's not *globaloney!*

CHAPTER 1

GLOBALIZATION? OR GLOBALONEY?

We are suffering just now from a bad attack of economic pessimism." So wrote the most famous economist in the world. "It is common to hear people say that the epoch of enormous economic progress . . . is over, that the rapid improvement in the standard of life is now going to slow down . . . that a decline in prosperity is more likely than an improvement in the decade which lies ahead of us."[1]

He was right, of course. The mood was indeed very dark. Understandably dark, given "the prevailing world depression, the enormous anomaly of unemployment in a world full of wants, the disastrous mistakes we have made. . . ."[2]

Disastrous mistakes. No doubt about that today. But the famous economist quoted here is not Paul Krugman or Ben Bernanke writing in 2009, as you might guess; it is John Maynard Keynes in his 1930 essay "Economic Possibilities for our Grandchildren." Keynes wrote in the darkest days of the financial crisis of the depression, trying to imagine what the world would look like when those disastrous mistakes were corrected.

We are the grandchildren whose economic fate Keynes tried to foresee. It is ironic that the words he wrote in 1930 should ring true once again eighty years later. Disastrous mistakes indeed.

This book is about the future of globalization and I don't want to keep you in suspense about the conclusion. The situation today looks a lot like it did when Keynes wrote his famous essay. The future of globalization in the short run is that there will be a lot less of it. Global flows of money, goods, and people all have collapsed. Even illegal immigration has declined as the opportunity gap that draws workers from poorer countries to richer ones has narrowed.

Globalization is down, but not out. Writing in 1930, Keynes could see that economic prosperity and global markets would revive, but in what form? Same again? Oh no, not that. Or transformed in ways that make them better able to serve the needs of the world's peoples and less likely to repeat the disastrous mistakes of the past? In a passage I will return to at the end of this book, Keynes distinguished between the immediate "economic problem" of recovery and the "permanent problem" of crafting human arrangements so that values higher than simple market values motivate our actions and the accepted purpose of economic activity cannot be summed up by the four-letter word "more."

We face the same challenge today. The globalization that returns as the world economy solves the "economic problem" will certainly be different from the global market of a few years past. It has to be different. The players have changed. Some have disappeared (Lehman Brothers, Washington Mutual) or been swallowed up (Merrill Lynch). The game has changed, too. The investment banking game has basically ceased to exist while the game that auto makers play is almost unrecognizable as demand shrinks, consumer preferences change, and consolidation proceeds.

The new globalization will be different from globalizations past, but what will it look like? My answer is: it depends. It depends upon how today's turbulent forces play out. And it depends upon how we react to them. In particular, it depends upon whether we make an effort to mold and shape globalization into a different form, one that is both feasible and sustainable.

Remaking the world—reshaping globalization—is a bold undertaking, but not an unprecedented one. It was a task that John Maynard Keynes and his international colleagues took up in 1944 when they met at the Mount Washington Hotel in Bretton Woods, New Hampshire, and drafted the outline of the postwar global economy. It is a challenge worth taking up again, if not for ourselves then for our grandchildren, who must live in the world that our actions and inactions bequeath them.

POWERFUL IDEAS

"The ideas of economists and political philosophers," Keynes wrote, "both when they are right and when they are wrong, are more powerful than is commonly understood. Indeed," he said, "the world is ruled by little else."[3] Keynes's point, in the conventional interpretation, is that while *interests* often dictate in the short term, it is *ideas* that rule in the long run. Just as important, but often overlooked, however, is the thought provoked by the phrase "both when they are right and when they are wrong" because it suggests that ideas do not need to be wise or correct to be influential. Sometimes it is just the opposite. Nothing can stop a bad idea whose time has come.

This book is about the ideas we use to understand globalization and the stories we tell to make those ideas persuasive. Globalization is so huge and complex that we cannot understand it by simply observing it—there is literally too much information. So we are forced to simplify and synthesize—to select bits of information about the world and put them into whatever patterns our idea of globalization sets before us. The result is always wrong in the details, since details are left out, and it can be either right or wrong in terms of the big picture it creates. When the picture is horribly wrong, by accident or design relentlessly distorting, I give it a special name: *globaloney.*

Globaloney matters. Distorted images of globalization and deceptively smooth stories about it can be both powerful and dangerous. They can be powerful because they can shape our actions and reactions. They can be dangerous when they are distorted blueprints that lead us to construct worlds that are unstable, unfair, and unsustainable. They can even guide us to make disastrous mistakes.

And so I wrote this book, *Globaloney 2.0.* I think that today's economic crisis and the collapse of globalization that we see around us are not just about misguided interests—*greed*—but also about the misleading stories that justified their actions and the public's response—*globaloney*. If the next globalization (and there will be one) is going to be better than the one we've just seen fall apart, it will need to be built upon a clearer vision of what globalization is and what must change to make it feasible and sustainable.

THE FATHER OF GLOBALONEY

It's important to learn the difference between globalization and globaloney and to find ways to spin tales that are a more realistic blueprint for the future. This means we need to learn more about what globaloney is, how it is produced, and why it is so darn effective. We need to steal globaloney's secret recipe and find out who is to blame for cooking it up in the first place. The blame game is the easy part.

When the time comes to assign guilt for the fact that almost everyone misunderstands globalization, I think the jury will not have to deliberate very long. If most people confuse globalization with globaloney, if they perceive the complex patterns of global markets as simple images of hamburger stands and soda pop cans, if they are so mesmerized by globalization rhetoric that they fail to see what's right before their eyes—well, you don't need to be Sherlock Holmes to deduce the reason why.

You can blame it all on Adam Smith.

Now, if this were one of those popular antiglobalization books, like *One World, Ready or Not: The Manic Logic of Global Capitalism*[4] by *Rolling Stone* writer William Greider, I might be blaming Adam Smith for going too far in his praise of free markets, and the next couple paragraphs would read something like this:

> Globalization is a vast turbo-powered machine that circles the globe destroying all that it touches. Who is in control of this unstoppable manic machine? No one. No one can control it. The best we can do is to offer up human sacrifices to try to satisfy the demands of the nameless, faceless market gods.
>
> Who created this twenty-first-century Frankenstein? You can blame it all on Adam Smith. Adam Smith created the myth of the Invisible Hand, which falsely justifies the ruthless pursuit of individual greed and personal power on the grounds that it is somehow in the

public interest for market forces to make children work in sweatshops. There is no Invisible Hand, just the fact of greed, exploitation, and the ultimate destruction of civilization as we know it.[5]

On the other hand, if this were one of those popular pro-globalization books, like *The Borderless World: Power and Strategy in the Interlinked Economy*, by business consultant Kenichi Ohmae,[6] I might be damning Adam Smith for not going far enough in his praise of market forces, and the next paragraphs would read something like this:

> Globalization is the new world of unlimited opportunity and unimaginable prosperity. Globalization essentially frees humankind from all of the barriers that have for centuries kept people from achieving their true potential. We are all connected by the vast global web where time and space are irrelevant and authoritarian rule is impossible.
>
> Why has it taken us so long to realize the unlimited potential that global markets offer? Adam Smith is to blame because he failed to appreciate the full potential of the Invisible Hand of Self-Interest. He wrote how the Butcher and the Baker, seeking no end other than their own profit, unintentionally benefit society as well, as if guided by the famous transparent appendage. Smith's examples are quaint and charming, and his conclusion is no doubt correct, but he missed the point. What the Invisible Hand really does is to push inevitably for one vast stateless, border-free world where friction-free capitalism can weave a seamless web of peace and prosperity.

But this chapter isn't going down either of these roads. Adam Smith is to blame because he taught both the antiglobalizers and the pro-globalizers how to sell bogus arguments and to make extravagant claims on the basis of the flimsiest evidence (or even in spite of evidence). Forgive me, Adam Smith. I am a trained economist, and you are the father of my discipline. But you taught the world how to manufacture globaloney.

PINS. IT'S ALL ABOUT PINS.

Adam Smith is the godfather of globaloney, although hardly anyone thinks of him that way, despite the work of Friedrich List and many others. He is more famous as the father of modern economics. His book

The Wealth of Nations, published in 1776, is one of the most influential books of all time.

Adam Smith wrote about a lot of things in *The Wealth of Nations*, but globalization wasn't one of them. The world of 1776 was still trying to figure out how *international* relations worked; they weren't ready for the idea of *global* affairs. Adam Smith's contribution wasn't so much that he created globaloney itself as that he popularized a way of thinking and writing that lends itself to globaloney. I guess you'd say he perfected the rhetorical technology that powers the modern globaloney factory. Here's how it happened.

For the most part, *The Wealth of Nations* was a work of synthesis, not something Adam Smith whipped up from scratch. Smith drew together ideas that had been in the air for decades and pieced them into a coherent system of economic thought. This systematic organization of economic ideas was a great achievement, and it made him famous.

Surprisingly, *The Wealth of Nations* contained only one truly original concept: the division of labor, the idea that you can break down a big task into specialized functions that can be more efficiently performed. Henry Ford's assembly-line system is a famous example of the division of labor at work. The division of labor is an important idea, and we should remember Adam Smith because of it, but of course it is not what we actually remember him for. For most people, Adam Smith stands for "laissez-faire"—free markets and free trade. But the division of labor is where it all begins and where globaloney technology was first put to use.

I suppose that Rule #1 in the globaloney guide is Be Bold! Don't dillydally. Make your claim loud and clear. Page one, chapter one, book one of *The Wealth of Nations* therefore starts out with a bang.

> The greatest improvement in the productive powers of labour, and the greatest part of the skill, dexterity, and judgement with which it is any where directed, or applied, seem to have been the effects of the division of labour.[7]

Adam Smith begins *The Wealth of Nations* with an incredibly broad generalization about the division of labor. Labor productivity owes more to the division of labor than to anything else, where "anything else" includes most of the factors we usually associate with increasing productivity—innovation, learning-by-doing, technology, capital investment, and so forth. You cannot fault Smith for understating his main point! And remember that this is the very first sentence in the book.

How can Smith possibly convince the reader that the division of labor, which hasn't even been defined yet, is the main factor in the production of prosperity? The claim is so broad and the notion so abstract that it would probably be impossible to support it using figures and statistics. But Smith isn't bothered by this, because he isn't trying to *prove* that the division of labor is the key to productivity growth, he only needs to *persuade* the reader that it is—and this is a much easier task. So instead of statistical analysis he tells us a story. Economists tell stories. That's what we do.

> To take an example, therefore, from a very trifling manufacture; but one in which the division of labour has been very often taken notice of, the trade of the pin-maker; a workman not educated to this business (which the division of labour has rendered a distinct trade), nor acquainted with the use of the machinery employed in it (to the invention of which the same division of labour has probably given occasion), could scarce, perhaps, with his utmost industry make one pin in a day, and certainly could not make twenty. But in the way in which this business is now carried on, not only the whole work is a peculiar trade, but it is divided into a number of branches, of which the greater part are likewise trades.[8]

This is the beginning of the famous "pin factory" story, which is, along with the "Invisible Hand," the most memorable part of *The Wealth of Nations*. The pin example is a clever choice. Pins must have been among the most common manufactured items in Smith's day. If he were writing today, Smith might pick pencils (as Milton Friedman did for his 1980 television series, *Free to Choose*), but pins worked fine in 1776. Common, ordinary, cheap. Smith is right, however; I cannot imagine making pins (or pencils) myself. If pins are so hard to make, why are they so cheap? Glad you asked, Smith says. The answer is the division of labor.

> One man draws out the wire, another straights it, a third cuts it, a fourth points it, a fifth grinds it at the top for receiving the head; to

make the head requires two or three distinct operations; to put it on, is a peculiar business, to whiten the pins is another; it is even a trade by itself to put them into the paper; and the important business of making a pin is, in this manner divided into about eighteen distinct operations, which, in some manufactories, are all performed by distinct hands, though in others the same man will sometimes perform two or three of them.[9]

The use of detail in this paragraph is very effective, don't you think? In my mind's eye I can see each of the steps he enumerates, and I am instantly convinced that the division of labor can be extended to at least eighteen steps or stages of production. How does Smith know so much about ordinary pins? Glad you asked, Smith replies. I once visited a pin factory myself.

I have seen a small manufactory of this kind where ten men only were employed and where some of them consequently performed two or three distinct operations. But though they were very poor, and therefore but indifferently accommodated with the necessary machinery, they could, when they exerted themselves, make among them about twelve pounds of pins in a day.[10]

Seeing is believing, it is said. The fact that Smith reports on a personal observation is very persuasive, more persuasive than if he reported industrial statistics of some sort. It is *so* persuasive, in fact, that it is the only actual example that he provides. It is all he needs, however, because it is such a great example. The global relevance of the division of labor, in terms of Smith's argument, rests upon ten men and a pail full of pins. How many pins is that, anyway? Glad you asked, says he. I counted them.

There are in a pound upwards of four thousand pins of middling size. Those ten persons, therefore, could make among them upwards of forty-eight thousand pins in a day. Each person, therefore, making a tenth part of forty-eight thousand pins, might be considered as making four thousand eight hundred pins in a day. But if they had all wrought separately and independently, and without any of them having been educated to this peculiar business, they certainly could not each of them have made twenty, perhaps not one pin in a day; that is, certainly, not the two hundred and fortieth, perhaps not the four thousand eight hundredth part of what they are at present capable of performing, in consequence of a proper division and combination of their different operations.[11]

Since Adam Smith cannot possibly *prove* his broad assertion that the division of labor is responsible for all improvements in labor productivity, he doesn't even try. Instead he tells the story of his own observations with just enough detail to establish his own credibility. If Smith is credible, that makes Smith's argument credible. By choosing an example that you can readily imagine, he makes his story almost as trustworthy as if you had actually been to the pin factory. The picture is vivid, so the example is persuasive.

It is a good thing that the story is so appealing, because the conclusion is astounding, and all the more astounding for being true. Working alone, ten men might make between 10 and 200 pins in a day altogether. But working together (and taking advantage of the division of labor), they produce 48,000 pins. The division of labor is responsible for a 240-fold increase in the productivity of labor. No wonder pins can be so cheap despite being so difficult for a person to make. The division of labor is indeed a miracle—in regard to pins, in any case, and ignoring any other forces that might be at work.

If you found the pin factory example convincing, then you have swallowed Smith's bait and he will now reel you in, because he means to draw a universal conclusion from this one particular example. Does the pin story apply just to pins? Glad you asked.

> In every other art and manufacture, the effects of the division of labour are similar to what they are in this very trifling one; though in many of them, the labour can neither be so much subdivided, nor reduced to so great a simplicity of operation. The division of labour, however, so far as it can be introduced, occasions, in every art, a proportionable increase in the productive powers of labour.[12]

This is a powerful paragraph because it smoothly extends the argument from pins to everything else. The division of labor has the same sort of effect as you saw at the pin factory in *every* other situation. No support of this claim is offered; it is just simple logic. Smith is saying, more or less, that what is true about pins cannot be false about the great majority of human productions. Pins are a "trifling" example; if the division of labor so powerfully increases the productivity of simple pins, it must be even more powerful when applied to matters of substance.

In short, Smith leads us quickly from a single memorable and convincing example to a general conclusion. The division of labor makes (or can make) all things as cheap and common and abundant as pins. The division of labor is the key to unlocking vast quantities of goods and services generally, just as it enables the production of uncountable numbers of pins. Say, who profits from this mass production? Glad you asked.

> It is this great multiplication of the productions of all the different arts, in consequence of the division of labour, which occasions, in a well-governed society, that universal opulence which extends itself to the lowest ranks of the people.[13]

Pins are so cheap that even the poor can afford to buy some and taste a bit of "opulence." And what is true of pins is generally true. So the division of labor benefits everyone in society, bottom to top.

Now if the division of labor is so beneficial, it should be maximized, expanded, exploited. What determines how much division of labor can take place? Glad you asked. It's the market. The division of labor is limited by the extent of the market.

> As it is the power of exchanging that gives occasion to the division of labour, so the extent of this division must always be limited by the extent of that power, or, in other words, by the extent of the market.[14]

Broader markets, finer division of labor, greater opulence; simple as that. Regulating markets, restricting their growth, or restraining international trade necessarily limits market extent, limiting the division of labor, hurting everyone, even the poor. If you wanted to maximize labor productivity, it is obvious that you would favor global markets—free international trade connecting free national markets—and the laissez-faire policies that are necessary to avoid limiting them.

So there you have it. Globalization (global markets and laissez-faire policies) increases opulence, providing benefits that reach even to the lowest ranks of society. Proof? Well, the whole argument is really built on just one single fact: ten men working *together* can make a lot more pins than if they work *by themselves*. It is really not much of an argument, evaluated objectively, but it is great rhetoric. Once you have that pin factory centered in your mind's eye, the conclusion of global laissez-faire is just a few steps away.

THE NEWTONIAN SYSTEM

The tight little chain of principle, example, assertion, and logical conclusion that starts on the first page of *The Wealth of Nations* is one of Adam Smith's best rhetorical achievements. It sure was effective at converting readers to Smith's point of view. And it didn't happen by accident. Smith knew economics, but it might be true that he knew rhetoric even better.

Adam Smith studied rhetoric in addition to jurisprudence and moral philosophy, and he even gave lectures on this topic in both Glasgow and Edinburgh. Although he never wrote a book on rhetoric, we do have good notes taken at his lectures, which reveal quite a lot about Smith's thinking in this field.[15] He was part of a movement called the New Rhetoric, which sought to rationalize argument. The Old Rhetoric was flowery and indirect; it relied upon allegory and metaphor more than cold facts and logic. The New Rhetoric was intended to be plain, rational, and almost scientific by comparison.

Three elements of the New Rhetoric, as explicated in Smith's lectures, interest us here. Smith argued for plain language, for the effective use of historical example, and for tight organization of an argument. Plain language, he said, makes arguments clear and persuasive. He cited Jonathan Swift in this regard. The use of historical examples, Smith argued, gives weight to an argument and provides it with a solid foundation. According to the notes, "It sets before us the more interesting and important events of human life, points out the causes by which these events were brought about and by this means points out to us by what matter and method we may produce similar good effects or avoid similar bad ones."[16] He cited Thucydides as a master of this method.

Finally, Smith championed a systematic approach to argumentation. The Old Rhetoric, which he associated with Aristotle, among others, was a leisurely pursuit. It examined all the various possible lines of reasoning one by one, drawing insights and making comments here and there as appropriate, until all possibilities had been exhausted. Smith contrasts this with what he called the Newtonian system, which is to identify a principle right at the start of an argument (say, on page one) and then to construct a chain of observations that are all connected by that principle. Smith did not invent the Newtonian system—his biographer Ian Simpson Ross indicates that it went back at least as far as Plato—but he vigorously championed its use.

Adam Smith had strong views about effective rhetoric, but he didn't always practice what he preached. He didn't always follow all of the principles of the New Rhetoric in *The Wealth of Nations*, for example, and even his lectures on rhetoric didn't strictly follow his rules of rhetoric, according to Vivienne Brown.[17] In particular, Smith could not resist violating the first rule, stick to straight talk. His writing is often complicated and indirect, and it can try the patience of modern readers (one reason why Smith is more read about than read today, I suppose). Smith didn't bend the rule about history, however. The whole of Book III of *The Wealth of Nations*, for example, is a survey of the "Progress of Opulence" from the ancient through the modern worlds. More generally, however, Adam Smith used examples and details very effectively, both to give weight to arguments and to capture the imaginations of his readers.

Where Smith really excelled, however, is in his use of the "Newtonian" form of argument, and this is why he is to blame for so much of the globaloney that is written. The idea of the Newtonian argument is to take a principle and use it to connect several observations in ways that entice and convince the reader. Smith took the principle of the division of labor and, in just a few paragraphs, made it a powerful image. Once this image was created, he encouraged the reader to see it everywhere in forms big and small and to see its influence at all levels. Smith exploited fully the psychological impact of the Newtonian system. "It gives us a pleasure to see the phenomena which we reckoned the most unaccountable all deduced from some principle (commonly a wellknown)," according to notes from one of Smith's rhetoric lectures, "and all united in one chain."[18] Readers of *The Wealth of Nations* are thus not only willing to accept universal conclusions based upon sketchy arguments and minimal evidence, they are in fact pleased to do so. Smith delights his readers by solving easily and at once these otherwise puzzling and troublesome problems of the real world.

So powerful is the Newtonian technique in *The Wealth of Nations* that Adam Smith can even disclose the limitations of his argument without undermining its effectiveness. He writes, for example, that the division of labor cannot be as complete in some products as it is for pins, but that really doesn't undermine his point that it has *some* effect in all products. He notes that the case of the pins is really a trifling matter (it is—man does not live by pins alone), but that doesn't really undermine the gee-whiz impact of the example (ten men, 48,000 pins). Opulence extends even to the lower classes, he writes, when a society is well governed, but poorly governed societies were probably the norm in 1776 and are in much of the world today. But, again, the main point or the image of that main point is so clear and strong and compelling that its impact is undiminished, indeed it is unaffected, by these notes and conditions.

In other words, Smith can have it both ways. He can paint a simple universal picture based upon the principle of the division of labor and at the same time be able to claim a more complex, nuanced argument. Nice work, Adam Smith.

THAT'S GLOBALONEY!

I am not the first person to accuse Adam Smith of globaloney. The nineteenth-century German political economist Friedrich List did it before me in *The National System of Political Economy*, first published in 1841, his mercantilist response to Smith's *Wealth of Nations*.[19] The story of List's attack on Smith's globaloney is instructive—it shows us that globaloney cuts both ways.

List is little known in the United States today, but his influence on European and Japanese economic policy has been profound. I think of List as a sort of German twin brother of the Frenchman Alexis de Tocqueville because both based major works on what they observed in the United States. De Tocqueville famously conned the French government into sending him to the United States in 1831 for the purpose of studying American prisons. He studied American society instead and wrote *Democracy in America*, still perhaps the best statement of American domestic political culture.

Friedrich List came to the United States just a few years before de Tocqueville, but under somewhat different circumstances. List was a professor and liberal member of the Representative Assembly of Würtemberg who was driven by the idea of free trade. He agitated and schemed and finally, in 1825, mounted a major legislative action to create a Commercial Union (a sort of European Union) among the German states of the time.[20] His forceful advocacy of free trade so offended the entrenched protectionist interests that he was expelled from the assembly, convicted of agitation, and sentenced to ten months' hard labor in prison. List escaped this punishment by fleeing German territory, going first to Paris and then, armed with letters of introduction supplied by a sympathetic Lafayette, to the United States, where he found work as a journalist.

Like de Tocqueville, List was deeply influenced by the relative peace and prosperity that he found in the United States. Unlike de Tocqueville, who was most impressed by the quality of America's "civil society," List was intrigued by the power of the federal government and the effectiveness of American economic policies that dated from Alexander Hamilton's era. A strong and forceful state, List decided, was needed to promote industry and build a nation. Free trade, however beneficial in theory, he argued, meant dominance by Great Britain in practice, since Britain already had such a head start and so many advantages. No one could catch up with Britain if exposed to unprotected competition.

List went public with his views in a series of newspaper articles on U.S. tariff negotiations with Great Britain, which were collected and published in 1827 as *Outlines of a New System of Political Economy*. Protectionist interests were drawn to List's elegant prose and effective argumentation. They saw to it that his articles were widely circulated. So well known did List and his views become that he was sent on a trade mission in 1830 by President Andrew Jackson, who appointed him as U.S. consul to Hamburg. List was still considered an outlaw in German eyes, however, and Hamburg refused to accept him.[21] Although List himself was unacceptable, his new American ideas were eventually embraced; Germany under Bismarck adopted many of the trade policies List's American newspaper articles advocated.

The foundation of List's case is a critique of Adam Smith. List contrasted his own theory of *political* economy with Smith's doctrine, which he called the theory of *cosmopolitical* economy. The difference between political economy and cosmopolitical economy, according to List, is the fact that the nation-state is a fundamental element of the economic system. Smith, he argued, assumes that there are no nation-states or that they are in a state of "perpetual peace." With states and nations assumed away, List said, one can approach economic problems from the pure perspective of the individual. *Sans* states and the power and conflict associated with them, the principle of laissez-faire and the policy of free trade are indeed valid in theory.

"A true principle, therefore, underlies the system of the popular school," List wrote, referring to the economic liberal school of thought, "but a principle which must be recognized and applied by science if its design to enlighten practice is to be fulfilled, an idea which practice cannot ignore without getting astray; only the school has omitted to take into consideration the nature of nationalities and their special interests and conditions, and to bring these into accord with the idea of universal union and an everlasting peace."[22] In assuming away nations and the state, and thus essentially assuming a borderless world of individuals, List said, Smith put the cart before the horse. Nations and nationality are facts of life and we cannot pretend that they do not exist, because they do.

"The popular school has assumed as being actually in existence a state of things which has yet to come into existence," List continued. "It assumes the existence of a universal union and a state of perpetual peace, and deduces therefrom the great benefits of free trade. In this manner it confounds effects with causes."[23] List firmly believed that political union was a necessary precondition for economic union or free trade and, given his personal history in Germany, it is easy to see why. Nations at war or facing the possibility of conflict put security ahead of potential economic benefits and reject free trade and economic union.

What are the consequences of free trade in a world of nations, national interests, and state power? Not perpetual peace, List argued, but rather domination.

> That, however, under the existing conditions of the world, the result of general free trade would not be a universal republic, but, on the contrary, a universal subjection of the less advanced nations to the supremacy of the predominant manufacturing, commercial, and naval power, is a conclusion for which the reasons are very strong and, according to our views, irrefragable.[24]

What should the state do? Free trade and laissez-faire invite disaster. The best course, both for the nation and for the society of nations, List argued, is American-style protectionism.

> The system of protection, inasmuch as it forms the only means of placing those nations which are far behind in civilisation on equal terms with the one predominating nation . . . appears to be the most efficient means of furthering the final union of nations, and hence also of promoting true freedom of trade. And national economy appears from this point of view to be that science which, correctly appreciating the existing interests and the individual circumstances of nations, teaches how every separate nation can be raised to that stage of industrial development in which union with other nations equally well developed, and consequently freedom of trade, can become possible and useful to it.[25]

List was right that nations and politics matter, of course, and he made the most of his opportunity to undermine Adam Smith's vision of a borderless world. He was also correct that Smith's rhetoric in this case did not so much assume away an important problem as simply ignore it. In other words, I think List accused Smith of globaloney and made it stick. But then List managed to sneak in some globaloney of his own.

It is not true, as List says above, that a system of protection really does or necessarily can place nations on an *equal* footing, except in the narrow sense that import prices are driven up to equal or exceed those charged by domestic businesses. The underlying differences between the countries may remain vast, creating a chasm that is in fact impossible to span, but List ignores these differences. Having just pointed out that Smith neglects the existence of nations, List is confident that the reader will not notice that he has neglected culture, geography, and history. No matter, List said, because there is no *real* difference. Even taking individual circumstance into account, he said, "science" teaches us that every separate nation can be raised by protection to a level approximately equal to the highest, and therefore trade on equal footing with them.

List's greatest globaloney achievement only becomes apparent when we step back and consider where he has taken us. Globalization—in the form of peaceful free trade among equal nations—is impossible without protectionism, which is its opposite. The way to tear down walls, therefore, is to build them higher. The way to promote equality is to reinforce difference. The way to achieve peace is to make war. It is an argument right out of *1984*. Or, more precisely, out of 1943.

List's critique of Adam Smith, you see, reminds me of Clare Boothe Luce's sarcastic criticism of U.S. Vice President Henry Wallace's 1943 plan for postwar freedom of the skies, which is the first known use of the term globaloney.[26] Wallace thought that freedom of the skies would lead to peace and prosperity. Having freedom of the air, Luce might have said, is all very well in Mr. Wallace's *cosmopolitical* theory, but we live in a world of *political* reality, where open borders put all our security at risk. The America of Friedrich List was afraid that Great Britain would dominate them with its technical superiority. The America of Clare Boothe Luce, which had achieved technological superiority, feared dominance by low-wage competition abroad. Such double-edged fears are common elements of the globaloney syndrome.[27]

MANUFACTURING GLOBALONEY

One of the most powerful Old Rhetoric images of contemporary globalization was created by William Greider in his best-selling book *One World, Ready or Not: The Manic Logic of Global Capitalism*.[28] On page one of chapter 1 he describes globalization as a "wondrous new machine, strong and supple, a machine that reaps as it destroys." He goes on:

> It is huge and mobile, something like the machines of modern agriculture, but vastly more complicated and powerful. Think of this awesome machine running over open terrain and ignoring familiar boundaries. It plows across fields and fencerows with a fierce momentum that is exhilarating to behold and also frightening. As it goes, the machine throws off enormous mows of wealth and bounty while it leaves behind great furrows of wreckage.[29]

This sure is a powerful image, easy to visualize and full of emotion. It is so powerful that the reader initially fails to consider that there is no particular reason to think of globalization as a machine or its domain as a farm field. You could just as easily use an organic metaphor (globalization is a cancer) or a geologic metaphor (globalization is an earthquake) or a meteorological one (it's a hurricane).

Choose the metaphor you like and it determines a particular way of understanding globalization.

If your metaphor is strong enough, you can even warn the reader that the image distorts without fear of undermining your argument. Caveats give such arguments the appearance of objectivity and thus actually reinforce the point. Thus Greider, for example, points out that

> The metaphor is imperfect, but it offers a simplified way to visualize what is dauntingly complex and abstract and impossibly diffuse—the drama of a free-running economic system that is reordering the world.[30]

People who talk or write about globalization use both Old Rhetoric (metaphors) and Adam Smith's New Rhetoric, where the key is to establish an organizing principle and then to push it as far as it will go. I think that Smith's "Newtonian" method of connecting a chain of observations is especially effective in making arguments about globalization. Globalization is such a large, ambiguous idea that it necessarily contains lots of examples of just about everything, so it is no challenge to link it up to whatever principle you like.

To choose a trifling example, suppose that I say that globalization is based upon the principle of the network, especially computer networks that share information. This is not a big stretch, it seems to me, since globalization is all about markets and markets are networks that link together buyers and sellers and other interested parties. Everyone knows that market networks are pretty dependent on computers these days, and there are computers almost everywhere, many of them networked. So if I provide one or two memorable examples, like Adam Smith did with his pin factory, then pretty soon you will be *looking for* computer networks wherever you go. And, because you are looking for them, you will see them. And every one of them will reinforce the idea that globalization is based on the principle of the network.

Once the globalization network principle is established, there are two ways we can go. One approach would be to examine how networks actually work and what real principles networks embody to see if there are insights to be gained from this analysis. This might be a fruitful path to take, but it would involve research, not persuasion.[31] It is the road not taken. Let's see where rhetoric alone can take us.

Once I've got you thinking about globalization in terms of networks, then I think I can manipulate the concept of the network to encourage you to interpret globalization in some particular way. Networks, like markets, can be very decentralized, with no strict decision-making hierarchy. Networks connect everyone in the system to everyone else, so you might say that networks are democratic, pushing power out to the grass roots. Since globalization is based upon the principle of the network, it follows that globalization is democratic, too.

Globalization is democracy: isn't this a crazy conclusion? Yes, I think so. But it is not much crazier than Adam Smith's chain linking the pin factory to global free trade via the principle of the division of labor. There is nothing particularly democratic about either markets or networks—at least not in the sense that Thomas Jefferson would use the word. Not according to Thomas Frank, either, who wrote a whole book to refute it.[32] But the Newtonian method of the New Rhetoric is powerful, so powerful that even Thomas Friedman, whose book *The Lexus and the Olive Tree* remains one of the better globalization reads, cannot resist concluding that finance, information, and technology—three critical elements of globalization—have been democratized.

Of course, the happy conclusion that globalization is democratic isn't the only way that the network principle can be applied here. Networks can be dangerous—they can crash and spread damaging viruses. So network globalization is a threat. Networks also have the effect of excluding those who are not part of the system (the digital divide). So network globalization is unequal and creates haves and have-nots. The network principle, it seems, can be used to make all sorts of arguments about globalization, and each can be made as logical and appealing as Adam Smith's pin factory story.

SEARCHING FOR THE SOUL OF CAPITALISM

As I was preparing for a discussion of Smith's rhetoric and List's critique at the Johns Hopkins Center in Bologna, Italy in 2003, I started reading another book by William Greider, *The Soul of Capitalism: Opening Paths to a Moral Economy.*[33] Perhaps it was just because I had been studying Smith's methods so closely, but I could not help but see

Smith's New Rhetoric strategy at work: principle, example, connect the dots, generalization.

William Greider is a longtime critic of capitalism, and it must be said that capitalism has a lot to criticize. Where Smith intentionally painted an artificially optimistic vision of global market expansion, Greider makes it his business to do just the opposite. Although Greider says in the opening chapters of *The Soul of Capitalism* that he just wants to reform capitalism a bit—to iron out the harsh creases, more or less—in fact his agenda is a lot more radical. But how do you make the case against capitalism at a time when it is seen by many as a great success? Oh, Greider says, you think capitalism is working because it generates economic growth and material abundance? Then you are obviously missing the point—capitalism steals your soul. Let me tell you a personal story.

The story Greider tells is of his grandfather Franklin S. McClure, who farmed the land in western Pennsylvania a hundred years ago. Greider treasures the memories of the summers he spent at the farm the way most of us, I suppose, embrace such recollections. Grandpa was a stubborn man, Greider says, and he resisted change pretty much across the board: no phone, no electricity, no indoor plumbing—he even continued to farm with horses long after everyone else turned to tractors and farm machines.

Why did Greider's grandpa give up all the comforts of life that global capitalism can provide? Here's where the globaloney part begins. "Though I never heard this said," Greider writes, "my hunch is that what my grandparents resisted was the encroaching loss of self-reliance, the steadily vanishing complexity of their own self-contained lives, the capacity to do many things well and provide well enough for themselves. Put in those terms, it seems a huge and frightening loss. They were unwilling to accept the trade-offs."[34]

Do capitalism and its comforts create a giant sucking sound of alienation that takes away our souls? It is a big jump from what grandpa *didn't* say to such an all-encompassing condemnation, but the right rhetoric makes it easy. You just say that it does, using grandpa's unspoken words as your only evidence. "The same alienating exchange is occurring in our own time," Greider says on the next page, "and not just for those workers displaced by new technologies."[35]

Now, Greider has a good point about capitalism's ability to alienate. Adam Smith even said that working in a pin factory could be pretty discouraging, and the pin factory was as close as Smith ever got to modern industry. What I want to point out is how closely Greider has followed the outline of the "Newtonian" type of argument that Smith advocated in his lectures on rhetoric and used so cleverly in the first chapter of *The Wealth of Nations.* Paralleling the pin factory example, Greider starts with a bold assertion, then follows with a single memorable example, complete with details about outhouses and farm livestock, which forms the basis for a universal conclusion. The fact that one example is pretty slim evidence doesn't matter; the fact that the key parts of that example are imagined rather than observed doesn't matter either. And, in fact, Greider even acknowledges that visiting that farm wasn't much fun after the first couple of days. He and his brother couldn't wait to leave.

None of this matters, because the rhetoric has done its job. The image of the soulful farm and noble farmer has been created and capitalism blamed for the alienation we feel today. Cause and effect, simple as that. Feeling alienated? Soulless global capitalism's to blame! Just connect the dots.

Although I disagree with a lot of what William Greider says and the way that he says it, I do give him credit for two things. First, he is a wonderful writer who can create powerful images and who wields both Old Rhetoric metaphors and New Rhetoric organization with equal skill. So strong are the images found on the pages of *The Soul of Capitalism*, for example, that the publisher, Simon & Schuster, were forced to pull out all stops to provide appropriate cover art: the Stars and Stripes is merged with the image of an old-fashioned apple pie. Two of the three most powerful symbols of American values are deployed to represent a book that argues that those values need fundamental reform.[36] And, of course, a piece of the pie is missing: its soul has been cut out.

I also credit Greider with being completely honest about what he is doing. Obviously he is not providing a fair and balanced picture of capitalism, and he doesn't say he is. That's very hard to do in any case and impossible if you also want to advocate an agenda for radical change. In the penultimate chapter, however, Greider explains his real purpose.

Societies don't use facts to define themselves, Greider argues, or to help them justify their actions. Social elites use myths, narratives, and stories to create what Antonio Gramsci would have called intellectual hegemony. It hardly matters whether the story is true or false. What matters is that people accept the story and use it to justify a set of actions and to further a set of interests.

Adam Smith's pin factory example provides such a narrative. Although on the surface it is nothing more than a tiny insignificant case study in preindustrial productivity, the story as told by Adam Smith has vast implications and justifies a world of free-trade, open-market, and pro-industry policies. Society should encourage pin factories and other factories and bear the costs associated with factories, factory work, and open markets, because the ends justify the means. And the ends, you will recall, are increased material abundance from the bottom to the top.

These narratives are important, Greider believes; they shape the world. Images are everything. "America needs to develop a new narrative for itself," he writes. "The old story is no longer working to the mutual benefit and general satisfaction of the society and, in fact, does great damage to many lives and to our prospects for the future."[37] Greider's aim, to put it more bluntly than it deserves, is to replace one globaloney with another. To replace one narrative—the pin factory's story of *more*—with another narrative—a story of *moral*. And that's what he tries to do in *The Soul of Capitalism*.

HOW TO FIGHT A FIRE

What's the best way to respond to globaloney? I've changed my mind about the answer to this question. In the first edition of this book I argued that

> You need to fight fire with fire, Greider believes. The only way to beat a story about capitalism or globalization is with a better story. Although he may be right, I still disagree. I think (or perhaps I only hope) that you can defeat distorting stories with facts—and that is what this book tries to do in the next several chapters. The problem with trying to shape or reform society by fighting stories with stories is that victory goes to the best storyteller, and that may not be you.

I drew support from probably the most famous economist in the world today. I wrote that

> This is the danger that Paul Krugman points out in the introduction to his book *The Great Unraveling*.[38] Krugman argues that many of the supporters of President George W. Bush, who say that they support traditional American values and social principles, intend, in fact, to produce radical social change—and not the kind of change that William Greider has in mind. They justify their policies with stories, not facts. Indeed, the stories they tell about many policies, such as the tax cuts and Social Security reform proposals, are almost wholly divorced from the facts of the situation, a point that Krugman makes again and again in his *New York Times* columns. Krugman never tires of pointing out the fallacies these stories contain. Krugman seems to think that the best way to fight fire is with facts.

That's what I thought back in 2005, but now I've changed my mind. I haven't given up on the facts, but I have come around to Greider's point of view about the stories. You can't fight a good story with facts. Facts just aren't powerful enough. The only way to defeat a good story is with a better story.

So that's what I'm going to try to do. In the chapters to come I'll examine the three types of globaloney that help explain the world economic crisis: Financial Globaloney, Golden Arches Globaloney, and Grassroots Globaloney. I'll use facts to reveal the flaws in these stories, but I won't stop there as I did in the first edition. I'll go further and, in the final chapter, outline the sort of new stories we need to start telling if the next globalization isn't going to just repeat the errors of the past. Globalization can be feasible and sustainable, but it won't happen by itself. And that's not globaloney!

Chapter 2

FINANCIAL GLOBALONEY

Safe as Houses

Looking back, it is hard to imagine that anyone really believed that the global financial system was stable, secure—"safe as houses." There was just too much contradictory evidence. But they did—why?

When I say "looking back" I'm not talking about looking back to 2008, when it seemed like the whole financial system started to unravel; or 2007, when statistics say the U.S. recession officially began; or 1998, when the Long Term Capital Management crisis hit; or Black Monday's stock market crash in 1987. If you want to see strong evidence of the financial system's persistent instability, you can find examples near and far. People naturally compare the world economic crisis of today to the Crash of 1929, but that's relatively recent history for students of financial panics.

The best book yet written about financial crises is economic historian Charles P. Kindleberger's 1978 volume, *Manias, Panics, and*

Crashes: A History of Financial Crises.[1] Kindleberger makes the unsettling frequency of economic crises very clear; he provides an incomplete accounting of financial crises in North America and Western Europe between 1720 and the Great Depression. He reports major financial collapses starting with 1720 (the South Sea Bubble) and continuing in 1763, 1772, 1773, 1797, 1799, 1810, 1815–16, 1819, 1825, 1828, 1836, 1838, 1847, 1848, 1857, 1864, 1866, 1873, 1882, 1890, 1893, 1907, 1920–21, and 1929.[2]

Looking at this long list of dates, it is hard to imagine that an intelligent observer in, say, 1866 would be surprised that another panic or crash was building. But they were and still are. Always. Kindleberger[3] quotes a series of "hyperbolic statements" that give a sense of how unexpected and unique each chaotic event was seen in its time:

- Britain (1772): "One of the fiercest financial storms of the century."
- Britain (1825): "A panic seized upon the public such had never been witnessed before."
- Britain (1847): "More reckless and hazardous speculation than any other known in modern times."
- Hamburg (1857): "So complete and classic a panic has never been seen before . . ."
- United States (1929): "The greatest cycle of speculative boom and collapse in modern times . . . "

And so on—I'm just scratching the surface here. In each case, the crisis seems to come as a surprise and to surpass anything in living memory. But memory is such a fragile thing. They say that those who don't remember the past are doomed to repeat its mistakes. If that's true, then the Sam Cooke classic "Wonderful World" must be the official anthem of the financial industry ("don't know much about history . . . "). Each emerging bubble or speculative scam seems new, an unprecedented opportunity. "This Time is Different" is therefore an appropriate title for the most comprehensive study so far of global financial crises.[4]

THIS TIME IS DIFFERENT

Carmen M. Reinhart and Kenneth S. Rogoff assembled a database of eight centuries of financial crises from all around the world that adds fuel to Kindleberger's fire, showing that financial panics are more the norm than the exception. Writing in early 2008, during what they saw to be a periodic pause in global financial turbulence (if only they had known what was to come!), they noted, "Aside from the current lull, one fact that jumps from [the data] are the long periods when a high percentage of all countries are in a state of default or restructuring."[5]

"Looking forward," Reinhart and Rogoff continued, "one cannot fail to note that . . . each lull has invariably been followed by a new wave of defaults."[6] And this time was no different.

The idea that financial markets are a stable foundation upon which to construct a global economic system is pure globaloney, judging by history. In fact, Princeton historian Harold James cites the economic insecurity associated with financial instability as one of three factors that caused the "end of globalization" in the 1930s.[7] (The other factors were fear of foreign trade competition and fear of foreign migrants.) And yet such optimism persistently reappears. Why are financial markets so unreliable—and why don't investors and public officials get it?

NOT SO DIFFERENT: THE SEVEN STAGES OF A FINANCIAL CRISIS[8]

I have a Japanese print on my office wall to remind me about how global financial markets really work. It is a copy of a woodcut called "The Great Wave Off Kanagawa" made by Katsushika Hokusai (1760–1849). Perhaps you are familiar with it. It shows turbulent seas tossing three small boats, and their unfortunate passengers, to and fro. One particularly large wave seems poised to crash down on a boat, presumably destroying it. In the background a snow-crowned Mt. Fuji silently observes the scene. The contrast between the violence of the sea and the serenity of the mountain is striking.

Financial markets are like Hokusai's sea.[9] They can be calm and serene at times, invitingly placid. But sooner or later they reveal another side of their personality. Financial markets are prone to two types of storms: panics like Hokusai's big wave; and chaos, a potentially more disturbing underlying current. Together they explain why much of what is said and done about global finance is really globaloney.

The leading authority on the theory of financial crises is Hyman P. Minsky, an economist who never received the respect he deserved within the profession because his theories challenged the orthodoxy that markets are generally quite stable (I will have more to say about this later).[10] Every financial crisis is different in the details (and not all bubbles or potential bubbles actually burst), but there is a family resemblance which Minsky explains as the seven stages to a financial crisis.[11]

The first stage is called *displacement*, and it represents a change in expectations. It could be a new invention, discovery, or government policy, or it could be simply a change in expectations about the future. Whatever it is, displacement creates a new object of speculation and at least some insiders rush in to take advantage of the news.

Displacement happens all the time, of course. That's why the stock markets go up and down every day and every hour of the day and every minute of every hour. People constantly react to real news, fake news, and changing expectations. So there are a million little potential financial bubbles filling the market like fizz in a glass of champagne, rising up and popping all the time. But some of them are a bit more substantial and gather the attention of both insiders and outsiders. It is hard to predict in advance when it will happen, but when it does a speculative bubble starts to form.

Minsky's second stage is *expansion*. More and more money begins to focus on the speculative object, whatever it is—gold, silver, real estate, or even tulip bulbs. The market can expand in several different dimensions. The most obvious, of course, is through money creation. When central bankers expand the money supply, as they sometimes do, they may expect that new funds will flow pretty much everywhere, but sometimes they are disproportionately diverted to particular investments fueling bubbles.

Leverage is another source of expansion. Leverage refers to the use of borrowed funds (*other people's money*) to increase the return on *your* money. Suppose you have a thousand dollars and you believe that XYZ Corporation's stock will double in value in the next month. You could invest your thousand dollars and, if you are correct, earn a thousand-dollar profit, a 100 percent return. Or you could take your thousand dollars and borrow nine thousand dollars to invest ten thousand dollars in total. This would be a leverage ratio of nine to one. If your expectations are fulfilled, the profit would be ten thousand dollars on your thousand-dollar investment (minus whatever interest costs you had to pay). Instead of a 100 percent return you would receive something approaching a 1000 percent return. Leverage is a wonderful thing when it works, but it is, of course, very risky. Just as you can earn much more than your initial stake you can also lose much more.

Expansion also takes place as the population of potential investors grows. Insiders (people with specialized investment knowledge) are joined by well-informed amateurs, and then rank amateurs who sometimes just follow the herd based on what they read on the Internet or hear from friends and coworkers. Water-cooler investors, I guess you could call them. The movement from professionally managed employee pension funds to individually managed 401k and similar retirement instruments has facilitated this sort of expansion in many countries. It is easy to belittle the ill-informed financial decisions that "blind capital" makes, but highly paid geniuses do not always outperform them.[12]

Finally, expansion can occur if the speculative object draws the attention of international or even global investment markets. Interconnected global financial markets are capable of focusing enormous sums on particular speculative objects, with predictable results. It is as if a giant magnifying glass focused the full power of the sun on some object or creature. Destruction seems assured, but first comes the heat.

Expansion does not always produce a crisis, because investors can be fickle. There is always something new to consider, always a million different things to displace expectations, and the funds that fuel expansion now can quickly withdraw and move on. The markets can achieve a state that Minsky calls *euphoria*, however, if attention remains focused and expansion sustained. Euphoria produces a sense that investors can do no wrong. It is impossible to make a bad decision, since the general rise of the market covers any poor individual choices.

Economic logic simply evaporates in the euphoria stage. Logic warns to buy less as price rises. Euphoria whispers that rising prices today are harbingers of even higher prices tomorrow—time to buy! And buy even more as those future price increases appear. The buying binge and the higher prices they produced are indeed self-fulfilling prophecies, which are the best kind. Sometimes euphoria just fizzles out, but sometimes it can be sustained, especially if expansion from whatever source is maintained.

Distress comes next in the classic seven-stage scenario. Distress is the moment when insiders begin to believe that the market cannot be sustained. Doubts creep in and alternative scenarios are reviewed. The market may pause or slow, or the collapse could begin.

Revulsion follows as some investors begin to act upon their doubts. Insiders head for the door first, often leaving with substantial profits in their pockets. Others follow, causing the *crisis* stage. The self-fulfilling rising price prophecy of euphoria is reversed as lower prices trigger sell-offs that drive prices even further down. Everyone wants cash in this market, but it is hard to come by. Who will lend in a falling market? Who will buy when prices are falling too fast? Someone does, obviously, but at much lower prices.

Crisis is often accompanied by the seventh stage, *contagion*. The crisis in one market spreads to others. Contagion can happen in several ways. Sometimes the bubble in one market expands to others and all collapse at once. This was the case with the Peso Crisis of the 1990s. Unlucky investors, drawn to Mexico by the prospect of NAFTA gains, ended up putting money into many Latin American markets, all of which surged and then collapsed together. They called it the "Tequila Hangover" effect.

Leverage creates another contagion vector. As prices fall, leveraged investments go "under water" and speculators are required to put up additional funds. Since credit is hard to come by in the crisis stage, there is often little choice but to sell off good investments to cover losses on increasingly bad ones. Thus the Russian financial crisis of 1998 triggered contagion in Brazil as speculators sold off Brazilian investments to cover their rouble losses.

Finally, contagion can take place as credit markets freeze up generally. Businesses that are accustomed to ready access to credit (for themselves or their customers) are shocked as liquidity disappears. Economic misery spreads from the financial sector to the so-called real economy as declining wealth and restricted credit affect buyer and seller behavior.

This is how a classic financial crisis unfolds. Not every crisis goes full term, of course, and the damage when they do is not always substantial. But as Kindleberger explained thirty years ago and Reinhart and Rogoff's study has more recently confirmed, major damaging financial crises happen often enough to be considered a common feature of international finance. So no one should be surprised when these markets behave as they so frequently do.

I'll apply Minsky's model to the world financial crisis in the next chapter, but before I do that I want to explain why speculative bubbles are not the only reason to suspect that financial markets are not always safe and stable.

A PERFECT STORM

Financial crises aren't always international or global, although the most serious ones typically are because international or global expansion can make any bubble bigger and any collapse more complete. During the days of the Bretton Woods financial system, in the 1950s and 1960s, international investment flows were highly regulated and most financial crises were distinctly national, as opposed to international, in cause and effect. Contagion was still a problem, but a smaller one compared to the era that began in the 1970s, when investment capital became increasingly able to travel the world in search of profitable opportunities. Tiny Iceland was somehow able to attract billions of dollars of global capital in this post-Bretton Woods era, with almost predictable tragic effect.

The globalization of financial flows introduces a second element of uncertainty, a second reason to doubt the stability of financial flows. This is the additional current of instability that comes from the foreign exchange markets. International investment in a world of national currencies requires the constant buying and selling of foreign exchange. Exchange rates were managed, regulated, or "pegged" during the Bretton Woods era, but they have been more subject to market forces ever since.

The impact of foreign exchange fluctuations on international investment is fairly straightforward. If you invest in a yen-denominated stock or bond, for example, then the value of your investment rises with the yen and falls with it, too. You face the risk of the original investment and also the risk of the changing currency. It is possible to hedge exchange rate risks using foreign exchange options and forward markets, and most multinational corporations do just this, but lower risk generally comes at a cost, and profit maximizers sometimes cut corners on things like this.

So the first chaotic current is due to exchange rate fluctuations. The yen will rise and fall because of the myriad of factors that affects its demand and supply. As it rises and falls, it carries your investment's profits with it.

A second current brings speculative forces. Although economists generally view currencies as a medium of exchange—something that businesses purchase in order to buy foreign goods, services, or investments—sometimes they can become an object of speculative attention themselves. This is what happened in the Thai financial crisis in 1997, which was a classic example of a speculative attack. The Thai government had guaranteed that the exchange rate would remain steady at 25 baht per U.S. dollar—a strategy to boost foreign trade and investment by removing exchange rate risks. Speculators correctly determined that the Thai government didn't have sufficient reserves to maintain this exchange rate in the face of pressures against it. When these pressures were brought to bear, the baht plunged to half its earlier value. Foreign investments in Thailand similarly collapsed. Thai firms that had borrowed abroad suffered enormous losses as the home currency cost of their debt doubled.

THE BUTTERFLY EFFECT

The third current is perhaps the most disturbing one because it is the hardest to perceive. Foreign exchange markets are at times subject to chaotic price movements qualitatively similar to the turbulent air and water flows that scientists need supercomputers and millions of data points to model and understand (but not always predict). Exchange rate movements during turbulent episodes are not exactly random, but they are essentially unpredictable, adding a new dimension of risk to every aspect of international investment.[13]

This insight actually came to me while I was watching a play in London's West End a few years ago. It was *Arcadia* by Tom Stoppard and one of the main characters, a young woman named Thomasina Coverly, was figuring out what would later be called chaos theory. As I watched the play, my mind wandered to exchange rates, the one part of economics I thought was most relevant to Thomasina's theory of nonlinear dynamical systems.

The mathematics of chaos theory is very difficult, but the idea of how it applies to foreign exchange markets is very simple. Imagine that two traders are speculating on the dollar/yen exchange rate. One is a "fundamentalist" who has calculated an expected exchange rate based upon economic fundamentals like GDP growth rates, expected inflation rates, and so forth. If the yen is above her expected rate she sells it "short" (a way of profiting when price falls), and if it is below her expected rate she buys the yen and goes "long."

Now imagine a second trader also speculating in this market who is a "chartist." Chartists look for patterns in price movements (using charts to graph the price, hence the name) and try to profit by buying or selling whenever the market price differs from the projected chart trend.

Our speculators buy and sell based upon two different exchange rate theories, which interact in the market place. If the fundamentalist perceives the yen to be overvalued, she may short it, driving down the price, which could trigger actions by the chartist that might push the yen's price further down or send it spiking back up, depending on how he reads the price trends. The chartist's action produces a counter-movement from the fundamentalist and so on.

In theory, the two traders might settle into equilibrium, where the current exchange rate matches both their expectations. In practice, however, this is unlikely to occur because there are more than two traders with more than two types of speculative models guiding their actions and many different interconnected currency markets. Add to this the fact that there is a constant flow of news and outside activity that alters the exchange rate and forces the traders to update their expectations. The result, as you might imagine, is that exchange rates are constantly humming at changing pitches, like a tuning fork gone mad.

Sometimes these chaotic vibrations are like background noise, but they can at times build to a crescendo, creating real risk and even triggering larger crises. Or at least that's what theory says. You may be familiar with the "butterfly effect" described in a famous paper called "Practicability: Does the Flap of a Butterfly's Wings in Brazil Set Off a Tornado in Texas?" by Edward Lorenz.[14] Once again, the math is complex but the idea is simple: small changes in "initial conditions" can snowball into much larger effects when they trigger increasingly unstable dynamic interactions.

When you add these effects together you can appreciate why I'm so attracted to Hokusai's woodcut of "The Great Wave." It's a terribly beautiful image of how global finance can unravel. The inherent risks of the investments themselves float on the currents of foreign exchange, rising and falling with the currency values. Those values are subject to everyday fluctuations to which markets are prone, plus the effects of bubbles and speculative attacks, plus the possibility of the chaotic effects I've just described. Add to this the fact that central banks and governments frequently try to alter exchange rate trends, either directly through market intervention or indirectly through interest rate adjustments. The result can be as dramatic and dangerous as Hokusai's famous image.

Let me be very clear: I'm not saying that global financial markets are always dangerously unstable. They are quite literally like the oceans most of the time, a useful medium for international investment and exchange. But storms can brew up unpredictably, and sometimes a "perfect storm" can emerge, when all of the effects line up so that the interactions become more and more intense before collapsing into equilibrium. These are the events that attract our attention because they are so destructive, but even the day-to-day variations in exchange rates add risk to what are in any case risky transactions. They do not prevent the construction of a global economy, but they must inevitably limit how complete it can be.

I hope I've persuaded you that economic globalization is a risky enterprise and that its foundation, global finance, is particularly suspect. As finance has become increasingly global since the end of the Bretton Woods era, the financial markets have become increasingly unstable and prone to turbulence, crises, and chaos. A perfect storm indeed. And no set of global regulations or safety net has emerged to match the scale and scope of the global markets.

How, if this is the case, is it possible for anyone to believe the globaloney that economic globalization is safe and secure? And, when new crises come, why are the lessons of the past so quickly forgotten?

SLICING THE GLOBALONEY:
THIS TIME IS DIFFERENT

Traditionally the answer to these questions has been that human nature itself prevents us from learning from our follies, at least when it comes to financial investments. Faced with an apparent sure thing, investors find they can resist everything except temptation and oops, I did it again!

Kindleberger cites Walter Bagehot, the first editor of the *Economist* magazine, in this regard. Bagehot lived through a series of financial crises in nineteenth-century London and became almost cynical about the propensity of his fellow citizens to fall once again into the same old hole. "At intervals, from causes which are not to the present purpose," he wrote, "the money of these people—the blind capital as we may call it, of the country—is particularly large and craving; it seeks for someone to devour it, and there is a 'plethora'; it finds someone and there is 'speculation'; is devoured, and there is 'panic.'"[15]

Certainly there is something to the idea that at times "a great deal of stupid people have a great deal of stupid money," as Bagehot wrote in the same essay. But surplus of wealth and shortage of common sense cannot be the whole story, although I am afraid that even today it still explains a lot of it. Even if we factor in the speculator's perennial optimism ("this time is different!") and the possibility of ADD-like attention spans, there is something left to be explained. Unsurprisingly, I blame the stories that economists and others tell and the interests that call these stories forth. Herewith three stories that help explain how financial crises bubble up and explode today after centuries of depressing experience.

The first story is also called "this time is different," but I mean that in a particular way. At some point in the prosperous years of the 1990s economists and policy makers began to believe that they had finally figured out the key to sustain noninflationary economic growth. If you were smart and followed the rules, economic prosperity seemed guaranteed.

Or at least that's what we thought in the United States. In fact times were *so* good that student interest in economics (particularly macroeconomics) began to decline. Inflation, unemployment, and economic crisis were the bread and butter of introductory macro courses, and *sans* crisis there seemed to be little to teach and less to study. Who cares about the national economy if it works so very well? Give us *real* problems to figure out. University economics enrollments declined around the country and many departments shut down their full-year introductory sequence, replacing it with a quick and dirty "greatest hits" course.

Now, the fact is that economic crises did not go away. There were plenty of countries that experienced rapid inflation or economic growth problems. And there were a whole string of financial crises of one sort or another. But it was easy to dismiss them and conclude that this time is different.

Some of the crises seemed to be the result of erroneous policy moves. This time is different—we would never make those mistakes. Other crises were seen as the inevitable consequences of failed economic systems. This time is different—our system is not the same. It seems like there was always a reason to think that any particular crisis was the result of a problem that we would never see repeated.

And so, one by one, the lessons of history were checked off . . . and ignored. The Sterling Crisis of 1992? Idiocy. The British were foolish to link the pound to those European currencies. The whole idea of a single European currency is pie in the sky anyway—that'll never work.

The Peso Crisis of 1994? That was just Mexico being Mexico—crazy Latin investors! What can you expect? We would never make the same mistakes.

The Japanese economic crisis (hard to put dates on this one—it seems to go on and on)? Easy to rationalize that—it's a structural problem. Everyone knows that the Japanese don't really let markets work. Their system is based on the iron triangle—the cozy relationship between big business, politicians, and the bureaucracy. It's really corrupt crony capitalism; no wonder it failed.

And so you can see that "this time is different"—we aren't unrealistic like the British, hot-tempered like the Mexicans, corrupt like the Japanese. The problem isn't with financial markets but the governments who try to run them. Global financial markets are safe and sane—if you just let them work and avoid the mistakes of the past.

The problem with this line of reasoning—the thing that makes it globaloney—is what it ignores. Japan shows that crisis can occur even in very rich creditor nations. If the Japanese can have a crisis, anyone can. Mexico's policies were not out of line with accepted practice in the 1990s, but the peso crashed just the same. And Britain's example suggests that even a very rich country cannot defend an exchange rate against a speculative attack.[16]

Taken together, in other words, the experiences of the recent past suggest that crisis and instability is always and everywhere a possibility. Even, as we have learned, in the United States.

WE HAVE THE TECHNOLOGY

The pace of technological change—new products, new processes, new technologically driven business and social arrangements—has increased dramatically in recent years. The advance of technology is seldom smooth; it is an example of what Joseph Schumpeter called "creative destruction" and the anticipation of the benefits of creation is generally matched by concern over what will be or might be destroyed in the process. Technology played a major role in convincing the world that globalization, and especially financial globalization, is safe as houses, which is ironic because the process of technological change is inherently risky.

Risk has always been an important constraint on the growth of the global market, and technological change can reduce risk in a variety of ways. In the Middle Ages, for example, the natural risks associated with ocean shipping was one constraint on international trade. A single lost ship could spell bankruptcy for the merchants who backed her. One reason trade advanced was that technology was found to reduce this risk. Better and safer ships were developed, of course, but so were more sophisticated shipping insurance contracts that allowed a ship's owners to hedge against disaster. You might not think of new financial instruments as technological innovations, but they are. Even without stronger hulls, better insurance would have made global trade safer from an economic standpoint.

The digital revolution promised to make globalization safer by making information flows faster, cheaper, broader, and deeper and by allowing for the creation of innovative financial instruments. Digital technology makes it not only possible but actually convenient for us to gather news from around the world and to "talk" (both figuratively via email and literally through online services like Skype) with people many time zones away. You can check your portfolio of global investments, update your global "friends" network on Facebook, and even make a microcredit loan to a Bangladeshi merchant on Kiva.org while still in your pajamas sipping your morning coffee. The sense that technology has eliminated the constraints of time and place can be very strong at times.

Instantaneous communications is a convenience in our everyday lives (at least up to a point), but it is also an important factor in the expansion of global business. Information is critically important in global trade and finance. Businesses need to monitor the performance of foreign partners and contract holders, track international shipments, and assess foreign market conditions. Investors need access to both financial information and market trading systems in real time in order to trade effectively. The technological advances in the last twenty years seemingly have removed the constraints of time and place and made gathering key data both faster and cheaper.

People who talk about technology often focus on speed, on how fast information travels these days, but this is not necessarily the most important factor. Doubling the speed of communications is nowhere near as important as important as halving the cost, and costs have fallen enormously. The lower cost of digital communication has allowed the information network to be both broader and deeper. It is broader in the sense that it extends to more markets and industries in more parts of the world. It is deeper in the extent to which this information and the technology that allows its production and access drills down into and throughout organizations and societies. "Thin" globalization was overtaken by "thick" globalization. This dynamic can be captured in a single word: outsourcing. Digital technology encouraged the global diffusion of production and investment and the creation of complex value chains and business relationships. Global arrangements that seemed impossible only a few years before became commonplace.

Technology played a second and perhaps more important role in the global investment boom. Advances in what is called "financial engineering" made it possible to construct more complicated synthetic financial products that could apparently maintain high returns while reducing effective risk. Financial engineering, we were told, could strip the risk from one sort of investment and combine it neatly with offsetting risks elsewhere. Ordinary financial products like stocks, bonds, and mortgages were mixed as in a food processor and the resulting dough was kneaded and massaged, baked to a golden brown and sold in slices (literally, the financial term is *tranche*, French for slice) that promised high return without high risk. Financial engineering, cheap and plentiful information, and the availability of computer trading in twenty-four-hour global markets made investing around the world seem safe and convenient.

"We have the technology" to make globalization safe and secure. But there were several problems with this belief, as we will see in the next chapter. The idea was that more and cheaper data necessarily produced better production and investment decisions, but this isn't always true. Economists define information as data that reduces uncertainty, but more data is not always more information, in this technical sense, particularly if its quality is uncertain or it cannot be sufficiently examined. One problem of the information age is that we sometimes have literally too much information in the ordinary sense of the word while not having enough when the technical definition is applied.

Then there's the problem of risk. Financial engineering products created new ways to slice and dice risk, but they did not eliminate it—particularly risk at the system level. Their complexity actually introduced new elements of risk as they sometimes proved too complicated to adequately evaluate using standard risk assessment techniques. People who thought they were taking less risk were frequently taking different types of risk and sometimes exposing themselves to greater potential loss.

The bottom line is that new technologies encouraged globalization by lowering cost and reducing risk. The cost-saving part of the story might have been real, but the risk-saving part contained a good deal of globaloney.

MARKET FUNDAMENTALISM

The strongest thread in the "safe as houses" globalization narrative was neither a misunderstanding of history ("this time is different") nor a misunderstanding of risk ("we have the technology"). Rather it was a faulty belief in the universal benefits of markets themselves which I call "market fundamentalism."

I prefer the term "market fundamentalism" to the more popular "neoliberalism" as a title for a belief that free markets can solve all problems. I am uncomfortable with neoliberalism because it seems to me that it slanders "liberalism." Liberalism, or Classical Liberalism as we call it in the United States, is a complicated ideology that focuses on individual rights. It is both economic and political, both Adam Smith and Thomas Jefferson. Neoliberalism seems to be missing the political element, substituting a fundamentalist belief in the market form of social organization and/or a great distrust of government. It would be better to call it half-liberalism (or maybe half-baked liberalism) than neoliberalism, in my view. But "market fundamentalism" fits just fine, so that's the term I prefer to use.

Much of the focus of market fundamentalists has been on free markets. Free markets are a means, an end, and a sort of religion to market fundamentalists. First came free markets within countries (think Reagan and Thatcher) and then free trade markets between countries (think NAFTA and the World Trade Organization). Now the best way to think about free trade is to go back to Schumpeter's idea of creative destruction, which I mentioned before when talking about technological change. Like new technology, freer trade creates many benefits but it also threatens to destroy old economic arrangements and jeopardize established interests. Trade creates anxiety, just like technology does, but there is an important difference. No one seriously imagines that it is possible to halt technological change at the border or even delay its effects for very long. Technology is destiny in this regard: you cannot escape it. This isn't true about freer trade, however. Governments have always shown a fairly deep concern for those who are hurt or fear they could be hurt by trade. The political push-back against trade's costs is a force to be reckoned with.

Market fundamentalists tend to dismiss this push-back and to understate both the costs of freer markets and the anxiety of those who fear they will bear those costs. This is a mistake, in my view. It is a political mistake, of course, because anxiety ignored can reappear as reactionary populism. It is an economic mistake, too, because the gains from freer trade are large enough in most cases to allow for some accommodation of damaged or threatened interests. It is perhaps not a bad rule to say that creation must be sufficiently greater than destruction if disruptive change is to take place, but the actual cost-benefit calculations are always problematic. The fear of loss is more commonly and deeply felt (when it comes to trade) than the expectation of benefits. And the gainers from trade are typically widely diffused throughout the economy, while the losers are more concentrated and thus better able to mobilize politically.

In any case, market fundamentalism was very much in fashion in recent years. It would have been one thing if the focus had been on international trade, but fundamentalist fervor soon spread to international finance (pushed along a bit, I would say, by financial industry interests who stood to profit). This proved to be very problematic because the creation/destruction balance for trade and finance are quite different. The gains from freer international *finance* are small relative to those from *trade*, but the costs can be much higher, particularly when free capital markets means exposure to global currency and financial crises.

The fact that global finance made globalization a risky business was no secret. The *Economist* (an unlikely champion of unfree markets) made this point clearly in a 2003 editorial:[17]

> If any cause commands the unswerving support of *The Economist*, it is that of liberal trade. For as long as it has existed, this newspaper has championed freedom of commerce across borders. Liberal trade, we have always argued, advances prosperity, encourages peace among nations and is an indispensable part of individual liberty. It seems natural to suppose that what goes for trade in goods must go for trade in capital, in which case capital controls would offend us as violently as, say, an import quota on bananas. The issues have much in common, but they are not the same. . . . Why is trade in capital different from trade in goods? For two main reasons. First, international markets in capital are prone to error, whereas international markets in goods are not. Second, the punishment for big financial mistakes can be draconian, and tends to hurt innocent bystanders as much as borrowers and lenders. Recent decades, and the 1990s most of all, drove these points home with terrible clarity.

Although you can argue with the *Economist's* optimist view of trade, where mistakes apparently do not occur, you cannot doubt their opinion of finance. Global goods markets may make mistakes, I think, but global capital markets are *prone* to mistakes, which is a different thing, a different and more serious sort of risk. The idea, which market fundamentalists sold hard, that all global markets were the same proved to be seriously risky globaloney.

THE WORLD ISN'T FLAT

Woven together, these three globaloney threads created a powerful narrative that assured citizens, investors, and government officials that globalization was safe and secure. Of the three arguments—this time is different, we have the technology, and market fundamentalism—I believe that the last was the most potent in pushing globalization ahead (and the most responsible, therefore, for the collapse that followed).

One reason I put particular weight on market fundamentalism here is its obvious connection to Keynes's famous quote about the power of ideas. The wrong-headed ideas embedded in the market fundamentalist creed have a lot in common with the some of the bogus syllogisms to which Keynes referred in his famous quote. But there's more to it than that.

What made market fundamentalism so powerful was that it actually combined all three of the types of globaloney I discuss in this book. First, it is what I call Financial Globaloney—the idea that globalization, even global investment, is fundamentally safe. It makes this case in a way that Adam Smith would recognize. Market for goods are stable (even the *Economist* seems to believe this); markets are markets (all markets are the same), therefore financial markets are stable, too. The fundamental belief in markets generally, as opposed to the nuanced analysis of the characteristics of different types of markets in different economic environments, is the heart of this globaloney.

You can see how this relates to Grassroots Globaloney, which is the idea that globalization is irresistible and diversity is impossible. Because market fundamentalists believe that markets are good and that all markets are fundamentally the same, their ideas conflicted with the notion of economic diversity—that different systems of state-market relations could make sense or be preferable in any way to pure market organization. The job of the grassroots was to get with the system—the free market system.

Finally, market fundamentalism is rooted historically in the experience of the United States and so draws upon the power of what I call Golden Arches Globaloney, which argues that globalization seeks to transform the world into a giant pseudo-American theme park. The United States is in many ways the model for the market fundamentalist vision of the world. It is a huge single market—one market for goods, services, capital, and labor. If you can sell a product anywhere in the United States, you can sell it everywhere.

This vision of America is badly distorted—America's unified free market is very incomplete. State regulations mean that some goods (alcoholic beverages, for example) cannot be freely bought and sold throughout the country; some services are also restricted by state licensing requirements of financial services regulation. There are few restrictions on labor movements, however. The United States is like one big market without actually being one big market. But since you see the Golden Arches of McDonald's pretty much everywhere you go in the U.S., it just seems like it must be.

The U.S. single market was the model for Europe's Single Market initiative of the 1990s which established four economic freedoms—free movement of goods, services, capital, and labor. The idea was to import the dynamism of the U.S. economy by adopting its single market formula. This worked, to a certain extent, although the diverse regional, national, and local social and economic arrangements were retained to a considerable degree. But since you could see Golden Arches pretty much everywhere in Europe, too, the illusion of a true single market was clear.

The market fundamentalist agenda is therefore to continue this expansion from the United States to Europe to, well, the world. All markets the same, all nations the same. A universal system.[18]

Perhaps the best unintentional statement of market fundamentalist ideas is *The World is Flat* by *New York Times* columnist Thomas Friedman.[19] In it Friedman tries to use the image of fiercely competitive emerging global markets to scare Americans into investing in the education and technology necessary to compete. That was his intent. Along the way, however, he painted a picture of a world flattened by technology and market forces, where everyone competes with everyone else on a level playing field.

Ironically, Thomas Friedman is probably the last person in the world you would think could believe that the world is flat and that local factors don't really matter. As a specialist in Middle East politics, he surely knows how varied the economic, political, and social terrain really is. And I don't really think he believes replacing local values with market values is a prescription for universal peace and prosperity. But some of those local differences have been the source of much conflict and grief—perhaps he imagines a flat world would be a better one.

The world isn't flat and won't likely be flattened anytime soon. The collapse of globalization will make the market terrain more rugged than before. The idea that globalization was safe and secure—as safe as houses, as stable as a table—has surely been revealed to be what is always was: globaloney!

We've learned a hard lesson about global instability, as I'll explain in the next chapter, but did it "take"? Or will we fall back into old habits, thinking this time is different, technology will triumph, and market fundamentalism rules?

CHAPTER 3

THE CRASH OF 2008 AND THE GLOBAL MARKET MYTH

This time it really *was* different. The Crash of 2008 wasn't based in some faraway place—Thailand, Brazil, Russia. Its impact wasn't limited to a third world country—Mexico, Argentina. It wasn't caused by an evil genius (George Soros and the Sterling Crisis of 1992) or a team of geniuses gone badly wrong (John Meriwether and Nobel laureates Myron Scholes and Robert C. Merton and the Long Term Capital Management Crisis of 1998). And it wasn't just a financial crisis, like many others, with limited effects on the so-called "real economy." The crisis on Wall Street was a crisis on Main Street. No one was spared.

And the effects really were global. International trade and finance collapsed, spreading the impact of the crisis far beyond the financial markets where it began. *Deglobalization*—the unraveling of global economic arrangements knit together over many years—was quickly set in motion as contagion spread from shore to shore like the wake of a speedboat.

This was time different—or *was* it? This chapter argues that the basic structure of the Crash of 2008—the pattern of cause and effect—was not new at all. In fact it is as old as the Dutch Tulip Crisis of the 1600s. What *was* different was the depth and breadth of the crisis and this is due, I argue, to Financial Globaloney, the stories that guided the construction of an elaborate global economy that we thought was safe as houses—but that proved to be instead as steady as a house of cards.[1]

SYNOPSIS: THE SEVEN STAGES
OF THE CRASH OF 2008

Looking back, it isn't very difficult to see how the Crash of 2008 unfolded and how its broad outline fit Hyman Minsky's pattern of financial crises. The process begins with displacement, a change in attitudes and beliefs, a shift in market focus, the birth of a new object of speculative attention. Arguably, displacement occurred in the wake of the "dot-com" bubble of 1995–2001. The collapse of Internet stocks sparked the search for a safer alternative and residential housing fit the bill perfectly. The conventional wisdom—unsupported by actual fact—was that housing prices could only rise. And even if they fell, you still had a solid asset—the property itself—to provide security. That made housing a much better prospect than Internet stocks. When they collapsed, as many of them did in the first years of the new century, investors were left with . . . well, nothing. The virtual companies virtually vanished, leaving behind only office leases and piles of secondhand Aeron chairs and cubicle furniture. Houses were definitely safer than that!

Expansion, as I will explain shortly, quickly followed and in every possible way. More people in more places found themselves acquiring direct and indirect interests in the housing bubble. Enormous sums were brought to bear on what was, in retrospect, a relatively narrow market. Certainly the global market for housing is vast and could conceivably absorb such sums, but the speculative object in this case was much more tightly defined. Although housing prices surged in many parts of the world, some areas were disproportionately affected: the Southwest and Southeast in the United States, for example, but the

Midwest not so much. In many ways it was the depth and breadth of the expansion and the tools that facilitated it that made the eventual crash so devastating.

Soon the pleasant feeling of euphoria (the fourth stage) set in as housing prices zoomed ever higher and profits rolled in from home sales and the financial services that go with them. The stories are legion of properties purchased with no intention to hold, then resold at a higher price before the first payment came due. Money for nothing, as Dire Straits sang; real estate was bigger than rock and roll.

Then, slowly, distress set in. As interest rates crept up a bit from the post-dot-com bust lows, some of those mortgage loans didn't look very secure. The conventional wisdom that there would always be a buyer ready to pay a higher price began to look a bit optimistic as well. Every Ponzi scheme hits a limit, where there are not enough new investors to bail all the old ones out with a profit, and it started to look like the housing limit was in sight. So insiders got out. Of housing, of course, but more importantly of mortgage securities.

Revulsion followed, but not immediately. A housing bubble has considerable mass and momentum and does not suddenly implode, especially one as large, complex, and uneven as this one. The mortgage security market, however, is different and that's where the dike broke. Security prices fell as investors realized that they had no idea what their complicated mortgage-backed paper was really worth.

And so came the crisis stage, with prices falling to fire-sale levels. First to fall were the financial securities, where the market is more centralized and fluid, but eventually the housing market started to collapse as well as funding for new loans dried up and interest costs increased. Borrowers who couldn't afford higher interest payments on their adjustable-rate loans felt distress themselves and then crisis and default.

Contagion followed and so the financial crisis became an economic crisis. It wasn't just the housing market or the mortgage market. The expansion had drawn resources from all parts of the global economy and the shock waves of crisis followed those threads all the way back, where they set off new shock wave sets. It was a bit like those science films you saw in school, the ones that illustrated how a nuclear reaction takes place by throwing a ping pong ball into a room full of mousetraps, each armed with a ping pong ball. Ping, ping, ping . . . kaboom!

SAFE AS HOUSES

The most fundamental principle of finance is that there is a trade-off between risk and return. Riskier investments must promise to pay higher returns because there is a greater chance that you might not get your money back, or not all of it, or get it back when you expect it. Higher risk, higher return—it is as close as you can come to a Law of Economics.[2]

As the dot-com bust of 2001 was evolving into a housing boom, there was a strong sense among investors that the economic law of risk and return had been repealed—that the investments they were making (and the high profits they received) really were safe as houses. The first reason was because, as I have already noted, the initial speculative object was housing—tangible assets—generally located in desirable or fast-growing areas. It just made sense, investors told themselves, that housing prices had to rise because of the simple forces of demand and supply.

The idea that houses were safe as houses is easy to appreciate even if it isn't always true. Housing prices will rise in a growing market, yes, when increasing demand moves ahead of rising supply. But how much? Prices that rise on speculative waves have room to crash back to long-run market fundamental values, much as they did in Japan in the 1990s and at various times and places in the United States in recent years.

The fact of the bubble added to the sense of weightlessness, as it generally does. As the expansion stage becomes euphoria it seems as if prices will never stop rising. Individual mistakes are quickly forgotten as the rising market raises all values. Pay too much for a house? Forget about it. Someone else will pay too much to buy it from you. It is literally impossible to lose money, or so it seems.

MORAL HAZARD

Something important happens when investors suddenly believe that they have been excused from the law of risk and return. Economists call it moral hazard. Moral hazard is quite simply the idea that if you don't have to bear the consequences of the risks you are taking, you will probably take more risks. The term dates back to the 1600s when it was used by early insurance companies to describe the tendency of businesses with fire insurance to have more suspicious fires than businesses without insurance coverage. The assumption was that some unethical behavior was involved when owners found their property worth more as an insurance claim than an operating enterprise—hence the "moral" hazard terminology. Or maybe they were just less diligent about fire risk when they knew they were covered. In any case, no moral judgment is implied by the term today. Moral hazard is simply a rational response to economic incentives.

Rational for the individual, that is, but as sometimes happens, rational individual actions can yield irrational collective results. As each individual takes more risk to get higher returns, secure in the knowledge that the risk really isn't there, the result is a bubble. Individual risk is replaced with systemic risk—the possibility that the entire market could collapse. This is a real problem because, while investors are sometimes able to assess accurately the risk of individual investments, it is very difficult to determine systemic risk. If it were easy, the history of financial crises would be quite short—lesson learned, won't make that mistake again—not long and endlessly repetitive as we have seen.

The housing market certainly seemed to be in the thrall of moral hazard. Everyone wanted to get in on the deal, even people who could not afford to purchase a house by conventional measures. Low-income households, without much savings and small and perhaps unstable income, would not normally think about making a major purchase. But the rising tide of housing prices took away the risk, since they would be able to sell out and earn a tidy profit before the consequences of their otherwise unsustainable actions hit home.

Thus moral hazard both fueled the intensity of market speculation and served to encourage expansion. The demand for housing expanded from families purchasing houses for their own use to speculators buying property simply to resell at higher prices. And the socioeconomic profile of housing buyers changed, too, from households with the economic means to make monthly payments to a larger group including so-called "subprime" buyers, who could only make ends meet if someone or something (in this case the trend of rising housing prices) stood by to bail them out.

As each individual made that sure-thing investment, the housing bubble inflated just a bit more and systemic risk—the risk of the bubble bursting—increased just a bit more. Wasn't someone supposed to be looking after the system, paying attention to the collective consequences of individual moral hazard?

The answer of course is yes, but the situation is complicated. The Federal Reserve, the U.S. central bank, is charged with evaluating the economy's overall condition. The fact of the housing bubble (and the dot-com bubble before it) was of concern to the Fed, but policymakers made an explicit decision to look away from the situation. The Federal Reserve's policy in recent years has been to encourage sustainable growth with low inflation. If new money went into creating jobs, that was good. If new money just pushed up product prices, that was bad. But if new money went into asset markets like stocks and houses—well, that just didn't seem to matter, since it didn't directly affect either inflation or growth targets. Fundamentally the Federal Reserve, while its governors might privately be concerned about a housing bubble, didn't see the bubble as its business, which was inflation and economic growth. That left the problem of monitoring for financial risk to the financial system itself.

IT'S A WONDERFUL LIFE 2.0

Most houses are financed with mortgage loans, where the house itself is collateral to back up the loan. Back in the day, as they say, banks had a very strong incentive to take into account both the risk of individual borrower default and the likelihood of a market collapse because they both made the loan and held it on their books as an asset. You'll appreciate this concept if you've seen the film *It's a Wonderful Life* starring Jimmy Stewart and Donna Reed. At one point the Stewart character George Bailey explains to panicked patrons of his bank that their deposits aren't in the vault, they've been loaned to friends and neighbors in the community so that they could buy or build houses. The bank had to make these loans carefully because both its own profits and the savings of its depositors were in the balance.[3]

Now fast forward to today and *It's a Wonderful Life 2.0*. George Bailey III finds himself is a much different situation. He doesn't worry about angry mobs of upset depositors because all their savings accounts are insured (up to a limit) by the FDIC. It doesn't really matter very much in a *moral* sense if his mortgage customers' loans turn out to be good or bad because the FDIC will bail out any deposits losses. He's not really putting their money at risk, just the bank owner's capital, which is much less. So he has little concern about a run on the bank.

But if a run did happen, he'd need to give a different speech than his granddad did in that famous scene in the old movie. He can't say that Mr. Smith's deposit is invested in Mr. Jones's home anymore, because the 2.0 system doesn't really work that way. Yes, Smith's life savings were initially loaned to Jones, but then Jones's mortgage was sold to investors and the proceeds were used to make another mortgage to Mr. Black. And Black's mortgage was sold to investors and the money used to make a new loan to Mrs. Miller. And so on and so on, so long as people could be found who want to borrow money to buy houses.

The whole role of the bank is changed in the 2.0 scenario of the years just before the Crash of 2008. Now the bank initiates mortgage loans, collecting a fee, and processes payments, collecting a fee. It is the visible link between a local borrower and ultimate owner of a mortgage-backed security somewhere in the global financial system. But in terms of accountability, there isn't much.

So local banks suffered the same moral hazard temptation as home buyers and speculators. In the bank's case, the profits came with mortgage fees, so the more loans they could make and resell the greater their profits would be. If those new loans were riskier than the ones before—well, that wasn't really their problem. It was all return, no risk.

UP THE DOWN STAIRCASE

So money flowed down from investors, investment banks, and government agencies like FannieMae and FreddieMac and the securitized mortgages went back up. Investors got high returns with low risk. Why did they believe that the law of risk and return didn't apply to them? In part for the same reasons as individual home buyers and the banks that sold them loans: houses were safe, banks were safe, and the euphoria of rising prices would cover any stupid mistakes. But they had more reason than this to feel that their investments were all but risk-free.

Financial engineers were busy making investment safer and more profitable. The first innovation was relatively simple: securitization. Mortgage-backed investments were packages of low-risk loans that were bundled together into standard, tradeable units (securitized) and sold to investors. Individual loans might be problematic—certain homeowners could unpredictably be late in making payments or even be forced to walk away from their loans—but the economic performance of the group would be relatively stable, predictable, safe. The packaged financial product was safer, or at least more predictable, than any of the individual loans—assuming, of course, that there was no systemic shock that made all the assumptions of the engineers' financial models obsolete.[4]

George Soros has pointed out that, while the securitization of mortgage loans reduced risk in some ways by spreading it out over the global financial market, it also introduced a new type of incentive risk that many investors failed to appreciate. The principals (the investors) had a strong interest in the security of these loans—their investments were based on the idea that they were safe as houses. The loan agents, however, got paid according to how many loans they made. After a certain point, the agents' incentives began to run counter to the principals' and risk began to rise, not fall, as more and more mortgage-backed securities were packaged and sold.[5]

Mortgage-backed securities actually proved to be a very efficient way to move mortgages up the down staircase in exchange for loanable funds, especially in a rising market and for borrowers with good credit. This left the problem of home buyers with low incomes, bad credit history, or both. Some of these "subprime" borrowers could get financing through various government-sponsored loan programs, but there was not enough of this money available to match the demand. So the financial engineers went to work again, making risky loans safe.

The innovation this time was a special type of investment called a collateralized debt obligation, or CDO, that was customized to meet the needs of the housing boom. Loans from a large group of subprime borrowers were put into a financial food processor and the resulting batter was baked into what you might think of as a big pie. The pie was sliced up into pieces with different claims on the payment stream and these slices were sold to investors for different prices. Even if the pie filling was full of very shaky borrowers, there is a high likelihood that *some* of the loans would be repaid in full and on time. So the first *tranche*, which had very first claim on loan repayments, was relatively secure and could be sold to risk-averse investors at a relatively high price. The second *tranche* would only be paid after the first set of investors were free and clear. That's a riskier situation, so the second slice had a lower cost to investors. The lower investment cost meant that they would get a higher return if all money came in as promised, but there was greater risk that they would get less or maybe even none at all. Risk and return. The third *tranche* was riskier still since these investors wouldn't be paid until the first two groups had their money. And so on down to the final *tranche*, which was enormously risky but incredibly cheap, and therefore potentially very profitable.

Financial engineering couldn't make risk disappear for subprime borrowers and the investors who provided their funds, but they certainly made it seem as if risk was tightly managed and under control. Absent a systemic shock, risk was low for most loans and manageable for the rest. Large investment banks jumped into the business of assembling structured investment vehicles both to sell to their clients around the world and to hold as their own investments.

LEVERAGE

The logical next step was to bring in more money. This was clear to everyone. For home buyers and speculators: the more houses you could buy, the more profit you could make. For the banks: the more mortgages you could arrange, the more fees you could collect. For the investment banks: the more investment packages you could construct, the more profit you could make. And so on.

The money came from all directions. The global expansion of the mortgage securities market came first. With a risk-return profile that was impossible to beat—and high liquidity because of the vast market—mortgage-backed securities found their way into private investment portfolios and pension fund accounts around the world. The globalization of the mortgage system was a big deal, but leverage was arguably even bigger.

Leverage is the principle of taking a little of your money and a lot of someone else's (borrowed) money and making a big investment. Let me illustrate this with a completely ridiculous example. Suppose you took $1 million of your own money and borrowed $76 million more to make a $77 million investment in housing, mortgage-backed securities, or anything else. Thus leveraged, any small change in the value of your investment translates into a huge investment gain for you. Suppose, for example, that the housing portfolio you've purchased rises from $77 to $78 million—a gain of much less than 1 percent. Well, that $1 million gain represents a 100 percent return on your investment, ignoring of course the interest on your loan. A 10 percent increase from $77 million to, say, $85 million would yield an $8 million return on your $1 million of capital.

Bottom line: you are smart to invest in the housing bubble, smarter to leverage your investment, and a genius if your leverage is as high as this example. By the way, my ridiculous example actually isn't totally ridiculous. Although investment banks at the time frequently leveraged up their investments at 20-to-1 to 30-to-1 ratios, one part of the now-defunct investment bank Lehman Brothers is said to have gone all the way to 76-to-1.

Leverage magnifies gains, but it also exaggerates losses. Using the same example, if your $78 million housing lost just 2 percent of its value (about $1.5 million) this would wipe you out! All of your $1 capital would be gone and you'd be bankrupt. A tiny loss has enormous consequences in the high leverage finance game.

FAIL SAFE

Why were banks and investors able to be so highly leveraged and to take what we now understand were such great risks? One reason is that they were allowed to because of holes in the regulatory structure. After the banking crises of the 1930s regulations were put in place to limit how much risk banks could take, a sensible reaction to the excesses that had helped trigger the Great Depression. The system was supposed to be Fail Safe, to repurpose an old Cold War term.[6] Banks were designed to have multiple safeguards in place, including minimum capital requirements, leverage controls, investment restrictions, and of course FDIC deposit insurance. Banks were supposed to be stable and a bit boring, but pretty safe. And the failure of one bank or even a few of them would not bring the system itself down.

But these regulations focused upon banks; that is, financial institutions that took in deposits and made loans. They did not contemplate the existence of institutions that were not banks (and so not regulated like banks) but provided some of the services of banks just the same. Investment banks, for example, raised money directly in the credit markets, using these funds to leverage their own capital to make huge purchases of mortgage-backed securities from "real" banks that effectively only made and serviced the initial loans. The advent of the un-der-regulated non-bank banking system (sometimes called the "shadow banking system") is one reason that the Fail Safe financial system of the 1930s failed.[7]

The existence of unregulated or less-regulated competitors put banks in the classic position of trying to compete on an uneven playing field. Regulators found themselves under pressure to restore equity not, as you might suppose, by finding a way to regulate non-bank banks more effectively, but instead by loosening the constraints on traditional banks. A regulatory race-to-the-bottom scenario unfolded, both within the U.S. and abroad.

There were not many concerns that the emerging financial structure would be any less Fail Safe than the one it replaced. The reasons for this confidence were both philosophical and practical. Market fundamental-ist belief always held that regulations stifled growth and innovation and made the system *less* safe, not more. There was widespread belief that financial engineering would make it possible for financial institutions to effectively assess risk and to manage it through new technologies and markets in increasingly sophisticated financial instruments.

There was also a strong sense that these large financial firms would not be allowed to fail in the unlikely situation that markets moved in the wrong direction. The belief was that they were TBTF and TCTF.

TBTF stands for "too big to fail"—that the big banks and non-bank banks were so large that their failure would bring down the entire fi-nancial system and with it the global economy. Someone—Fannie Mae, the Federal Reserve, the U.S. Treasury, the IMF—*someone* would step in and prevent a collapse.

TCTF stands for "too connected to fail" and it is the idea that the financial system had evolved in much the same way as your computer. Old mainframe computer systems of the 1960s evolved into desktop units that have now been integrated into highly diffused Internet-based "cloud computing" systems (think IBM then, Google docs now). Highly regulated banks were the financial version of the mainframe computer. Complex webs of financial transactions involving banks and non-bank banks are the networked replacement. The worldwide bank-ing web was enormously powerful, profitable, and convenient, but it exposed everyone to unfamiliar types of risk. One risk was that a large investment bank might be so connected to others (through complex financial markets and instruments) that a single failure could lead to a catastrophic cascade of bankruptcies and insolvencies. It was only logical, therefore, that a TCTF bank would not be allowed to fail. The cost of crashing the financial network was just too high.

Too big to fail, too connected to fail—really? Would anyone really rescue a failing financial institution on that basis? Well, that was the premise of the emergency rescue of Long Term Capital Management in 1998. It was believed that LTCM's losses—just a few billion dollars, small by the standards of today—could have produced the dreaded domino effect that might threaten the financial system as a whole. And so a rescue was arranged, conditioning expectations from that day forward.

JUST ADD MONEY (AND STIR)

All that was missing was money to complete the scenario for a perfect storm. Adding money to highly leveraged moral hazard, I tell my students, is like pouring gasoline on a forest fire. Boom! And the money came pouring in.[8]

It came from many sources. In the U.S. the Federal Reserve pumped money and credit into the financial system, initially to deal with the recession associated with the dot-com bust and then to finance economic expansion. The flow of funds continued so long as inflation remained low, which it did since soaring housing and stock prices do not directly affect the Consumer Price Index.

Money also came from all around the world. There was talk of a global "savings glut" centered in rapidly growing China. High savings rates in Asia and the Middle East were effectively transformed into mortgage-backed securities and other highly leveraged investments in the U.S., Europe, and elsewhere through the dynamic web of TBTF and TCTF financial firms. The global reach of the financial firms, combined with market-friendly policy reforms in emerging market countries, assured that the crash, when it came, would produce truly global contagion effects.

THE CRASH OF 2008

The crash—when it came—was both predictable and surprising. It was predictable that the housing bubble would eventually have to end. Stein's Law, named for presidential economic advisor Herbert Stein, holds that if something cannot go on forever, it will stop, and the housing boom was clearly unsustainable. What surprised most observers was how severe the reaction was—how deep into the economy the shock waves penetrated: beyond housing, beyond finance, deep to the core.[9]

The housing boom peaked in 2005 and prices began to decline somewhat, at least in the most speculative markets. Small price decreases would not have been enough to cause a crisis in the old-school banking world of George Bailey. George's customers were buying houses for their own use and had substantial home equity because of large down payments to absorb a price decrease. They would not easily have been dunked "under water," with a home value less than the remaining loan balance. At worst, George's bank would have negotiated some sort of interest or principal adjustment to cushion the blow and prevent default and especially foreclosure, which tends to drive prices down even further.

Things were different all around in 2005. Many recent home buyers had little equity, some borrowing more than 100 percent of the purchase price, so they quickly sank beneath the surface and had to face facts: better to stop payment and walk away than to continue with a $400,000 loan for a $350,000 (or less) house. Housing speculators, of course, were very highly leveraged and hit especially hard by falling prices. Some never expected actually to take ownership of properties, buying simply to resell in a few weeks or months at a higher price. For them, even a pause in the bubble's growth was a problem; falling prices were catastrophic.

As housing prices fell and mortgage payments slowed, the value of the mortgage-backed securities also fell, and many of their owners found themselves under water, too. Their highly leveraged investments paid huge profits when the market was headed up, but even a small, proportionate fall in value was enough to wipe out capital or force quick sale of both the mortgage securities themselves and other investments to cover the loses. A general collapse in financial markets began, with losses in one market causing fire sales in other markets and so cascading through the system.

Given that the initial housing price declines were relatively small, why didn't George Bailey III's bank just renegotiate the loans as

Granddad would have done? The simple reason is that, while Bailey III made the initial loan and probably continued to collect monthly payments, his bank didn't own the loan anymore. The ultimate ownership of the loan was now widely scattered around the globe among investors with pieces and slices of mortgage securities. There was no practical way to bring borrower and lender together to cut a new deal on a case-by-case basis as in the past. So the loans simply collapsed, damaging both sides severely.

YOU CAN'T UNSTIR A PUDDING

The policy response to the crisis was both heroic and pathetic. It was heroic in the sense of the bold moves and positions that government and central bank officials around the world took. It was pathetic in terms of the mistakes that were made and the strong sense at key moments that no one really knew what to do, what would work, what would be enough.

No one should be surprised that the reaction to the crisis was so chaotic and disorganized. There was and is great disagreement about the causes and effects of the crisis, so it isn't a surprise that consensus was hard to find. Even as the crisis unfolded some still believed that global finance was safe, safe as houses, while others saw the mess as the crisis of capitalism that Marx predicted so many years ago. Moderate views were criticized from both sides.

The problem, I argue, is one that the Tomasina character uncovered in the Tom Stoppard play *Arcadia*. Under the influence of Financial Globaloney, the world had stirred together three volatile elements: money, moral hazard, and leverage. Mixed together, these three ingredients exploded with devastating effect. The problem that policymakers faced while the crisis was raging is that, according to Tomasina, you can't unstir a pudding. That is, simply reversing the causes doesn't reverse the result.

Start with money. If money is the problem, why not cut the supply? The answer is that this makes the imperative to sell to cover losses even greater, and the crisis deepens. Any hint of falling liquidity from any source was met with the smell of fear and falling values. So it was important to keep the money flowing in.

What about moral hazard? The false belief that risk was on holiday was one root of the crisis, but would a sudden return of reality fix the problems its seeming disappearance caused? In the United States there was concern that bailing out big investment banks would both deepen this crisis and encourage the next one, so in September 2008 the decision was made to allow Lehman Brothers, a big, connected, highly leveraged investment bank, to fail. The stunned markets panicked and the crisis deepened. After Lehman Brothers it was clear that the system could not afford another collapse. The point about moral hazard having been made, policy-makers reversed course. Short-term stability was more important than making a stronger statement about the nature of risk.

Finally, there is leverage. Although it is possible to "unstir" leverage—deleveraging is the technical term—the process is necessarily contractionary. Moving from 20-to-1 leverage to 10-to-1 means a halving of demand for whatever products or assets you are buying. Deleveraging means tighter credit and shrinking markets. It *was* necessary to deleverage the financial markets to make them less dangerous (they were doing it themselves, of course, as the sell-off proceeded), but it was important to prevent the full damaging effects from striking the economy.

The solution was simple. As the private sector deleveraged and contracted, the public sector leveraged up to fill the gap. The public sector's version of leverage is public debt, where relatively small government assets (anticipated tax collections, central bank reserves) are magnified to provide more aid, spending, and credit through the use of borrowed funds, mainly from abroad. The contractionary effect on the economy is reduced as the leverage (and associated risk) is shifted from one part of the economic system to another.

The policy response to the crisis showed that even very smart women and men were unable to safely unstir the toxic pudding of money, moral hazard, and leverage. So they stirred it faster and harder, hoping to stir the danger away.

DEGLOBALIZATION

It *is* possible to unstir globalization—the process is called deglobalization—but it isn't a pretty thing to watch. Harold James wrote about how it happened in the 1930s in his fine 2001 book *The End of Globalization*, and the world of 2010 and beyond gets to watch the sequel from a front-row seat. When the final accounting is done, the Crash of 2008 will have a long list of consequences and deglobalization will undeniably be one of them. Many people thought that globalization itself was a rough and rugged process, with lots of losers to match the winners. Deglobalization is worse.[10]

The basic outlines of deglobalization were pretty clear even before the dust had settled from the Crash of 2008. The first effects were transmitted through the financial system. As banks, financial institutions, and credit markets in the U.S. and Europe found themselves under great stress they pulled in reserves from far and wide to try to strengthen their balance sheets. The credit crunch at home was therefore passed along to borrower countries, with particular focus on heavily indebted Eastern Europe and the Baltic countries. As investors sold Latvian lats and Hungarian forints to convert them back to dollars and euros, those currencies and the financial systems based upon them were subject to even more pressure.

The carry trade unwound. The carry trade is a type of international investment where you borrow money in countries where interest rates are low (Japan is a frequent choice) and lend or invest the funds in countries where interest rates are higher (Australia and Iceland were good choices in the boom years). Investors get high returns and the movement of funds drives down the Japanese yen and drives up the target country currencies like the Australian dollar as money is exchanged. Japan's export sector benefited from this pattern as a cheaper yen translated into lower prices for Japanese products abroad.

As the financial crisis unfolded, carry trade transactions needed to be reversed, or unwound, as they say in the business. The outflow of funds from Australia, Iceland, and other places pushed their financial systems and exchange rates close to the breaking point (and past it, in the case of Iceland). The surge of funds back to Japan drove up the yen, raising Japanese export prices abroad and dramatically cutting foreign sales. Globalization for Japan had been a system where the country sold products abroad and invested the resulting surplus in foreign markets, exporting goods and importing investment holdings. Both sides of the balance collapsed as deglobalization hit home.

The collapse of credit flows *between* countries mirrored what was happening *within* them. As credit disappeared (and, in some cases, the banks and financial institutions that had previously supplied them), the outlines of a deep economic decline were revealed. The economic system had learned to operate on cheap, secure credit lines. As access to credit dried up as investors searched for *real* security, business and consumer spending fell dramatically. Trade finance—loans to finance imports and exports—was particularly scarce and so the pace of international trade slowed as well.

Consumer spending fell as families adjusted to the effect of the stock market crash and housing price collapse on their wealth. Add this all together and you have a scene aptly captured by Paul Krugman's 1999 book, *The Return of Depression Economics*, which itself returned, in revised form, in December 2008.

Collapsing demand within countries translated into collapsing demand for imported products and, since my imports are your exports, substantial declines in international trade generally. The countries that were most heavily reliant on exports (Germany, Japan, China, and even India) were the worst affected.

Global businesses became keenly aware of counterparty risk, the risk that someone you have made a contract with cannot or will not honor the deal. Counterparty risk means that you might not get paid for your sale, you might not get the part you've been counting on, you might not get the loan you need, or you might not get the repayment you are due. Counterparty risk increases as economic transactions become more complex and as nations and businesses become more interdependent. The globalization boom was fueled in part by the idea that technological advances made interdependence more secure because more information about business partners and markets was instantly available. The real nature of counterparty risk was revealed as globalization collapsed and the benefits of interdependence, in complex commodity chains for example, were stripped away to reveal hidden dangers.

All that was left to make deglobalization complete was economic nationalism—"beggar thy neighbor" protectionist policies, and these did appear, although not in the extreme forms of the 1930s. In the U.S., for example, newly elected President Obama's initial proposals for "Buy American" policies were met with harsh criticism from foreign leaders. A later Chinese proposal to favor that country's home producers drew frightened responses from trade officials around the world. The most overt forms of protectionism were avoided, but the fear of a trade war remained and this concern alone was enough to limit new international initiatives.

LESSONS OF THE CRASH OF 2008

The Crash of 2008 and its aftermath provide the raw material for many lesson lists and there will inevitably be years of debate about which set of conclusions is correct. Some will argue that the Crash shows the resilience of finance capitalism—its ability to rebound quite quickly from a severe global blow. Others will take the opposite view, arguing that Marx and Lenin were right and capitalism is fatally flawed.

My lesson list avoids either of these extremes and focuses on the role of globaloney in the crisis. As I have argued in these chapters, Financial Globaloney, the belief that financial markets are fundamentally safe—safe as the houses that were at the center of the crash—was a strong contributing factor both to the expansion of globalization and its recent collapse. Financial Globaloney encouraged risk taking by making it seem as if those risks simply did not exist. Remove risk, add leverage, and shake with lots and lots of money and you have the recipe for financial crisis, economic collapse and deglobalization.

When globalization returns we will need to have something to replace Financial Globaloney—a new set of stories and beliefs that encourages us to take the risks of global markets seriously. Feasible, sustainable globalization is possible, but not in its current form. We need new economic and political arrangements and new stories to guide us in constructing them. Financial Globaloney needs to go, but that won't be enough. Golden Arches Globaloney is part of the problem too, as I'll explain in the next chapter.

CHAPTER 4

GOLDEN ARCHES GLOBALONEY

Who invented globalization? The way you answer this question depends on how you think about globalization. If you think of globalization *literally* you might answer "Christopher Columbus" or someone else from the great era of (European) discovery. If you want to know who "invented" the world as a single geographic unit, all connected to the European center, there are several names you might give, but Columbus is as good as any of them.

If you think of globalization as the *idea* of an economic *process* that unites and transforms the world, creating a single global system, the inventors' names are Karl Marx and Friedrich Engels. They said it all in

The Communist Manifesto, first published in that great year of revolutions, 1848. The bourgeoisie, Marx and Engels wrote,

> has through its exploitation of the world market given a cosmopolitan character to production and consumption in every country. . . . In place of the old wants, satisfied by the productions of the country, we find new wants, requiring for their satisfaction the products of distant lands and climes. In place of the old local and national seclusion and self-sufficiency, we have intercourse in every direction, universal interdependence of nations. And as in material, so also in intellectual production. The intellectual creations of individual nations become common property. National one-sidedness and narrow-mindedness become more and more impossible, and from the numerous national and local literatures, there arises a world literature.[1]

Marx and Engels were writing about capitalism, of course, but they were really describing globalization in this passage. Like many visions of globalization, theirs was rooted in technology. The bourgeoisie, which we may think of as the masters of globalization, "by the rapid improvement of all instruments of production, by the immensely facilitated means of communication, draws all nations, even the most barbarian, into civilization."[2] Resistance is futile; globalization "compels all nations, on pain of extinction, to adopt the bourgeois mode of production; it compels them to introduce what it calls civilization into their midst, i.e., to become bourgeois themselves. In a word, it creates a world after its own image."[3]

Marx and Engels provide us with an analysis of the process of economic globalization that might have been written yesterday. Indeed, someone somewhere probably did write it yesterday, or something much like it, totally unaware of Marx's prior claim to the idea.

Marx wrote about globalization, but he didn't call it that. The term *globalization* (or *globalisation* if you are British) seems to have come into use in the 1960s, according to the *Oxford English Dictionary*. Many people credit the Harvard political economist Raymond Vernon for inventing the concept, even if he did not actually coin the term. Vernon was famous for two things. The first was his pathbreaking research on multinational corporations from the 1970s to the 1990s, which made him the "father of globalization," according to Daniel Yergin.[4] His second great achievement? The Peanut M&M, which he brought to market in the 1950s while working for the Mars candy company.

BIG MACS, FRIES, AND GLOBALONEY

There is one product that is so closely associated with globalization that it has become a symbol for the process that Columbus got started, Marx and Engels described, and Raymond Vernon studied. According to popular accounts, globalization was invented, more or less, by two brothers named Richard and Maurice when they opened a tiny drive-through restaurant in Pasadena, California, in 1937 and named it after themselves. Surely you have heard of "Richard and Maurice's"? No? Of course not; why choose an awkward name like that when your last name is McDonald? Perhaps you've heard of that? In 1940 they opened a larger operation—six hundred square feet!—in San Bernardino.[5]

McDonald's. To some it means cheap, tasty, fast food. Others see a darker side—colorful clown characters luring innocent children into a salty, fat-filled nutritional wasteland. McDonald's, people say, is where you go for standardized, homogenized, corporate-branded food products including such delicious fare as the McSkillet Burrito with Sausage, Chipotle BBQ Snack Wrap, McRib sandwich, and of course Big Macs, Chicken McNuggets, Egg McMuffins, fries, shakes, and Coke. Everyone knows McDonald's; almost everyone has eaten at one—we all have our opinions. What's yours?

People who tell stories about globalization almost inevitably find themselves using McDonald's to explain what they mean. If globalization is McDonald's then it is simple, everywhere the same, and utterly American. And the global expansion of fast food in general, even if it is not McDonald's, is a metaphor for the transformation of the world into America's image.

But that's globaloney—Golden Arches Globaloney. The world—even the fast food part of the world—is really a much more diverse and interesting place than the McDonald's metaphor suggests. To deny this diversity (even in its defense) is to destroy it and to disguise the real significance of McDonald's for the future of globalization. To understand Golden Arches Globaloney and why it is important we have to go back, way back. Back to Richard and Maurice McDonald and their great invention.

ADAM SMITH MEETS RONALD MCDONALD

The McDonald brothers did not invent hamburgers. In fact, their first store didn't even sell hamburgers—hot dogs and milkshakes were its specialties. Burgers were introduced in San Bernardino, but the McDonald's innovation wasn't putting meat on a bun, it was turning bread and meat into dough—profits, that is. Drive-in restaurants like McDonald's were caught in a profit pinch, selling low-priced food using traditional methods, which were labor-intensive and expensive. The brothers' contribution to globalization was their decision to rationalize the food production process. They stripped down their twenty-five-item menu to its core—hamburgers accounted for 80 percent of their sales—even though this meant dismantling their authentic hickory-fired pit barbeque. They closed shop for three months in 1948 and remodeled the whole operation to be fast and efficient. Eventually the McDonalds designed new types of kitchen equipment for their maximum-efficiency operations.

McDonald's reopened with a product that was cheap but standardized. The old thirty-cent burger now sold for half that amount, but it came just one way. "If we gave people a choice there would be chaos," Richard McDonald said.[6] They were not an immediate hit, but eventually speed, consistency, and low price found a market.

The secret to the McDonalds' success was their mastery of Adam Smith's famous division of labor. In a traditional drive-in restaurant, one or two chefs might make the food from start to finish and sometimes they would serve customers, too. The McDonald's system applied the division of labor: three countermen took orders at two windows and issued orders to the production crew: three grill men, two shake men, two fry men, and "dressers" who assembled and added condiments to the hamburgers. They could take and fill an order in thirty seconds—or less.[7]

Today McDonald's is a multinational corporation that operates (in association with 5000 franchisees) 32,000 restaurants employing 1.5 million workers in 118 countries to serve 58 million customers each day. Its flagship product, the Big Mac, is so nearly universal that the *Economist* magazine uses it to calculate the relative purchasing power of foreign currencies.[8] Some people love McDonald's and others hate it. In the 1990s McDonald's became the defining symbol of globalization. No McDonald's store is a safe harbor during an antiglobalization protest.

The place of McDonald's in the center of the globalization debate is due mainly to the work of three men: Thomas Friedman, Benjamin Barber, and George Ritzer. All three use McDonald's and its ubiquitous Golden Arches as an icon or metaphor for the transformative force of contemporary globalization. Two of their versions of globalization-McDonaldization are globaloney pure and simple. One offers real insight into what globalization is today and where it may be headed. None of the three tells the whole story.

GOLDEN ARCHES: THE GOOD GLOBALIZATION

New York Times columnist Thomas L. Friedman is a globalization optimist who uses McDonald's to motivate a hopeful American vision of globalization past, present, and future. Friedman's idea of McDonald's and globalization is a distinctly American view, one that only an American who constantly travels abroad might naturally develop. McDonald's appears with nearly numbing regularity in Friedman's book *The Lexus and the Olive Tree* (as it does in many books on globalization). The entry for McDonald's in the index looks like this:

> McDonald's, ix, 9, 169, 248–254, 258, 263, 268, 271, 274, 292, 294, 296, 301, 303, 305, 311–13, 344, 358, 374, 379, 382–84, 464 [9]

Why so much McDonald's? Probably because it is such a useful rhetorical device—McDonald's is an instantly recognizable symbol of America to Friedman's readers, who are mainly Americans living in America. Frame a foreign problem in terms of McDonald's and your audience connects the dots immediately. But it is probably also true that Friedman, like many Americans who spend months and months abroad, is always looking for reminders of home. And since his home is the United States, his eyes search for branded goods, which are the way Americans think of things: not hamburgers, Big Macs. Not beer, Budweiser. Not soft drinks, Coca-Cola. And McDonald's has more than thirty thousand locations that display their trademark logos and designs, of which more than seventeen thousand are located outside the United States.

McDonald's is easy to spot—the company goes out of its way to be visible. And it is almost everywhere. McDonald's says that in 2002 its global restaurant system was arrayed across the world map as follows: United States, 13,491; Europe, 6,070; APMEA (Asia-Pacific, Middle East, and Africa), 7,555; Latin America, 1,605; and Canada, 1,304. The top five countries, ranked by numbers of stores, were the United States, Japan, Canada, the United Kingdom, and Germany.[10] So it is easy to understand why Thomas Friedman so often sees the Golden Arches in his travels and has a quiet little "globalization moment."

Looking at the world and seeing Golden Arches is a distinctly American kind of vision. It's not obvious that other people see globalization the same way. Imagine for a moment an Italian version of Thomas Friedman—call him Tomaso. For Tomaso, McDonald's restaurants are all but invisible. They are everywhere, you run into them all the time on the way to the airport, but they disappear into the visual noise of the background. They are unimportant because they are not what Tomaso is looking for, which is decent Italian food. Tomaso is looking for signs of home—good Italian restaurants—and he sees them everywhere. They are even more ubiquitous, if that's grammatically possible, than McDonald's. According to the Italian culinary magazine *Gambero Rosso*, there are about twice as many reasonably authentic Italian restaurants *outside of Italy* as there are McDonald's restaurants *in all the world*, including the United States.[11] So it's not hard to see them if that's what you are looking for.

Gambero Rosso estimates that there are about 15,000 decent Italian restaurants in the United States and Canada, which is about the number of McDonald's you will find there. Japan has more than 3,500 McDonald's and only about 2,000 Italian restaurants (both numbers insignificant, of course, compared to the number of Japanese food shops there). *Gambero Rosso* puts the number of Italian restaurants in Latin America at 7,000; in Africa at 1,000; in the Middle East, 300; and more than 28,000 in the European Union and Eastern Europe. McDonald's numbers are much fewer in each of these regions and especially in Africa, where McDonald's is all but unknown (except via satellite television commercials).

Except in Japan, Italian restaurants seem to be far more common than McDonald's stores. Surely you have seen Italian restaurants wherever you have traveled in the world? Yes, but you have not taken account of them the way that Tomaso Friedman would. Why is that? Branding is part of the story. McDonald's stores all have the same name, use versions of the same trademarked logo, and serve somewhat similar food items, so it is easy to use them to connect the dots that form a global pattern. McDonald's franchises are everywhere—must be globalization. But Italian restaurants have a stronger claim to globalization, even though their visual variety makes them blend into the background to American eyes. If Tomaso Friedman were writing a book about globalization, he would be having tagliatelle al ragù moments (not Big Mac attacks) and seeing Italian influences everywhere. It would be a different book, but it would be just as valid as Thomas Friedman's.[12]

Tommy Friedman's book (Tommy is British) would be filled with examples of British influence abroad, and he would have no trouble finding it, let me tell you. The legacy of Britain's global empire guarantees that Tommy would constantly encounter familiar people, places, and things, including the food. He'd run into Britain's signature fast food everywhere he went and build clever global metaphors from the experience. Do you doubt it? No, I am not thinking of fish and chips or bangers and mash or bubble and squeak, as you might assume. Britain's fast food of choice is "curry"—Indian food. Curry is the most popular food in Britain. Britain has taken Indian curry to its heart much as Americans have adopted hamburgers and hot dogs (frankfurters)—food with Germanic origins obvious to anyone who thinks even for a moment about their names (Hamburg, Frankfurt). The global Indian diaspora practically guarantees that Tommy Friedman would be able to find a familiar plate of chicken tikka masala nearly everywhere he goes.[13]

For my money, Tao Friedman would write the most interesting book. I probably do not have to persuade you that Tao, who is Chinese, would be able to find familiar home-style dishes wherever she goes, and the experience would raise important questions for her about Chinese influence abroad and about globalization's effect on China.[14] Are traditional recipes and preparations preserved in foreign Chinese restaurants, or are they adapted to local tastes and ingredients? Is "authenticity" preserved? Are culinary norms maintained—or are they lost forever as regional Chinese cuisine is melded into international "fusion" foods? Tao Friedman is a fictional invention, but there are real scholars who study these questions and publish volumes with titles like *The Globalization of Chinese Food*.[15]

Thomas, Tomaso, Tommy, and Tao constantly encounter images of home as they travel the world, and they associate them with their particular visions of globalization. Their reactions to what they find are likely to differ, however, because, although they see the same world, they process the images through different cultural filters, which yield predictably different conclusions. Thomas assumes that the fast food he finds abroad is the same as at home and takes comfort from that.[16] But he's wrong. In fact, McDonald's menus are not all the same, although they tend to be as similar as local markets will allow. McDonald's tries to have each location carry some of the "classic" American items, but please remember that McDonald's really isn't about particular foods, although that's what the branding process leads you to believe. What made the original McDonald's distinctive was price and efficiency, and this is still true today.

McDonald's must compete with local retailers wherever it operates (and with local Italian, Indian, and Chinese restaurants), so its restaurants necessarily adapt to local tastes in terms of food recipes and preparations—only the efficiency remains the same. After trying and failing to sell all-beef burgers in India, a country where the majority of the population considers cows sacred, McDonald's now has a 100 percent vegetarian menu in Hindu regions, featuring items such as Pizza McPuff, the McAloo Tikki spiced potato sandwich, Paneer (Indian cheese) Salsa McWrap, and McCurry.[17] Because Chinese food is popular in India, there is even a vegetarian Crispy Chinese burger. McDonald's menus in most other countries have not adapted to local taste to quite this degree, but all show the combined influence of local preferences and competition from local restaurants that know those preferences well. Interestingly, some Indian items have been earmarked for introduction in China, Hong Kong, Great Britain, and the United States.[18] That's globalization, I guess.

The world has become a culturally complex space, both in terms of food and more generally. As Tyler Cowen has noted, as local areas become more diverse (with more kinds of ethnic foods, for example), the discontinuities between places fade and the world as a whole feels less diverse.[19] What each of us makes of this depends on how we approach it. People who love America will see it and smile. People who hate America will see it and scowl. People who look for Italy or India or China will find them, too. Thomas Friedman's perspective, with McDonald's everywhere, is that of an American looking for America and finding it.

This is what makes Thomas Friedman's version of McWorld a globaloney theory. It presents as universal a view of the world that is strictly American, using American symbols to tell an American story. I call it the Good Globalization because it is an optimistic viewpoint. Friedman can at least appreciate why people would be happy to embrace the image of McDonald's and globalization that he creates.

McWORLD: GLOBALIZATION GONE BAD

McWorld is perhaps the most powerful image of globalization yet conceived. Significantly, it is a very negative image. Thomas Friedman's optimism aside, McDonald's has an image problem. If you want to express your informed disrespect for anything that the masses seem to enjoy, the best way is to make it a Mc, as in McMansions (suburban housing), McDoctors (HMO health-care providers), McWine (wine that lacks distinctive character), and volumes like this one (McBooks). Mass-produced, interchangeable, undistinguished—crap—that's what a Mc-prefix says.

So you don't need much imagination to guess that McWorld is a description of globalization gone bad. Benjamin R. Barber invented McWorld in a 1992 *Atlantic Monthly* article titled "Jihad vs. McWorld."[20] The article inspired a 1995 book, also called *Jihad vs. McWorld*, with the subtitle, "How the World Is Both Falling Apart and Coming Together—And What This Means for Democracy." A paperback edition appeared in 1996 with a different subtitle, "How Globalism and Tribalism Are Re-shaping the World," and a revised volume was released in 2002, subtitled "Terrorism's Challenge to Democracy."[21] McWorld is a flexible concept, apparently, equally relevant to the collapse of communism in 1995, the rise of ethnic violence in 1996, and terrorism after September 11, 2001.

I fear that Barber's McWorld has become a McIdea—an undistinguished product cynically crafted to appeal to an undiscriminating mass-market audience, which is a shame. The migration of titles gives it away: Barber's publisher seems to be trying to sell the book by appealing to the market's "fear du jour"—tribalism, terrorism, whatever. Barber's core *argument* is not crap, however, and it is worthwhile to separate the two and appreciate their differences.

Barber believes that globalization is a threat to democracy, which is a legitimate concern (the book's title should be *Globalization versus Democracy*, not *Jihad vs. McWorld*). The argument is that globalization twists the world in two ways at once. On one side it bends the world toward markets and business, which tend to organize along certain lines, guided by the ideology of globalism. This is McWorld, an America-centered, media-driven version of global capitalism. I don't even have to tell you what McWorld looks like—it is McDonald's and the culture, media, technology, and values that critics associate with it.

At the same time the world is twisting toward McWorld, however, it is also turning toward Jihad. Globalization magnifies ethnic, religious, and racial divisions, producing Jihad. Jihad is not literally an Islamic holy war in Barber's lexicon any more than McWorld is literally the global McDonald's empire. Barber doesn't intend to pick on Muslims when talking about "Jihad," and he is very careful in this regard in the book's text. Unfortunately the regrettable image of an apparently Muslim woman in full head-scarf holding a Pepsi can on the cover strongly reinforces at every glance the very Islamic Jihad connection that Barber says he wants to avoid.[22] Jihad, properly understood in Barber's argument, is the reaction to or retreat from globalization and back toward the security of tradition, religion, and tribe or nation.

Now the problem, Barber says, is that both Jihad and McWorld are essentially undemocratic and perhaps even antidemocratic. Therefore this global torsion is a threat to democracy. Jihad places tradition or religious teachings ahead of popular opinion and legitimizes autocratic rule. Hard to grow democracy on that rocky field. McWorld privileges money over people, replacing one-person, one-vote with one-dollar, one-vote. As market fundamentalist policies shrink the state and market forces expand, democracy becomes at best a meaningless ritual and potentially a threat to global competition. If the world disintegrates into Jihad and McWorld, Barber asks, what chance is there for democracy?

The future of democracy in a globalized world is a very important question, although I must point out that is a distinctly American question. Worship of democracy is America's civil religion—we are raised from the ground up to view the United States as a nation built upon democratic principles and to honor the Founding Fathers who symbolize a commitment to democratic ideals. A European might ask a different question, such as whether Jihad and McWorld are consistent with peace, not democracy. Americans, I believe, simply assume that democracy produces peace. Europeans worry that it might not. Others might be concerned with inequality, economic development, or environmental sustainability—there are many critical values potentially threatened by globalization. To privilege democracy in the pantheon of principles is not unreasonable, and I would probably do it myself, but we must recognize that it is a distinctly American thing to do.

Benjamin Barber is someone who takes democracy seriously. No wonder he is worried about it. Jihad and McWorld are not the only threats to democracy, however, nor perhaps even the most important threats. Jihad and McWorld are sexy concepts that quickly focus our attention on democracy and its discontents, and I think that's why Barber wrote the original *Atlantic Monthly* article. In a world where people don't worry very much about democracy, Jihad and McWorld made a lot of people think about it more seriously, which is a good thing. The book that packages the argument is another matter. In order to gather sympathy and support for democracy, Barber seems to try to make McWorld and globalization as evil as possible—a force that destroys not only democracy, but everything else of value in modern and traditional societies, too. This is where the globaloney comes in.

If you read it uncritically, *Jihad vs. McWorld* is very persuasive—nearly as persuasive as Adam Smith's argument in the first chapter of *The Wealth of Nations*. Like Smith, Barber uses the "Newtonian" principle of the New Rhetoric—he states a grand principle, provides a few memorable and well-chosen examples, then leaps to a universal conclusion. The readers, you and me, are pleased to connect the dots. Soon we see examples of the argument all around us and we notice that they fit the rule even as we ignore everything that breaks it. Thus does unscientific observation make believers of us all.

Democracy has lots of problems, as I have said, and globalization is probably one of them, but it is not the only one nor perhaps even the most important one. And many people (ask Thomas Friedman) think that markets might even promote democracy by undermining undemocratic authority. So I am suspicious that the threat to democracy is as simple as this, or that saving it is just a matter of stopping globalization.

One of the best ways to understand why McWorld is more about globaloney than globalization is to look at what it has to say about its most representative component: McDonald's. McWorld is named for McDonald's, of course, and the Golden Arches show up almost as regularly in *Jihad vs. McWorld* as in *The Lexus and the Olive Tree*.[23] Here's the story, pieced together from Barber's book.

- McDonald's (and McWorld) stands astride the globe like a Colossus, more powerful than modern nation-states. "McDonald's serves 20 million customers around the world every day," Barber tells us, "drawing more customers daily than there are people in Greece, Ireland and Switzerland together."[24]
- McDonald's ideology is more powerful than even the great revolutionary thinkers. "The McDonald's way of eating is a way of life: an ideology as theme park more intrusive (if much more subtle) than any Marx or Mao ever contrived."[25]
- McDonald's is the vanguard of global capitalism. "Following McDonald's golden arch from country to country, the market traces a trajectory of dollars and bonds and ads and yen and stocks and currency transactions that reaches right around the globe."[26]
- Resistance is futile. "We have seen . . . how McDonald's 'adapts' to foreign climes with wine in France and local beef in Russia even as it imposes a way of life that makes domestic wines and local beef irrelevant."[27]
- We have sold our souls to McWorld . . . "When McDonald's sells *Dances with Wolves* and *Jurassic Park* videos with sundry movie tie-ins in a vague celebration of multiculturalism or environmentalism or extinct reptile preservation, or hires Michael Jordan to link its products to celebrity sport, simple service to the body . . . is displaced by complex service to the soul."[28]
- . . . and destroyed democracy in the process. "If the traditional conservators of freedom were democratic constitutions and Bills of Rights, 'the new temples of liberty . . . will be McDonald's and Kentucky Fried Chicken.'"[29]
- And if you think otherwise, you are just wrong. "There are stylistic differences between McDonald's in Moscow, in Budapest, in Paris and in London by which they all can be distinguished from the first McDonald's," Barber says. "But squint a little and all the small differences vanish and the Golden Arch is all that remains, a virtual ghost haunting our retinas even on Champs

Élyseés in Paris, where the actual display is no longer permitted.
. . . [The] 'world where there is only one image' has already come
to pass."[30]

What is wrong with this argument? Well, you already know. Almost
everything.

McDonald's has more customers than whole nations have citizens?
That's comparing apples and oranges. It is wrong to compare lunch
counters with nation-states—unless you think that national citizenship
is the patriotic equivalent of pulling into a restaurant's drive-through
line.[31]

McDonald's has a more subtle and intrusive ideology than Marx or
Mao? Doubtful, although I see Barber's point and expand upon it in
the next section. This seems overblown, however. I wonder how many
people have gone to their deaths with the words "Big Mac" on their
lips? Some, probably, but nothing compared with the effect of Marx
and Mao.

McDonald's is the Trojan horse for global capitalism, clearing the
way for bond markets and advertising agencies? Sorry, but McDonald's
is a business, not an economic evangelical organization. McDonald's
comes in *after* the property rights, legal institutions, markets structures, ads, and money, not before. McDonald's needs those things to
survive.[32]

McDonald's *imposes* a way of life that makes local products irrelevant? That's strong language, and strong language invites abuse. To
impose a way of life is to take away choice, but it seems to me that
McDonald's actually does the opposite. I don't see how McDonald's
imposes anything. I suppose there is one case: if you believe that people
should have no options and make no choices, then adding McDonald's
does change everything—it *imposes* the necessity to choose. It seems
to me that an argument rooted in a concern about democracy ought
to lean on the side of the right to choose—the McDonald's side—not
against it, even if the choices made are sometimes poor ones.

McDonald's customers are seeking a soulful experience, not just
a quick meal? Yes, I agree, but so what? We shouldn't be surprised
that the people who eat at McDonald's think about their meals as
more than just food. "Unlike other species," anthropologist Sidney
W. Mintz notes, "human beings invest their food with secondary

meanings that transcend nourishment. We eat to live, yes, but hardly ever *only* to live."[33]

"Temples of Liberty?" Is it even possible to compare McDonald's to the Bill of Rights? And the final straw—if you see anything that seems to contradict this argument, just squint and it will go away. This lacks the elegance of Adam Smith's solution to the problem of inconvenient counterexamples. Smith would have covered his tracks like this: "What is true of a single McDonald's cannot be false about the entire system, so tightly 'twined are branch and root, and what is true about McDonald's cannot be false about McWorld, its logical extension."

Benjamin Barber's argument about democracy deserves better than this. You don't need to use globaloney to argue his point about democracy and the forces that threaten it. That globaloney is useful, however, is clear because it covers over the fundamental flaw in *Jihad vs. McWorld*: that it is, like Friedman's argument, an argument about America, not the world. It is based upon American values and is concerned, ultimately, that America is not true to its uniquely American principles.

One particular problem with the McWorld scenario is its reliance on the power of the media, especially the electronic media—Barber calls it the "infotainment telesector." The working assumption seems to be that this sector has such power over people that it is virtually irresistible. Once the infotainment telesector has local consumers in its crosshairs, indigenous culture is dead meat. And, of course, it is under the command of American multinationals like McDonald's.

There are several reasons to doubt that the world really works this way and to believe that the infotainment telesector is globaloney. The first is that many multinational firms fail to penetrate foreign markets even with the help of their evil media persuaders. Even the McDonald's record is blemished.[34] These failures are invisible, of course, because they have failed and so disappeared. You only see the success stories, so that's what is reinforced. The failures can be found, however, in MBA case-study books.[35]

McWorld believes that foreign consumers cannot resist these forces—it denies them agency and assumes that, absent media coercion, their own cultures would remain permanently fixed. They indiscriminately absorb the products and values that are pushed in their direction. This is a sad view of humanity, which is sadder still because it may be based on the belief that this is true about American consumers, too. If people are really such hollow vessels as this, then it is unclear why we should care about them. The world would be better off without them. We should fill them with large orders of fries until they explode!

But when you look closely at these people, they are not at all like their globaloney image. A group of anthropologists examined McDonald's customers in Asia, for example, and what they discovered didn't bear much resemblance to McWorld. The results were published in a fascinating 1997 book called *Golden Arches East: McDonald's in East Asia*.[36] The authors studied how McDonald's customers related to the products and brands and to each other over time and compared results across countries. Here is a small smattering of their findings.

McDonald's has enabled (*imposed* is too strong a term) small changes in foreign cultures. In Japan, for example, few people ate food with their hands before McDonald's came along.[37] McDonald's and other fast-food stores are displacing local "street foods" to a certain extent, but research indicates that this is due in part to greater concern, especially by parents, over sanitation and food safety. As incomes rise, these factors become more important and restaurants with better sanitation gain market share.

On the other hand, there are many examples of how local consumers have transformed McDonald's, shaping it to play particular roles in their societies. In Beijing, Seoul, and Taipei, for example, many people use McDonald's as a refuge from urban chaos. Middle school students in Hong Kong hang out at McDonald's for hours, talking and doing homework. Both of these uses are diametrically opposite to the McDonald's system, which stresses efficient production and consumption of food, "turning" tables over to new customers every few minutes.[38] "Suffice it to note here," James L. Watson says, "that McDonald's does not always call the shots."[39]

McDonald's is given many meanings by its patrons, who seem to have the ability to do this (they are not *all* empty vessels, it seems). Some women in East Asia, for example, seem to use McDonald's stores as a "sanctuary" from male domination. As the multigeneration nuclear family has disintegrated into separate households, McDonald's has become a gathering place where children and grandchildren are especially celebrated. (McDonald's plays this role in the United States, too.)[40] McDonald's is the home of "conspicuous consumption" for some, who flaunt their wealth and foreign tastes, but it is also a great leveler. Low prices and restricted menu choice mean that everyone eats about the same food and pays about the same amounts, so no one is likely to "lose face" in McDonald's. Eating a Big Mac can even be a political statement. In Taiwan, for example, the choice of McDonald's (versus a restaurant owned by a mainland Chinese family) makes a statement about independence from mainland influence.

McDonald's in East Asia doesn't seem to be very much like McWorld. But maybe it was a bad idea to use McDonald's as a model for McWorld. McDonald's may be much more local than most multinational firms. McDonald's restaurants in East Asia are at least partly owned by local firms and families; they are run by local managers and staffed by local people. They mainly buy their supplies from local businesses. A good deal of their profits stay at home, too, and are reinvested. As already noted, local food tastes and dining habits are accommodated, at least in part, within the overall burger and fries framework. It's ironic, but McDonald's might be one of the worst examples of the McWorld model—if McWorld were really about the world and not, at its core, a commentary on the United States.

But is McWorld even a true representation of America? If we use McDonald's as our analytical guide, I believe the answer is probably no. I really don't believe that a big media push—the dreaded infotainment telesector—accounts for McDonald's success even in the United States. In support of my position I cite evidence on obesity in the United States. The fact that Americans are gaining weight quite rapidly is well known and often associated with fast-food consumption. McWorld is McFat. The same infotainment telesector forces that push McWorld down our throats are to be blamed, it is said, for our McFat. It's not just the same principle, it is literally the same thing.

Harvard economists David M. Cuttler, Edward L. Glaeser, and Jesse M. Shapiro have asked the question, "Why Have Americans Become More Obese," and their findings are indeed revealing.[41] They test a number of hypotheses using data for the United States and other countries. They conclude that the best single explanation of rising obesity is that technological change—increased efficiency—has reduced the cost of food in terms of both the money it takes to buy it and the time it takes to prepare and consume it. Time and money are the two main constraints upon economic behavior. Fast food is both fast (time) and cheap (money)—and has only become faster and cheaper over the years. No wonder there has been a shift in favor of such products as their relative prices have fallen.[42]

Now, what is most interesting to me about these findings is that they point *away* from clever marketing and media power as the driving forces behind McFat, McDonald's and, by extension, McWorld and instead highlight the principle that the McDonald brothers recognized in their little San Bernardino store: efficiency, technology, and the division of labor. Cheaper. Faster. More. To understand the implications of this fact, we need to leave McWorld behind and move on to a simpler, but far scarier, vision of globalization.

RATIONALIZATION: THE UGLY GLOBALIZATION

Capitalism's tendency to reward and therefore promote efficiency is well known. It is the secret behind Adam Smith's pin factory and invisible hand. For Marx and Engels, it is the force that enables global capitalism to transform foreign countries, not simply penetrate them. Capitalism's drive for greater and greater efficiency causes it to do for society in general what it did for Adam Smith's pin factory in particular: break it down into basic components and reassemble it in the most starkly efficient fashion. There is not much harm done (and much benefit produced) when the division of labor is applied to the manufacture of pins. The stakes are higher when whole societies are involved, as some have suggested. *This*, not the superficial influence of advertising and electronic media, is the truly ugly side of globalization.

Efficiency, and the process of rational calculation that is necessary to achieve it, reaches its zenith inside a McDonald's restaurant. The American sociologist George Ritzer observed this fact in his 1993 book, *The McDonaldization of Society: An Investigation into the Changing Character of Social Life*.[43] If you make even a casual study of a McDonald's restaurant you will see Ritzer's point. McDonald's makes efficiency the top-most goal and consciously organizes its assembly line accordingly. This is not news, of course, since the McDonald brothers began doing this way back in the 1950s, even before they sold their name and business to Ray Kroc. What is interesting, however, is how McDonald's has managed to rationalize both sides of the counter. This is where Ritzer comes in.

It is easy to see the production side of McDonald's efficiency. Specialized technology and a highly organized division of labor produce standardized menu items quickly and efficiently. Service may not be quite as fast as in the San Bernardino store, where orders were filled in thirty seconds, but the menu is much larger and competitive factors have forced McDonald's to permit customers to make some special orders. All in all, it is a highly structured, very efficient production line for food of reliably consistent quality and relatively low price.

What may be more significant, however, is how McDonald's has transformed the way that its customers behave. In traditional restaurants, customers are relatively passive participants in the food service operation. They arrive, are seated, and given menus. Wait staff deliver water and other beverages, take the order and deliver it, assuring that everything is exactly as requested. Staff typically check on the customers at several points during the meal, which may be multicourse and require changes in cutlery, glassware, and so forth. Finally, the bill is delivered and paid, change given, and table cleared and reset before it can be turned over to the next group of customers.

Compare this to a typical fast-food experience. Customers arrive and stand in line to give their orders at the counter, choosing from the standard items listed on the backlit overhead display. The order is given, payment made, and the customer waits for the food to arrive at the counter. (In fast food, customers, not staff, do the waiting.) The customer gets her own condiments and eating utensils, fills her own cup, finds her own table, and then clears it when finished. Customers do much of the work of running the restaurant, work that would otherwise be performed by paid staff. (Over at the drive-through window, customers are actually making their own home and office deliveries!) And they do this work rapidly, efficiently, and without apparent displeasure. Actually, McDonald's customers don't seem to be aware that they are doing the restaurant's work; they just go through the paces automatically. The miracle of the modern McDonald's is that its customers work for the firm but draw no wages. The experience of cooking a meal and eating it is thus transformed from an art to a highly engineered, precisely coordinated production process.

McDonald's is an excellent example of the process that the great German sociologist Max Weber (1864–1920) called "formal rationalization." According to Weber, Ritzer explains, "*formal rationality* means that the search by people for the optimum means to a given end is shaped by rules, regulations, and larger social structures. Individuals are not left to their own devices in searching for the best possible means of attaining a given objective. Weber identified this type of rationality as a major development in the history of the world."[44] Weber's analysis of formal rationalization focused on bureaucracy as an institution that organized a certain segment of society to achieve certain goals quickly and efficiently. A successful bureaucracy is able to process large numbers of people relatively quickly and in a highly predictable manner. Individual variations are tightly controlled, with rules and regulations generally relied upon rather than variable (and therefore unreliable) human judgment within a tightly defined division of labor. There are few "surprises," especially unpleasant ones.

A successful visit to a modern health maintenance organization clinic illustrates a bureaucracy at work. The division of labor, both within offices and among specialties, is obvious. The steps of making appointments, gathering information, making diagnoses, planning treatment, performing tests, filling prescriptions, and so on, are all discrete and handled by specialists. Information technology is used to share information and coordinate the stages. The patient (you) moves efficiently through the production line, through various locations, until you are discharged, instructions in hand, into the parking garage. The term *patient* is well chosen because, as in the fast-food restaurant, the customer does all of the waiting, while the assembly-line workers are kept in constant, efficient motion. Other public and private bureaucracies, including income taxation and pension and insurance systems, work much the same way.

George Ritzer gave the name *McDonaldization* to the way that formal rationalization organizes contemporary society, especially in the United States, I think. McDonaldization is characterized by efficiency, calculability, predictability, and the use of technology to control human behavior. McDonaldization is not about McDonald's, Ritzer says; it is about the transforming force of rationalization.[45] Rationalization has many advantages, Ritzer notes.[46] More goods and services can be made available to a larger segment of the population with greater convenience with respect to time and place. Lower cost increases affordability. Workers and customers alike confront a standardized process that is therefore stable and familiar. Uniform treatment means that discrimination due to gender, race, age, or ethnicity is reduced.[47] Standardization means that many products are safer. A high degree of coordination means that technology is rapidly diffused.

McDonald's is a good example of each of these characteristics. When you go to McDonald's you know that there is little chance that you will have an unexpectedly good meal. The sandwiches, fries, and drinks will be just what you expect and no better. But no worse, either. The flip side of standardization is that bad surprises are systematically reduced (although the certainty of occasional human and equipment failures mean they can never fully be eliminated). If you've ever had an expensive meal with poorly prepared or unsafe food served (slowly) by a surly waiter, you know what I am talking about. There are few high points in a Big Mac value meal, but few lows, either.

I think this is why McDonald's was so popular when it first appeared in formerly Communist countries, despite prices that were high relative to weekly income. Under communism, people could be pretty sure of poor food and worse service in most cases, but sometimes they were pleasantly surprised. McDonald's is the other way around. The food is consistently decent. You provide most of the service yourself, so you are not dependent on the whims of a disagreeable waiter. Not a bad deal, compared to the alternative.

If formal rationalization and McDonaldization were limited to McDonald's I don't think we would have very much to complain about. Ritzer's concern, which is shared by many others, however, is that what is true about McDonald's may also be true more generally. It's not about the burgers. It's about the lives behind the burgers and the limited and automatic roles we play as efficient producing and consuming agents. What is the final consequence as formal rationalism spreads from McRestaurant to McMall to McCinema to McHospital to McUniversity to . . . to what? To McChurch?

This is what seems to worry Benjamin Barber. Barber sees the rationalization process (and writes about it in *Jihad vs. McWorld*), but he is apparently more concerned with who has the power in the system (hence his misplaced concern with the infotainment telesector's influence), not realizing that the power *is* the system. The power lies in the rationalization process itself. This is true even in the most unlikely places, such as the infotainment telesector.

Many people see increasing concentration in the print and electronic media and worry about the potential for abuse of influence. This is a legitimate concern, but it assumes that these firms want power, that they want to control what we believe, whereas I think they really want our money. What I see is increasingly fierce competition among the media giants, which drives them to ever bolder acts of rationalization. On television, for example, the reality show essentially gets audiences to produce their own programming just as McDonald's gets customers to fill their own drink cups. A true monopolist could become lazy and just show reruns or cheap game shows. It is competition and the quest for efficiency that drives them to extremes. It's not the manipulative power of the media giants that I fear; it is the possible effects of their drive to rationalize.

Thomas Friedman both recognizes the rationalization process inherent in globalization and, I think, embraces it. This accounts for Friedman's sunny but realistic attitude toward globalization. As a political reporter covering the Middle East and other troubled regions, Friedman has seen more than his share of irrational acts. I think he'd take economic rationalism over political or social irrationalism any day. He is hopeful that global capitalism will help people learn how to coordinate their actions and behave rationally—which means that they would try not to go to war, for example—even when they are not in a McDonald's. I sure hope he's right, but it is a long shot. Many people have argued that war is irrational because it is too expensive, but this doesn't seem to have stopped war. Perhaps McDonaldization—a deeper cultural process that starts with production and consumption and then eventually is absorbed into a society's DNA—will work where mere hunger for money has failed.

CREATIVE DESTRUCTION

I am a globalization optimist, although I argue in this book that globalization is unsustainable in its current form. But I take seriously the rationalizing force of capitalism and globalization that is driven by capitalism, so there are limits to my optimism. I am especially mindful of the argument made many years ago by the Austrian American economist Joseph Schumpeter in his book *Capitalism, Socialism, and*

Democracy.[48] Like Benjamin Barber, Schumpeter feared that capitalism would destroy democracy, but he was not worried about Jihad, McWorld, or the infotainment telesector. Rather, Schumpeter was worried about the effect of rationalization on society.

Schumpeter, you see, believed that society advanced due to the efforts of bold, heroic figures. This was especially true in business, where the figures are called entrepreneurs, but the idea also holds in politics, science, and the arts. Most of us take small risks with life and mainly play it safe. But a few people take bigger risks, and some of them achieve breakthroughs that really make a difference. These risk takers, even when they fail, are the real sources of social drive and change—he called it "creative destruction"—in Schumpeter's view. Without them, the world is a pretty stagnant, uninteresting place.

The problem, Schumpeter believed, is that capitalism's drive to rationalize is really quite intense, and he thought it would eventually destroy the culture that produces entrepreneurs. Capitalism, as a dynamic force, will slowly fade into stagnant socialism, Schumpeter thought, as rational calculation replaced entrepreneurial risk taking. Thus, he said, socialism will overcome capitalism, just as Karl Marx predicted, but not through a worker revolt. Nope, the culture of calculation will swallow up capitalism from the inside out, leaving meek and mild socialism behind.

Looking at Schumpeter's argument from today's perspective, we can see that he didn't anticipate some of the effects of rational capitalism. He assumed that rationalization would drive the risk out of capitalism. We saw in the last two chapters, however, that while the appearance of risk seemed to disappear, the reality of risk did not. Rational calculation encouraged investors to falsely believe that risk was a thing of the past. Moral hazard is a rational concept and the bubbles and booms we've studied here were always rational processes when viewed from within and in real time, regardless of how idiotic they seem looking back and from outside. In fact, you could argue that finance has become riskier as the human concern with trust has been replaced with rational calculation.

Schumpeter's view of politics is less well known, but he tended to see it in the same way he viewed the economy. He saw democracy as a competitive political marketplace. Like the economy, progress came through the actions of bold political entrepreneurs who took the risk of providing real leadership. And he thought that democracy, like capitalism, would be destroyed as a dynamic social force as bold political entrepreneurs were replaced by vote-calculating political managers, content to follow voters rather than leading them. Thus does democracy die, in Schumpeter's world, the victim of rationalism, not Jihad or McWorld.

GOLDEN ARCHES GLOBALONEY

Where does our study of globalization and McDonald's leave us? I don't know about you, but I feel like I have learned a great deal about McDonald's but not very much about globalization. This is the problem with using McDonald's or any single product or industry as a metaphor or image for something as complex as globalization. We quickly become caught up in the particular case and risk making false generalizations. Meanwhile, the true general globalization case, if it exists, remains unstudied for the most part.

McDonald's may in fact be an especially poor example to use in studying globalization. McDonald's seems to have a special meaning to Americans that it may or may not have to others. You can almost tell how an American feels about her country by what she has to say about McDonald's. We end up, as I have argued here, with an American view of America, not an objective analysis of globalization.

That said, studying McWorld is not entirely a waste of time. Ritzer's analysis of McDonaldization usefully highlights the rationalizing force of markets and makes us aware of the potential of cold calculation to benefit and (perhaps especially) to harm.

The bottom line is that it is hard to believe that globalization is really Americanization if the argument doesn't hold in the strongest (or at least most cited) case, McDonald's. The belief that globalization systematically removes the world's differences, replacing them with homogeneous mush of some sort, American, Italian, Indian, or Chinese, strikes me as globaloney. I believe that globalization both is diverse and ought to be. That's why the next chapter uses global sports to argue that globalization-Americanization is *not* "The Only Game in Town."

CHAPTER 5

THE ONLY GAME IN TOWN

David Beckham is the best-known player in the world's most popular spectator sport: soccer (or football as most of the world calls it), aka "the Beautiful Game."[1] Every day, in season and out, his image is pushed and pulled into homes, schools, and businesses around the world through all known forms of modern communications media. If global professional sports has a human face, it's probably Beckham's.

Do you know who Beckham is? The basic facts are these: David Beckham's career with the Manchester United soccer team began at age twelve (as a "trainee" or member of the club's youth squad). He played his first Premier League game in 1995 at the age of twenty and played midfielder in 394 games for Manchester United after that debut, winning six league titles. He was captain of England's national team. He was transferred to Real Madrid, another elite soccer club, for a fee of £25 million in 2003 before moving to Los Angeles in 2007 to play for the Major League Soccer team the Galaxy. He was "loaned" to AC Milan of the Italian Serie A in 2009. His face is one of the most recognized images on earth.

David Beckham wears the symbols of global capitalism comfortably; they are embroidered on his chest. At Manchester United his playing jersey featured the logos of Nike and Vodafone (the team sponsor—professional soccer players are human billboards to a degree not allowed in America's major professional sports leagues). At Real Madrid he was a walking advertisement for Adidas and Siemens, the German industrial giant. In Los Angeles it was Adidas again and Herbalife, a maker of nutrition and weight-management products. "Becks," as he is called by fans, displayed the symbols of Adidas and Bwin (Europe's largest online gambling and gaming website) in Milan.

The transfer from Manchester United to Madrid (and on to Los Angeles and Milan) resolved an awkward commercial conflict: Manchester was signed with Nike as its shirt sponsor, but Beckham himself was Adidas property—the beneficiary of a £100 million lifetime endorsement contract. The Beckham/Manchester mixed message (Nike shirt, but Adidas soul and contract) is now reconciled: he is Adidas through and through.

David Beckham is a global media superstar, whose face appears on magazine covers and newspaper pages every week. And not just on the sports page, either. His wife, Victoria, is better known as Posh Spice of the Spice Girls singing group. His, her, and their every action, emotion, and personal appearance is captured, analyzed, and promoted by the global tabloid press to an unimaginable extent. A Google News search of Internet sources on June 23, 2009, found more than eleven thousand Beckham news stories that had been posted during the previous few days.

BANK IT LIKE BECKHAM

David Beckham is so famous—and so bankable from a commercial standpoint—that the mere use of his last name was enough to guarantee an audience for *Bend It Like Beckham*, a 2002 film directed by Gurinder Chadha, which was the highest grossing British-financed, British-distributed film in history.[2] The film tells a soccer story, but it is really about globalization, of course, and so worth a brief digression.

David Beckham's signature play on the soccer pitch is the free kick—a focused moment of high drama in a game that otherwise features a flow of continuous motion. He is known for his ability to strike the ball so that it rises and bends around the opposing side's defensive wall, then arcs downward quickly, zooming into the net just beyond the goaltender's frustrated grasp. In the film, a teenaged girl named Jess Bhamra dreams of playing soccer and bending her shots like David Beckham, but she faces two obstacles: she is a girl, and therefore subject to gender prejudice in sexist English sports; and her parents are ethnic Indian immigrants who are uncomfortable with the prospect of assimilation. She is expected to behave like a proper Indian girl and obedient daughter, which makes bare-legged sports out of the question. An interesting subplot concerns her father, a cricket player back home, who quit the game after experiencing humiliating prejudice in England.

The critical question that this film asks is not whether Jess can really bend it like David Beckham (she can), but rather whether she and her teammates, coach, and family can become "globalized"; that is, whether they can transcend or overcome the obstacles that prevent them from becoming equal competitors. It is tempting to say that the question is whether they can be assimilated and "Americanized," so to speak, for a reason that will become clear shortly.

Jess is invited to join the girls' youth squad of the local soccer club. With the other girls she experiences English sexism and bonds with her coach, who is no stranger to English prejudice—he is Irish. The film ends happily, which is to say it ends with globalization triumphant. Jess's Indian family accepts her as a competitive female soccer player (her father even takes up cricket once again). Jess wins a big game by bending it like Beckham (in my favorite scene, she imagines that the defensive wall is made up of all her adult female relatives, dressed in colorful saris—an extra incentive to kick past them). Jess and teammate Jules gain the ultimate prize: they receive scholarships to play soccer in America, at the University of Santa Clara.

I call *Bend It Like Beckham* a globalization film because it is about how the forces of international or global competition empower individuals and allow them to overcome prejudice and cultural constraints. They transcend race, gender, and nationality. They become globalized. And they do it in Adidas logo soccer gear with the trademark of the AXA financial group emblazoned across their jerseys. David Beckham, who makes a brief cameo appearance as himself, a celebrity being chased and photographed by a frenzied media throng, is the perfect picture of this vision of globalization. Or at least that's what I think, but I admit there are differing views.

I believe that David Beckham is the perfect symbol of postmodern globalization. His game is global, his importance to it is frankly commercial, his role and his existence are media-driven, and his image sells, sells, sells. Plus, of course, he is a rich white male from an imperialistic country who models a high-end, cosmopolitan, metrosexual postmodern lifestyle.[3] What more do you want in a postmodern globalization poster boy?

Some people disagree, however—a true soccer fan would probably say that Beckham cannot be the symbol of globalization, or at least of global soccer, because, unlike, say, Michael Jordan in his prime, he is not the most skilled player in his game. If skill on the field counts (and soccer fans can be excused for thinking it should), then Beckham's name should be replaced with one of these: Cristiano Ronaldo, Lionel Messi, Fernando Torres, or Xavi. These are the players who were finalists for the 2008 FIFA World Player of the Year award (Ronaldo won the prize). Beckham was not among those nominated for the award.

Soccer fans have a point—the most famous player *should be* the *best* player, but soccer is a global business and other factors matter, too. There is power, for example, and Beckham has some due to his fame. He ranked number sixty-four on *World Soccer's* 2008 list of the most influential people in soccer (the second-highest player after the brilliant Brazilian Kaká at number forty-six).[4] The most powerful people in soccer, according to *World Soccer* magazine, are the club owners and international officials. AC Milan's owner, billionaire media-magnate Silvio Berlusconi, came in at number seventeen. He served as prime minister of Italy, another powerful position, when not checking soccer scores.

And then there's money. "Becks" holds down the thirty-eighth spot on *FourFourTwo* magazine's "Football Rich List 2009," the top player in the rankings.[5] Beckham's net worth was estimated to be £125 million, a lot of money for someone who plays a game for a living, but apparently the going rate for a global media superstar. Beckham's yearly pay was estimated to be £25.6 million, of which £5.1 million came from LA Galaxy and the rest from endorsements and other activities. As this chapter was being written, Becks' image was everywhere on the web in revealing photos created for a Beckham-centered Armani underwear advertising campaign. Sheik Mansour bin Zayed Al Naya, owner of the Manchester City team, was number one on the 2009 money list. He's apparently worth £15 billion, or more than one hundred times Becks and Posh.

Whereas basketball star Michael Jordan's great popularity and the power of his image was built on the foundation of his unmatched excellence as a player, Beckham's celebrity is due much less to his sports skills (which are not insignificant, it must be said) and much more to image creation and media manipulation—to his ability, in short, to extend the influence of global sports to people who are not sports fans.

Indeed, Beckham is perhaps as famous for his on-field errors in critical moments as for his outstanding performances. These would be damning errors for an ordinary soccer player, but they are just another part of the endless, highly publicized saga for a tabloid media celebrity. We demand perfection from athletes, but celebrity misdeeds are not just tolerated, they are expected. The tension between athletic value and market value is inevitable. "The Spanish sports press and many of the players are fearful of the impact Beckham, his entourage and the media circus that follows him may have," Sid Lowe reported when Beckham first joined Real Madrid. "His off-pitch lifestyle may encourage press intrusion into areas that are traditionally left alone; it simply isn't accepted practice for journalists to camp outside players' homes or follow their wives out shopping. With David and Victoria, that could all change."[6]

NOT THE ONLY GAME

The belief that there is just one version of globalization and that it is "the only game in town" is just plain globaloney. It is easy to see only what is familiar or only what you want to see as you travel the world, skimming its surface as the Four Flying Friedmans (Thomas, Tommy, Tomaso, and Tao) did in chapter 4, but deeper down local cultures and practices can be incredibly resilient and able to resist global market forces or bend them and adapt them to meet local needs. Market fundamentalists in Margaret Thatcher's Britain used to assert that "There is No Alternative," but there is. And it's everywhere. Just look around.

Is David Beckham the perfect symbol of globalization—of soccer or tabloids or anything else? Yes, according to the world media, but in the United States the answer might be different. David Beckham? Globalization? No, of course not. *Who* is David Beckham? How can he represent globalization (and therefore, according to the conventional wisdom, Americanization) if we have never heard of him?[7]

America is the exception to the rule that soccer is the global spectator sport. Soccer is certainly played in the United States, but despite several attempts and millions of dollars (and even David Beckham's efforts in a Galaxy uniform), it is a sport that only a relatively few follow compared to baseball, basketball, and (American) football. And those few are disproportionately immigrants and well-paid and educated elites. Americans, who *define* globalization in many eyes, are just about the least likely people on earth to know the name David Beckham.

I hope you appreciate the elegant irony of this situation. If globalization is Americanization, then the David Beckham image of globalization embodies even more of the stereotypical "American" elements than does the iconic Michael Jordan. Yet America is the one part of the world where Beckham's sport is not wildly popular because, as we will see, it is considered by some to be so un-American.

This chapter uses the specific case of the world's most popular sport—soccer—to argue the general case for global diversity—for many globalizations, not just one. An argument based on soccer doesn't prove anything about globalization—but neither do arguments about hamburgers (McDonalds) or coffee shops (Starbucks) or anything else. Remember, I'm telling stories here, that's what economists do, but I hope my soccer story makes you suspicious of other people's stories about alleged globalization's one size fits all pattern. What is global soccer's shape? Hmmm. I see at least three distinct silhouettes.

THREE WAVES OF GLOBALIZATION

Soccer didn't become the global game overnight. It took three waves of globalization to spread the beautiful game across the map. The first wave was global imperialism, in both its classic and modern forms. Rome's military might spread a kicking game something like soccer throughout the empire—even to Britain. Eventually Britain's nineteenth-century "informal empire" of trade and finance extended far beyond the Roman Empire's old boundaries and the British public school game, Association Football, was almost everywhere embraced from below (by local workers emulating British sailors) and from above (by British-educated local elites).

The second wave of soccer globalization was borne on the tide of nationalism starting in the 1930s, when FIFA (Fédération Internationale de Football Association, the global soccer governing body) created the World Cup, a competition among national teams designed to replace the Olympics as the world championship of soccer. The Olympic competition was for amateurs only; the World Cup welcomed paid professional players. Nations and their leaders seek status, recognition and legitimacy through competition on the World Cup's global stage. No wonder that they do: the World Cup final is watched by more people than any other event in human history.

The popular success that the World Cup achieved paved the way for even greater commercialization of the sport in general—the third globalization wave.[8] The World Cup created a truly global audience for soccer and provided global exposure to top-level international players. It is, however, contested just once every four years by national teams called together from the professional clubs. The vast World Cup audience was an obvious target for sports entrepreneurs who have sought to exploit it through the creation of super-clubs, such as Manchester United, Chelsea, Juventus of Turin, Bayern Munich, AC Milan, Barcelona and Real Madrid, and through the creation of an elite international super-league competition, the Champions League.

The teams that I call the super-clubs are more transnational enterprises than soccer clubs. Unlike the quaint image of a local soccer club, where young men (and women?) from the town play for their own enjoyment and to entertain their friends and families, the super-clubs mean business. They are owned, for the most part, by a global array of business and media giants. They buy players from around the globe and sell their products (the games, of course, but a wide array of other items including especially the logo-encrusted jerseys) to a global clientele. The super-clubs in the super-leagues are part of a "winner-take-all" global economic system, where disproportionate rewards go to the teams and players at the very top while others, only slight less talented or lucky, earn much less money and recognition.

As I look at global soccer today, I see three patterns that are distinct enough to persuade me of global soccer's diversity. I wonder if they are just patterns that are unique to soccer or if they reflect a diverse world more generally? Let me tell you about them and then see what you think.

First, the global soccer player market seems to display a classic core-periphery structure, which is often associated with exploitation in political economy. But, second, if we look closely at the periphery, it appears that there is something else going on besides simple exploitation. Soccer seems to be used as a tool to build local identity in resistance to globalization and exploitation. So this relationship seems complex and interesting. And, finally, there is the American exception to consider—what should we make of soccer's persistent inability, even during the era of strong market forces, to penetrate the United States as a spectator sport? The remainder of this chapter tries to understand the causes and consequences of these three images of globalization and soccer today.

CORE AND PERIPHERY

If you look at the top five professional soccer leagues in the world—England, Spain, Italy, Germany, and France—you will see the top players in the world at work. Not just the top English, Spanish, Italian, German, and French players, but the top players from everywhere: Africa, Asia, North America, South America, the works. The top teams in the top leagues bid talent away from the countries and teams in the soccer periphery and then sell the finished products—games, shirts, images—back to them. This pattern has all of the qualities of a classic core-periphery relationship in political economy. The core of the system controls the key elements of economic power (in this case, it is the privileged position within the winner-take-all system) and uses its advantage to purchase cheap natural resources from the periphery, selling back finished products at advantageous prices. That is a basic core-periphery relationship, considerably oversimplified, as originally conceived by Immanuel Wallerstein.[9]

The intensity of the core-periphery relationship in soccer is quite amazing. You can get a sense of it by examining team rosters of the two most-watched soccer games of 2009, the UEFA Champions League final played in Rome between club teams Manchester United and Barcelona and the FIFA Confederations Cup final played in South Africa between the national teams of the United States and Brazil.[10]

Manchester United and Barcelona are nominally teams from England and Spain (or Catalonia, if you ask Barça fans) but their players come from far afield. Manchester's squad included players from England, The Netherlands, France, Portugal, Brazil, Bulgaria, Wales, South Korea, Serbia, Ireland, Scotland, Poland, Argentina, Italy, Northern Ireland, Germany, and Belgium. The Barcelona side was a mix of players from Spain, Uruguay, Mexico, Iceland, Cameroon, Argentina, France, Mali, Brazil, Belarus and Côte d'Ivoire. I hope you can see the core-periphery effect here, with players drawn from soccer-rich but money-poor countries in Africa, the Americas and Eastern Europe to play for the big-money clubs.

The effect is even clearer when we consider the squads for the 2009 Confederations Cup final. The United States upset Spain to get to the tournament finals. Most of the players for Spain actually played their club soccer close to home in Spain, at Real Madrid, Barcelona, Villarreal, Valencia and Athletico Bilbao. The rest played at European super-clubs Liverpool and Arsenal in the English Premier League and Fenerbahçe of Istanbul. The players on the American squad, on the other hand, mainly earned their soccer incomes far from home. Only a handful of them actually played club soccer in the United States. The rest worked in France (Rennes, Monaco), Belgium (Standard Liège), Germany (Kaiserslautern, Hansa Rostock II, Borussia Mönchengladbach), Denmark (AGF, Midtjylland), Mexico (Pachuca), England (Everton, Fulham, Watford, West Ham United, and Aston Villa), Sweden (Hammarby), Spain (Villareal), and Scotland (Rangers). The Brazilian squad they faced in the final game told a similar story. A few played at home in Brazil while the majority worked for professional clubs in Italy (Internazionale Milano, Roma, Fiorentina, and AC Milan), England (Tottenham Hotspur, Manchester City), Portugal (Benfica), Spain (Barcelona, Real Madrid, Sevilla), Germany (Wolfsburg, Bayern Munich), and Greece (Panathinaikos).

In general, skilled players from the economic periphery end up playing for core clubs—the pull of the money is nearly inescapable. National team players from Brazil, Argentina, Cameroon, and Ghana are more likely to encounter each other in Champions League games in Europe than on their home turf.

The famous Brazilian Pelé is a great exception to the rule that the top soccer players from South America and other countries on the economic periphery are always exported to Europe to play for super-teams in the super-leagues. Why didn't he leave Brazil during his playing days? Because it was against the law! He was declared a national treasure by the Brazilian parliament and forbidden to play for a foreign team. (Pelé did eventually play abroad—for the New York Cosmos in the United States—but only after he retired from the Brazilian national team.) He was too valuable to export, both as a player and as a symbol of Brazilian achievement and Brazil's racial and ethnic diversity.

To restate my point, the economic core of soccer is in Europe's super-leagues, even though the playing core (when you consider the national teams) is frequently centered in South America, with emerging pockets of excellence in Africa, Turkey, and Eastern Europe. The economic forces of winner-take-all markets mean that clubs in Brazil, Argentina, Nigeria, Turkey, Croatia, and other countries cannot possibly compete with the super-clubs for the services of their own players. So, to a certain degree, they assume the role of minor leagues or youth leagues. Players with outstanding potential are identified and trained and then sold to European clubs. Sales of players take the place of ticket or television rights sales in their economic structures.

The very best periphery teams can be remarkably successful, although not in the same way as the European super-teams. Boca Juniors of Argentina, for example, frequently enjoys both economic and soccer success. In 2003 it won the Argentine league championship, the South American club competition, and beat European Cup champions AC Milan in Tokyo to claim the world club title. All this success on the field, with corresponding television rights earnings, meant that Boca was able to hang onto some of its best players for perhaps an extra season before selling their contracts to European clubs. But Boca Juniors is the exception. In 2003 it enjoyed its own version of the winner-take-all payoff. Boca's situation as the number one team was miles ahead of the average team in the Argentine league, which leaks money like a sieve, like most clubs in most countries.

Brazil is perhaps the world's leading exporter of soccer players. Brazilian players are said to have a particularly fluid and creative style and it seems like every team wants to have one. About five thousand Brazilians play professional soccer outside of Brazil, according to Alex Bellos, author of *Futbol: Soccer, the Brazilian Way*.[11] He explains Brazil's position as a huge net exporter in simple supply and demand terms. Many Brazilians, inspired by the success of Pelé, Ronaldo, and others, want to play soccer (a predictable problem in a winner-take-all market). There are too many for Brazil to absorb, even with its five hundred professional clubs employing about twenty-three thousand players. With so many teams, the individual club economic markets are small for all but the top teams and the pay low. (Bellos says that 90 percent of Brazilian players earn less than £100 per month.) Poor clubs, poor pay—and a high demand abroad. No wonder Brazil exports soccer players to the world.

Argentina's situation is of particular interest to me because of the way soccer reflects life and globalization more generally. Argentina experienced a severe economic crisis in recent years—a currency crisis, a banking crisis, and an international debt crisis all in one. Deteriorating domestic economic conditions affected the country's soccer clubs, too. Ticket and television revenues dried up, and even sponsorship funding fell. The two best teams, River Plate and Boca Juniors, were able to switch to international sponsors (Budweiser and Pepsi respectively) to shore up their revenue base, but most other teams did not fare so well. Desperate for funds, they flooded the world transfer market with players, pushing up supply at the same time that financial problems in Europe were cutting demand. The result: even their most valuable assets, the players themselves, could not be sold for enough money to make ends meet (Boca Juniors aside).[12] The plight of Argentine soccer mirrored in this case, as in many others, the sad economic situation of the country itself.

SOCCER AND LOCAL IDENTITY

If exploitation of the periphery were the whole story of soccer globalization it would be a sad story indeed, but it is not. Soccer is more than global capitalism acting upon countries like Argentina and Brazil; it is also a tool that people use to define themselves and, implicitly at least, to resist the forces of globalization.

The relationship between soccer and national or local identity has many layers, and my brief discussion here can only scratch the surface.[13] It begins, I suppose, with styles of play. Although soccer is a simple game, there are endless variations in styles and strategies. "The Brazilians play like they dance; the Germans play like they make cars, with lots of technical efficiency and not much left to the imagination; the English run hard all the time, maybe because of the weather; the Spanish are a mosaic of regional styles, which has yet to find a national pattern," according to Jorge Valdano, a member of Argentina's 1986 World Cup champion team. "And the Italians, they are a paradox. In every other area they export style and flair to the world; but in football they've allowed the ideal of collective organization to crush individual talent."[14] The way a player or team approaches the game makes a statement about their identity, or at least it can seem to do so.

The next layer is this: soccer can be used to establish or reinforce a national or local identity. Soccer is not unique among sports in this regard—Hitler famously tried to use the 1936 Berlin Olympics for particular nation-building purposes. FIFA's World Cup was, as previously noted, inaugurated during an era of growing nationalism and has been used ever since as a way to reinforce national identity. Soccer is an "us versus them" game and therefore can be an especially effective way to define identity, both who we are and who and what we are not.[15] The case of the Brazilian Pelé is an especially interesting one in this regard.

Pelé was the greatest soccer player of his generation, perhaps of any generation. He was born in 1940 and played for most of his career with Santos, Sao Paulo's richest team. A personal sponsorship contract from the Brazilian Coffee Institute allowed him to resist the financial incentives to play in Europe.[16] Pelé was a black player at a time when Brazilian teams still discriminated against blacks. Pelé's amazing skill and creativity changed that and, to some extent, changed Brazil, too.

Brazil's government quite purposefully used Pelé to shape the country's identity and to legitimize its own hold on power. When a military regime seized power in Brazil in 1964, it immediately turned its attention to the most famous Brazilian, Pelé, the man who defined Brazil to many people. "For the generals," Bill Murray writes, "Pelé became a resource to be shamelessly exploited in their own interests. He was encouraged to speak on behalf of their dictatorship, claiming that Brazil was not ready for democracy, and in a country with more soccer pitches than schools pointed to himself as an example of how the poor and blacks could do well."[17] Race was an important issue. When Pelé married a white woman it was promoted as a symbol of racial harmony and integration. Pelé was an especially powerful symbol because he was, like David Beckham, a ubiquitous presence. Media and commercial interests made sure that his face was everywhere, and his image was designed to sell more than just soccer and coffee—it was designed to sell a particular view of Brazil's government and a very particular image of Brazil itself: the harmonious multiracial land of opportunity.

We know that governments will use whatever tools they can find, soccer included, to advance their interests and shape national attitudes, but I am most interested in how people themselves use soccer to create or reinforce their identities. There has been a good deal of scholarly work written about how fan groups have used their association with soccer to build distinctive local identities.[18] One very interesting personal account is *A Season with Verona* by the novelist (and literature professor) Tim Parks.[19] Parks is a fan of Hellas Verona, his local team, and spent one season attending every home and away Verona game in the company of a group of *ultras* or extreme fans. Parks's book obviously lacks scholarly distance and objectivity, but it does provide an interesting perspective on this identity-creation process as seen from inside. The particular case that Parks reports is also interesting because Hellas Verona fans were thought to be especially racist and for a time Verona was forced by the Italian league to play its home games on neutral grounds due to the alleged racist environment. Soccer identities can be negative as well as positive and Parks helps us understand that the meaning of soccer within an *ultra* group may be different than the meaning assigned by outside observers.[20]

The basic "us versus them" structure of soccer seems to enable team followers to assign many different meanings to the teams they support. We might expect national identities would be at stake (France versus Germany), but it is more complicated than this. A game between the English teams Aston Villa and Birmingham City, for example, assumes the identity of a class war. Both teams are based in Birmingham, but City's fans identify themselves as blue-collar working class—gritty and hard-working—versus the bourgeois suburban Villa fans. Marx's class war is played out in surrogate form inside the stadium (and sometimes in real form outside it) each time these teams play.[21]

The rivalry between Glasgow's two Scottish Premier League teams, Celtic and Rangers, is even more complicated. The identities of these two Scottish teams reflect Irish religious tensions as transferred to Glasgow through industry and immigration.[22] Rangers is the team of anti-Catholic Protestants and Celtic is the pro-Catholic team. Rangers are "closely tied to the Unionist majority of Northern Ireland, whose livelihood was strongly associated with the shipyard industries of Belfast and Glasgow," according to Richard Giulianotti. "Celtic were founded in Glasgow's east end . . . as a benevolent club for poor Irish Catholics immigrants. It soon became a symbol of sporting and cultural success of the disadvantaged minority."[23] If Catholic–anti-Catholic sentiments define Scottish soccer at its highest level, you need only imagine what goes on in Ireland! Fortunately, religion and soccer do not *always* mix in conflictual ways. Giulianotti also reports a belief held by some Greenland Inuit people that the "northern lights" (aurora borealis) appears when the spirits of the dead play soccer.[24]

One of my favorite movies is all about how soccer can be used to construct an identity among oppressed peoples. It is *The Cup*, a 1999 film by Khyentse Norbu, a Bhutanese writer and director.[25] It was filmed in Nepal. All of the dialogue is in Tibetan (with subtitles, of course). It was the first Bhutanese film ever to be nominated for an Academy Award. It is the story of Tibetan refugee children who are smuggled into a monastery in Nepal. Separated from their families and friends, some of the boys get it in their heads that they need to watch the 1998 World Cup being played in France so that they can root for the French team (lead by Zinedine Zidane). Why? Because France is the only country that recognizes Tibet as a sovereign nation. A victory by France is, in their minds, a victory of their own and validation of their identities as Tibetans. The movie is the tale of how they found a way to watch the game and what, if anything, France's actual victory meant to them.

Soccer's ability to help nations and individuals construct their own identities is a very hopeful sign. We hear constantly that globalization destroys local culture, replacing it with the meaningless consumption culture of the American suburb, and if soccer is part of the globalization process, you'd expect it to do the same. But if soccer also builds distinct local identities, then it is also a force opposed to homogenization and commoditization.

Thus, for example, when the great Diego Maradona left to play in Europe, one effect of his transfer, it is said, was to strengthen the identity of the fans of his Argentine club, Boca Juniors. As far as the fans were concerned, or at least some of them, he was still their Boca player and his successes and failures were theirs as well as his. To the extent that this effect holds more generally, and I don't think that it can be as true for most exported players as it was for a famous player like Maradona, then I think the net effect of soccer globalization may be to strengthen local identity in opposition to whatever global forces may be weakening it.

That said, I also think that the relationship between global economics and local culture is a bit like a mousetrap, delicate and dangerous. I find it difficult to be confident about causes and effects, even when operating within a relatively simple framework such as soccer globalization. I'd like to say that global soccer strengthens local identity, but I worry that it just isn't so.

The economic tension between the professional clubs and the national teams seems to make this problem even worse. Players are paid by their clubs, of course, who are expected to release players for international competition (World Cup qualification games, for example) during league seasons. The clubs and their leagues are creatures of FIFA, the sanctioning body that organizes these competitions, so their cooperation is expected. But FIFA's interests and the interests of a club are often at odds when, say, an important league match coincides with an international game. The players are often caught in the middle between their clubs and fans in the super-leagues and their national teams and fans back home—a difficult situation either way. Some European-based players declined to join their national teams for the 2004 African Cup competition, for example, actions that caused many reactions—none of them good—in the home countries and teams.[26]

If you want to see the power of soccer to define local communities but also perhaps to destroy them, come to Buenos Aires. A city of thirteen million, Buenos Aires is home to literally dozens of professional soccer clubs. Thirty-six clubs, each with its own stadium, are found in the city proper, and the suburbs are home to another thirty-seven clubs (with thirty-seven stadiums).[27] Taken together, the seventy-three teams divide up the territory and population into large and small pockets of soccer identity. If local identity is an asset, then Buenos Aires fans are perhaps the wealthiest soccer fans on earth, wealthier even than the residents of London, who have twelve professional teams from the top three divisions to choose from, not counting teams from the outlying suburbs.

The sad fact of this is, however, that a population that could support three or four teams adequately in this winner-take-all world is spread too thin. Each club has its own stadium, so none of them are very good facilities (none of them would meet the standards for a World Cup match, for example). Many of the stadia are shoddy, some dangerous. Most of the clubs are financial basket cases, a fact partly due to their organizational structure: Argentine clubs are really clubs, which sponsor youth teams, women's teams, and teams in other sports such as basketball. Fans join and pay monthly dues, which give them the right to attend home matches for free. (This practice is not uncommon in Europe, which accounts for the low gate receipts they receive.)

The logical thing for the Buenos Aires clubs to do would be to consolidate, share facilities, share costs, and in this way evolve into an economically sustainable structure. But such changes—even sharing a stadium—are intolerable ideas because they challenge what it means to be a local club member. They threaten the identity that these soccer teams have helped their fans and supporters create. They would rather that the stadium be a shambles and the best players quickly sold than compromise the identity of the team.

In winner-take-all markets like soccer has become, team loyalty fragments the market and may doom the very clubs with which the fans identify. Or, if not doom them exactly, keep them firmly in the economic periphery of the game, despite their place at the core of the game of soccer itself.

THE AMERICAN EXCEPTION

Globalization is seldom really global. Africa, for the most part, was left out and left behind in the hot money investment-fueled, technology-driven rush to profit from economic globalization. It is the huge hole in the globalization ozone. If we look at globalization through soccer, however, Africa is right in there, and it is growing in significance as the 2010 South Africa World Cup indicates. But the United States is missing. It is the "Africa" of soccer globalization.

This is not a trivial fact. There is a lot of money behind professional soccer, lots of commercial interests and media stakes. In the super-leagues, soccer has been thoroughly commercialized and tailored to a high-end consumer market. All these factors are supposed to be distinctly appealing to Americans—factors that define Americanization, in fact. So what gives? Why the American exception?[28]

Before I try to answer this question, let me remind you what is at stake. Globalization-Americanization is supposed to be an unstoppable force, but if Americans, who are most comfortable in this environment, and presumably most susceptible to it, are immune in this case, then perhaps other people in other countries may be immune as well. That is, perhaps the idea that globalization-Americanization is the only game in town is—you guessed it—globaloney. Briefly, here are five ways to try to explain the American exception to soccer globalism.

Explanation One: There is no American exception. Soccer has been thoroughly embraced by America and Americans (even if most of them could not pick David Beckham out of a lineup). Soccer is, indeed, the most played sport in America. More school-age Americans play soccer than baseball, football, or anything else. But whereas young people who play baseball in school (and even those who don't) tend to follow the professional teams as spectators or fans (and many who do not play do also), young people who play soccer often grow up to be "fans" of other sports. Americans seem to identify with soccer more as participants, not observers. This answer has accuracy in its favor—soccer really is the number one participation sport —but it really raises more questions than it answers.

Explanation Two: Soccer is not currently a major American sport, but it will be. And soon. Nike and Adidas will see to it! The argument runs like this. Nike has a strong interest in the global sports market and originally intended that Michael Jordan, the U.S. Olympic Dream Team, and basketball would sweep (or maybe "swoosh" is a better verb) the world, starting from the United States and expanding steadily outward. But they did not take into account the strength of soccer, which steadfastly held onto its position as the world's number one sport. So, it is argued, Nike decided to reverse its strategy. It signed major soccer stars and teams to lucrative contracts and then set about both conquering the soccer world and extending that domain to include the United States. Having failed to conquer the world with basketball, Nike aims now to conquer the United States with soccer—an inside-out conquest.

Adidas, which has a long history as a soccer sponsor, has now invaded Nike's home turf through its sponsorship of the U.S. Major Soccer League. Together Nike and Adidas will conquer the world and even the United States.

Any argument set in the future is impossible to prove or disprove, but Nike certainly seems to be taking soccer seriously. One building on the Nike corporate headquarters campus is named for Michael Jordan, but another honors Mia Hamm, the most famous U.S. female soccer player. Nike has indeed vigorously entered the world soccer market, signing its share of the super-teams and super-players in the super-leagues. It does have competition in this, however, from companies with longer histories in soccer such as Adidas, Puma, Lotto, and Kappa. So Nike's success abroad, although likely, is not assured.

Explanation Three: The third explanation for the American exception suggests why Nike's initiative might work where previous attempts to inject soccer into the American sports culture have failed. Answer three is taken from a book called *Offside: Soccer & American Exceptionalism,* which was written by a politics professor (Andrei S. Markovits) and a former sports journalist turned politics professor (Steven L. Hellerman).[29] Markovits and Hellerman explain that there have been several attempts to introduce professional soccer in America and all have failed, at least so far. One reason they cite for the failure (there are many) is that soccer has generally been presented as a foreign sport and professional leagues, at least at the beginning, have relied upon foreign players. This strategy was effective in attracting an immediate audience of immigrants from soccer-playing countries and some well-educated Americans who sought status and elevated self-esteem by identifying with an international sport (that would be me, I suppose). But a focus upon foreign players to appeal to immigrant fans did little or nothing to develop a distinctly American constituency for the game. The teams and leagues just died away.

My personal experience as a fan of North American Soccer League (NASL) and Major Indoor Soccer League (MISL) soccer teams in the Pacific Northwest bears out this point. I remember the 1977 NASL championship game between the Cosmos, with Pelé and a squad of mainly aging European internationals, and the Seattle Sounders, which featured a number of players from the 1966 England World Cup squad. Each team had a several American players besides the "internationals," but the fans clearly came to see the exceptional skills of the foreign players, even if they were a little past their prime. The NASL folded relatively quickly, despite substantial financial backing, in part I think because the fans identified with the foreign players, who inevitably had to move on or out, not with their "home" teams themselves. How many fans came to see a Cosmos game? How many came just to be able to say that they had seen Pelé play?

Perhaps because the Pacific Northwest is soccer-mad, at least compared to the rest of the United States, interest remained after the Sounders faded away with the rest of their league. Indoor soccer (soccer played, basically, on an Astroturfed hockey rink) caught on, at least for a while, and I attended the finals series between the Tacoma Stars and the Dallas Sidekicks. There were many more American players on these teams, but the stars were still foreigners. Steve Zungul, from Yugoslavia, was the most famous and productive player in the league, followed by another young Yugoslav named Preki. (Preki later acquired U.S. citizenship and played on U.S. World Cup teams.) Only one player on the top ten all-time MISL points scorers (Dale Mitchell of Tacoma) was American, for example.

If you want an audience to embrace a sport as their own, it seems that the worst way to do this is to present it as a foreign game played by foreigners, yet this is what soccer promoters did in the United States until very recently. It is interesting how careful the National Basketball Association (NBA) has been about this as more and more non-U.S. players have arrived in the league. The NBA calls them international, not foreign, players (at least in that part of their publicity focused on the U.S. audience). But there are other problems. The structural organization of soccer is, in many respects, foreign to American audiences. Most American professional sports leagues are organized in a very simple way. Teams play each other within roughly geographical divisions (designed to minimize travel costs) to determine a play-off field. Several play-off rounds determine a league titlist. The more games a team plays, the more money it earns, which exacerbates the "winner-take-all" element of the business.

Soccer in other countries has a much more complex structure. Most soccer countries have a multiple hierarchy of leagues (in Italy the leagues are A, B, C1, C2, etc.). Teams compete to be at the top of their leagues, of course, but there is also interest at the bottom because the worst teams in league A, for example, are relegated to league B and replaced by the best teams from league B, with similar movements from leagues B to C1, C1 to C2, and so forth. So there is something at stake in games at both ends of the league table, which of course gives all of the games more meaning. Good teams want to advance and be promoted; bad teams try to avoid relegation. In theory it is possible for a team from a lowly C2 league town to advance via several excellent seasons to one of the super-leagues. This actually happened in Italy in the 1990s, a story that was documented by Joe McGinnis in *The Miracle of Castel di Sangro*.[30]

Teams in the middle may also compete for positions in international competitions, giving their fans a reason to care. In Italy, for example, the very top teams qualify for the Champions League competitions, but others who finish in the top half of the league table may enter the UEFA Cup competition or earn the right to compete with teams from other countries for a spot in these competitions.

Each soccer nation also features a national cup competition that includes teams from several of the national leagues, providing a C1 team the opportunity, in theory at least, to play an A team and win a major trophy (and a place in the next year's international competitions). The result of this is that fans of most teams always have something to hope for or to fear with each game. In a given week a team may play one league match plus an international or national cup game, and in general competition proceeds on several different levels at once. This system is confusing to the outsider and represents another "foreign" barrier to American acceptance.

If Markovits and Hellerman are right, then the current strategy is trying to have it both ways—to get attention through international super-teams and star players while also developing a distinctive American soccer identity. Perhaps it will work. But maybe it is too late.

Explanation Four: Markovits and Hellerman are optimistic about the chances of soccer finally catching on in America (see answer five below), but the timing is bad, they say. They note that the major spectator sports cultures around the world emerged during the period of the 1890s through the 1930s. This was the period when the urban middle class emerged in the industrial democracies and when the "space" of sports culture was created and filled. In the United States, they argue, this space was occupied by "the big three and a half" sports—baseball, basketball, American football, and, to a certain extent, ice hockey. Together these sports spanned the four seasons and provided a year-round outlet for the sports consumers' interest, enthusiasm, loyalty, and money. It is very difficult, they argue, for new sports to invade this space either in the United States or elsewhere around the world. What about basketball, you might ask (thinking about the theory that Michael Jordan and Nike have created a world hoops culture)? It was already there, as I explained in the first edition of *Globaloney*, thanks to YMCA missionaries. What about baseball in Japan? It was introduced in the 1940s and 1950s. Yes, but it was introduced through the forces of U.S. military occupation, which perhaps indicates how unusual the circumstances must be for a new sport to enter the arena.

Why didn't soccer take a place in the U.S. sports space a hundred years ago? Markovits and Hellerman suggest that it could have done so, but didn't. The "foreign" element worked against it, of course, but there is a better reason. American football emerged during this period instead. Elite colleges in the Northeast began to play a form of soccer in the nineteenth century, but it was the rough rugby-type game that was popular in England. It could have developed either way—into the Beautiful Game of association football or into the more violent game of rugby. Harvard seems to have been the key here. Just when it looked like Harvard would adopt rules like those in soccer today, the team played a series with McGill University in Canada, which played the rugby-style game. The team preferred this approach and published rules that evolved into American football. Ironically, American football, like "American" basketball, owes its emergence to Canadian influence. Professional football leagues eventually developed, building on but not replacing the college game, and the space that could have been occupied by soccer in the United States was filled instead by American football.

Explanation Five: Is it too late for soccer in America? Answer five is: maybe not. Markovits and Hellerman are optimistic that soccer can succeed as an important spectator sport this time around by developing a homegrown product and finding ways to span the gaps between youth, college, and professional strata. They are hopeful that current attempts to develop domestic soccer leagues that feature and develop American talent will be successful. A new professional league structure was launched in the mid-1990s, shortly after the successful U.S. World Cup. Major League Soccer (MLS) is the top U.S. league with fifteen teams as of 2009 (New York; Columbus; Chicago; New England; Washington, D.C.; San Jose; Dallas; Toronto; Los Angeles; LA-area Chivas USA; Salt Lake City; Colorado; Houston; Seattle; and Kansas City) and three teams in the expansion queue (Philadelphia, Portland, and Vancouver, Canada). The MLS includes many cities with relatively strong local soccer traditions (former NASL cities such as Seattle, Portland, and Dallas), strong college soccer traditions, or relatively high foreign or international fan bases. Competition is strictly American-style: no relegation and promotion.

If it is to be successful, the MLS must master several delicate balances. One goal is to develop American players and create a following for an American game, but foreign players are useful both on the field and to attract fans.

Perhaps Markovits and Hellerman are right: the time is ripe and the MLS can avoid the problems that have doomed earlier attempts—but I have my doubts. People thought that the 1994 World Cup, which was played in the United States, would give this process a jump start, and it did not. And then there is the core-periphery factor. If the new American leagues are indeed successful in developing local talent, it seems inevitable that they will be swept away into the super-leagues, depriving the U.S. teams of their feature players. I note that most of the U.S. national team that played in South Africa was based abroad. And the Beckham experiment in Los Angeles shows that MLS owners do not entirely reject the "foreign star" strategy that failed to keep the NASL alive.

Perhaps, however, there is hope—for women's soccer. The U.S. women's soccer team competes consistently at the highest level internationally, a statement that cannot be made about the men's side. The Women's Professional Soccer league began play in March 2009 with teams in Boston, Chicago, Los Angeles, St. Louis, New Jersey/New York, Washington, D.C., and the San Francisco Bay Area. The players are mainly Americans, but with a strong international presence. Marta, the Brazilian who is said by some to be the world's best soccer player (male or female—search for her on YouTube.com), plays for the Los Angeles Sol. Perhaps the United States will embrace women's soccer and be the center of the professional women's game. Perhaps, but that would require a greater change in U.S. sports culture than just accepting a foreign game with foreign players. It would require U.S. society to accept female athletes on the same terms as it does males. That may be a challenge even greater than globalization.

SPORTS GLOBALONEY

What have we learned by looking at globalization through soccer? Answering this question is necessarily an exercise in globaloney, if only because any attempt to generalize from just one example is an obvious distortion of the truth. That said, here goes.

History matters. The shape of global soccer today was determined, to some extent, by century-old events and processes. Globalization is path dependent, to use some economics jargon; where you are depends upon where you've been. If the past had been different (if Harvard had rejected McGill's rules), the present would be different too. There is no single line of globalization.

It is commonplace to assume that globalization is Americanization, but sports examples don't seem to support that notion very well. I am not saying that America or Americanization is not a factor in globalization, but that there is more to it than that and some globalization may be unrelated to Americanization or even antithetical to it.

To the extent that globalization creates winner-take-all markets, it is a real problem. It is very difficult to take an optimistic view of the effects of winner-take-all markets. These markets do not seem to be beneficial to the players, the teams, or the fans that support them (aside from the winners who take all, Michael Jordan and David Beckham). Not all global markets are winner-take-all markets, however, which suggests that globalization's effects will vary.

Resistance to globalization is certainly possible. It is too early to conclude that global capitalism will simply mow down any opposition. There is no better example of successful opposition than the United States. Local cultures can assimilate global influences and construct distinctly local identities from them.

So there is reason to be hopeful about globalization's diversity. Yet I do find it hard to be entirely hopeful because of what we saw in Buenos Aires. There the strong local soccer cultures—successful resistance!—fragmented the sports market, making teams too small to compete. Fan loyalty crippled their teams in the winner-take-all markets. Strong resistance, in this case, seemed to doom economically the local identity that it was trying to preserve. Diverse globalization seems to be feasible, but not necessarily sustainable in this situation.

🌀

This chapter ends by raising the question of Grassroots Globaloney—is it really true that people on the ground have no choice but to accept global market outcomes, or do they have the power to resist globalization or—more important—shape it to suit their needs? This survey of global soccer makes it clear that there is more than one side to this question. What's the answer? Turn the page to find out.

CHAPTER 6

GRASSROOTS GLOBALONEY

Everyone knows that clothing and apparel is a global industry. The sight of a foreign label is no longer a novelty to clothes buyers of the world. Indeed, our closets have become a sort of United Nations of wearable goods. No matter who you are or where you are in the world as you read this paragraph, the chances are very good that if you are wearing clothes at all, you are wearing at least one article of imported attire. Do you know where your clothes come from? If you don't, now would be a good time to look.

Start with your shoes. Please take off your shoes and look to see where they were made. Chances are quite good that the answer is China. Over the years I have asked thousands of students and audience members to take off their shoes and most come from China, with smaller numbers from Thailand and Vietnam and some (the designer shoes) from Italy. The one exception to this rule was when I spoke in Juneau, Alaska on a slushy winter day. A surprising number of the audience's shoes said Made in USA. Rubber boots!

Now look at your shirt. (If you are reading this is a public place, please don't take off your shirt to see where it's made—ask someone nearby to check out that little tag you usually find inside the neck band). Where does your shirt some from? China, perhaps, but chances are that it comes from somewhere else—perhaps somewhere unlikely. Western Europe, if it is a fashion garment, Eastern Europe, Northern Africa, the Middle East, India, Central America, South America, Southeast Asia, and beyond. If you go through your closet at home I suspect you will find that you own a shirt from at least one of these unexpected places: Bangladesh, Lesotho, or Mauritius. Bonus points if you can locate all three on a map!

MANY LOGICS, NOT JUST ONE

Why do shoes mainly come from one place and shirts from, well, almost everyplace? The answer is that one logic doesn't dictate global flows. Globalization is too complicated for that. Globalization obeys many different logics, which is why I don't believe in Grassroots Globaloney—the notion that individuals, communities, and nations are powerless to resist and to shape globalization. But you don't have to take my word for it. Just listen to the stories that your shoes and shirts have been trying to tell you.

Our clothing travels so far and has such a complicated path on its way to our wardrobes that it accumulates a certain personal history—a transnational biography, in the words of Karen Tranberg Hansen, an anthropology professor at Northwestern University.[1] The biography of a silk blouse, for example, begins where the silkworms were raised and the silk harvested through the production of the fabric, the design and production of the blouse, and its passage through the commodity chain to a store where someone buys it for herself or as a gift. The biography does not end there, but continues as the garment is worn and thus attends meetings, goes to weddings, and so forth.

Although each biography is different, there are perhaps some generalizations that can be made. Everyday (non-designer) shoes come disproportionately from China, for example, because these mass-produced items follow an economic logic that Adam Smith would have appreciated. Cost, economies of scale, division of labor—these all matter a lot in the shoe business, so shoe production tends to be centralized in China. So long as trade barriers are low and China retains its comparative advantage in this sort of manufacturing, your shoe rack is likely to remain Chinese export territory.

If you want to make and sell shoes elsewhere, you have to beat the China Price, which may be problematic, or you need to do something that's different—make a product that isn't mass produced, that doesn't rely upon the logic of Smith's pin factory for its existence. Such shoes and their alternative logics do exist (I cite my funny-looking Italian-made breathing-sole Geox sneakers as evidence) but cost is apparently a powerful factor when people purchase shoes. So China rules your feet.

The rest of your outfit is a different matter. The market for textiles and clothing is highly structured and segmented, and this serves to differentiate the biographies. Designer clothing, like designer shoes, is more likely to have European stamps on its passport—France or Italy, for example—and to have felt the touch of handwork, not just machines, at some point along the way. True designer original garments are mainly born in Paris, Milan, or New York—but mainly Paris. Their biographies intersect repeatedly because of the particular customs and rituals of the social class they adorn (couture more commonly appears at the opera gala than a Wal-Mart grand opening, for example).

The biography of a cotton sport shirt or blouse of the sort you see in a Lands' End catalogue is much different. These are the real global travelers of the textile world—they seem to come from everywhere and go everywhere, although this is not literally true. My own closet, which is unexceptional in this respect, includes sport shirts with these original ports of call: Bangladesh, Cambodia, Peru, Malawi, Egypt, Malaysia, United Arab Emirates, Pakistan, United States, and the Philippines, among others. There is no central provenance—no Paris or Milan—for sport shirts and the like. This is due in part of the most important international agreement that you've never heard of.

Between 1974 and 2005 world trade in textiles and clothing was governed by the Multi-Fibre Arrangement (MFA). Under the MFA, textile and clothing exporting countries had to agree to limit their foreign sales to specific quantities (export quotas). Textile producers in, say, Korea could not collectively export more than the agreed national quota. The quotas were negotiated on an individual country basis and so were grossly unequal and inefficient. Some countries were able to hold out for large quotas while others had to settle for tiny ones.

The purpose of the MFA was to regulate trade in textiles and clothing and thus to contain somewhat the rabid protectionism of textile workers and factory owners in Europe, the United States, and other rich countries who in the 1970s were fearful that, without regulation, soon all clothes would be made in Japan. Now of course, it is China that first-world industrial workers fear. I think the idea was that trade agreements in general would be easier if textile protectionism could be isolated this way, just as agricultural subsidies effectively took the farm lobby out of the debate. Minus these two strong political interests, the movement toward free trade made good progress for many years.[2]

What happened if a country wanted to exceed its export quota? Well, it could always produce above the quota limit and sell the excess under the table, in the international black market. Some of the suspiciously cheap clothing being hawked by street merchants may bear black market biographies. The one *legal* way around the limit was to build a factory in a country that had room to spare under its quota, which is exactly what happened. Textile producers, especially those in East Asia, fanned out across the globe in search of unused export quotas. They built factories abroad because they could not export more clothes from their existing factories. You could say that these factories (and your multinational collection of "made in xxx" labels) were built by the MFA.

Between 1974 and 2005, therefore, the biography of most common clothing items was determined less by the tension between function and fashion than the conflict between politics and economics. Politics—the desire to regulate textile trade to control political pressures—had the effect of scattering the seeds of the textile industry quite widely. When the MFA was phased out in 2005, these export quotas were supposed to disappear, but protectionist pressures remained, so clothing factories outside of China didn't suddenly vanish. Instead a new but still distinctly diverse type of globalization has emerged, with politics, economics, technology, and taste all playing a role.

If you are interested in all the factors that influence where your shirt comes from, how it is made, by whom, and under what circumstances, you need to read a nifty little book with a T-shirt on the cover. It is called *The Travels of a T-Shirt in the Global Economy: An Economist Examines the Markets, Power and Politics of World Trade* by Georgetown University economist Pietra Rivoli.[3] Rivoli follows a T-shirt she purchased on a Florida holiday back to its origins—back to the factory in China that made it, back to the farm in Texas that produced the cotton, and back in time to the history of how politics, economics, and changing technology have shaped the global "rag trade." It is a fascinating tale—and you will never look at your T-shirts in the same way again.

RECYCLED CLOTHING: THE STORY CONTINUES

Now it's time to complete the story. Clothes do have biographies, or at least we can think of them that way, and these biographies are increasingly transnational or global in both the supply chains that bring these items to us and the patterns of travel and migration that carry them along as we wear them. This much is correct. Here's the missing part: we assume that the global biography of our slacks and shirts ends with us. We see clothes and the clothing trade as a process that reaches its peak, or perhaps just its conclusion, when it reaches us. Sometimes I admit this is true. An old shirt is worn out; it gets tossed in the trash, its remaining biography brutally short: dumpster, garbage truck, landfill, oblivion. Frequently, however, a new global journey begins. Your discarded clothing enters the grassroots side of globalization—the global market for secondhand apparel.

Worn clothing is an important first-world commodity export. According to the U.S. Department of Commerce, the United States exported more than 350 million kilograms (about 385,000 tons) of used clothing in 2003. Total U.S. earnings were almost $240 million or about 30 cents per pound.[4] U.S. exports have risen steadily since 2003, hitting $413 million in 2008 according to government statistics.[5] The top ten markets for U.S. used clothing exports are Canada (which imports them mainly for re-export), Chile, Mexico, Guatemala, Tanzania, Angola, India, Honduras, Kenya, and Japan (which is a market for high-end "vintage" apparel).

When you see big containers coming off a ship and going onto trucks or railroad cars on their way to Costco or Wal-Mart, remember this: they come into the United States full of new products and go back stuffed full of your old clothes, or at least many of them do. Other major exporters of worn clothing are Germany, Great Britain, the Netherlands, and South Korea. The United States is number one in the used clothing trade, but there is a lot of competition.

This trade goes by many names. You can call it worn clothing or used clothing or secondhand clothing. The term *recycled clothing* is often used in the trade, and I don't see anything wrong with it, because it emphasizes the fact that the clothes are reused and not wasted. I sometimes call it the "rag trade" but I do not mean it in a derogatory way. It isn't that the clothes are rags (although some—the worst-quality ones—become rags), but because this is a slang term for the clothing trade generally that inevitably comes to mind when you see a 1,000-pound bale of mixed clothing.

Who buys our worn clothing? The people who are otherwise mostly left out of globalization—those in sub-Saharan Africa—are the largest market for used U.S. clothing (although in many cases the clothing's biography includes an intermediate stop in Canada, India, or Pakistan for sorting, rebundling, and transshipment). Other important markets include Eastern Europe, Central and South America, and South and Southeast Asia.

Worn U.S. clothes are number one globally, in quantity terms, but they are not the most desired in all markets. European clothing discards are preferred in some markets because of their higher quality. Exports from Japan and Korea are more popular than U.S. goods in Southeast Asia, however, because similarities in body sizes mean better fit. I saw used clothing for sale when I lived in Bologna, Italy. Bologna is a rich city that considers itself a fashion center, but about once a month an open-air used clothing annex would appear next to the usual Saturday market, and people would come out to pick through the piles of merchandise. I don't know where these clothes came from and I didn't think to ask, but some of the men's coats had an unmistakable Austrian cut. My favorite find (although I didn't buy it) was a marching band uniform from an Oklahoma high school. What an interesting biography that outfit must have had!

SECONDHAND CLOTHES: THE NAME GAME

People in rich countries refer to the garments by many different names. "Thrift store merchandise" is common American usage, and thrift stores and charity shops are important outlets. In Britain you'd call them "jumble sale clothing." There is nothing even vaguely international about these names because the goods, although often produced abroad, are seen as "domestic" goods. In third world countries, however, the real provenance of used clothes is hard to ignore, so slang terms for them have evolved to help explain their passage from abroad. In Haiti, for example, worn clothing imports were once called *Kennedys* because of an association with aid shipments of used clothing during the Kennedy administration. In eastern Zaire the term *Vietnams* was sometimes used because of the urban myth that the bundles contained the personal effects of soldiers killed in the Vietnam War. In Ghana the name is "dead white men's clothes." When rich white men die, the reasoning goes, their closets are purged and sent to Ghana. There is some truth to this, as we will see.

In Zambia, the term *salaula* applies, which means to pick or to choose in the Bemba language.[6] I especially like this term because, whereas the other names offer explanations for how foreigners' clothing came into the local market, *salaula* emphasizes its appeal to the buyers: choice. Used clothing, although not always cheap, is less expensive than new apparel and often better quality than home-produced goods. It gives customers an opportunity to choose, to be buyers, and to exercise consumer sovereignty in a world where such economic freedoms are often proscribed by poverty.

FOLLOW THAT T-SHIRT

How do millions of pounds of worn clothing get from here (the first world) to there (everywhere else, but especially Africa)? Here's a real case—an authentic biography—as reported in *The Guardian* to help you see how the dots connect. Michael Durham traced the ten-thousand-mile journey of a £50 rayon woman's blouse (made in USA, as it happens) from Leicester, England, where it parted company with its original owner, to the Zambian market where a high school teacher bought it for 10,000 kwachas (Zambia currency units) or about £1.50.[7]

The blouse, which had been bought on a whim and never worn, was dropped off at a charity collection bin at a Tesco parking lot along with a pile of other unwanted items from the back of the closet. A lot of worn clothing passes through charity collection bins. Sometimes these bins are owned and operated by a named charity (Goodwill Industries, Salvation Army, etc.), but this particular one was actually run by a commercial firm, Ragtex UK, which paid the associated charity, an organization for cerebral palsy patients called Scope, for the right to use its name. Scope did benefit from the donation to some extent but did not actually handle the goods, which were trucked directly to a Ragtex sorting facility nearby. There is nothing unusual about this relationship between Scope and Ragtex except perhaps that Scope received a fixed one-hundred-pounds-per-bin payment from Ragtex for use of their name; in other cases with which I am familiar the donation is made on a per-pound basis instead. Sometimes, I understand, the donation bins have no charitable connection whatsoever and exist purely for the receipt of clothing for resale. Donors may suppose that *all* such bins benefit a charity, but this is apparently not the case.

Once at the Ragtex warehouse, the blouse and all the other donated clothing and household items began a complex sorting process. A conveyer belt carried the clothing past workers who picked out items for different market segments. Designer or "vintage" clothing is often sorted into a special bin for resale at local specialty shops. For the most part, however, the clothes are sorted by gender (male, female), age (children's versus adults), type (underwear, jeans, blouses), weight (tropical, which excludes heavy items like coats, and mixed), and quality (items with obvious holes or stains sorted apart from newer-looking goods). Unwearables are sorted as "mixed rags" which have value, although obviously less than wearable attire. Mixed rags become industrial rags, used in foreign factories.

The sorting and bundling of clothes is an important process. Recyclers like Ragtex must be keenly aware of what types and sizes of clothing are popular in different foreign markets. The rag trade is a competitive one, and poorly sorted bales are guaranteed to lose customers. No buyer wants to open a bale and find it filled with unsellable items—too big, too small, too heavy, too light, too worn. *Salaula* means choice, and in this competitive market even beggars can be choosers, in the literal sense, so sorting must be carefully done.

I visited a recycler in Fife, Washington, because I wanted to see for myself how the sorting room operated.[8] But the Savers Company warehouse where I went no longer operated a sorting line for clothing. Sorting is a very labor-intensive process, as you can imagine, and they could not compete with foreign operations. So Savers shipped 1,000-pound bales of unsorted clothes to foreign operatives who sort, rebundle, and resell. I did see sorting lines for other products, however, such as housewares and shoes. A Japanese client was doing his own sorting from a big pile of shoes and boots during my visit. He comes to the U.S. every year, I was told, to pick out choice vintage products for his fashionable shop back in Japan.

Savers operates a chain of thrift stores in the United States and Canada that are associated with local charities. Donations are received directly at the stores, and the charities receive a per-pound payment without having to handle the goods. Items that aren't sold at the thrift shops are trucked to a regional sorting facility like the one I visited, where they enter the global market.

The blouse that we are following was in good shape and quickly found its place in a shrink-wrapped, 45-kilogram bale of similar items, inside a 40-foot shipping container aboard a merchant ship bound for Africa. Two months later it arrived at the port of Beira, Mozambique, where it was loaded onto a waiting truck and sent on its way to Zambia. The blouse passed through several hands before the school teacher bought it. Typically one merchant purchases the container full of baled clothing, buying perhaps one container per month. The individual bales are then sold individually to smaller merchants, who may sell the goods themselves in market stalls or sort them and repackage for sale to traveling sellers.

The container of blouses and other items we are following was purchased by a merchant named Khalid, according to Durham's account, who resold this particular bale to a trader named Mary, who operates a stall in the Kapata open-air market. Mary paid 950,000 kwachas (about £150) for the 45-kilogram bale—an unusually high price that indicates the high expected quality of the goods. As we learned at the beginning of this story, Priscilla Msimuko, the school teacher, bought the blouse from Mary for 10,000 kwachas (£1.50) or the equivalent of a day's pay. I can't help trying to calculate profitability—how many rayon and polyester blouses do you suppose there are in a 45-kilogram bale? At least a couple hundred, I'd guess; maybe more. At £1.50 each you'd only need to sell about half of them to come out ahead. Even if most of them sold for less than the initial 10,000 kwachas offering price, and some do not sell at all, this could be a fairly profitable business in the context of what opportunities Zambia may offer to someone with limited capital.

THE COMMON THREAD

This story—donor to charity to sorter to middleman to market stall to buyer—is the common thread that binds the forgotten biographies of our discarded clothes. The story is repeated endlessly with only a few variations. George Packer traced "the long chain of charity and commerce [that] binds the world's richest and poorest people in accidental intimacy" in an article he wrote for the *New York Times Magazine* in 2002. (The article was titled, "How Susie Bayer's T-shirt Ended Up on Yusuf Mama's Back.")[9] The garment in question in this U.S. case study was a thoroughly used and slightly stained gray T-shirt with "University of Pennsylvania" emblazoned in red and black across the front. The shirt was a tax-deductible donation to a local charity thrift shop that could not possibly find buyers for all the old T-shirts it receives. It, along with other unmarketable goods, is sold for three cents a pound to a textile recycler, Trans-Americas Trading Company. Packer reports that as much as 80 percent of the 2.5 billion pounds that Americans donate to charity each year end up in the recycling system, at Savers or Trans-America or any of the hundreds of other firms in the business.

Incredibly, even a beat-up T-shirt has an international market, but it is near the bottom of the food chain: tucked into one of the 540 "mixed Africa A and B grade" bales in a container bound for Uganda. Like the British blouse, the University of Pennsylvania T-shirt passed through several hands, and it is interesting to see where the money went. The wholesaler who bought the container paid about thirteen cents per shirt, including the freight costs, according to Packer, and sold them off to smaller traders for about nineteen cents per shirt. (No one trades individual shirts at this stage, however, so the price is only illustrative; all of the business is done by the bale.) The bales are then sorted once again and repackaged for smaller traders, who paid the equivalent of about sixty cents per shirt. These traders take their goods to rural village markets, looking for a buyer until one is eventually found. The T-shirt changed hands for the equivalent of $1.20 and started a new chapter in its biography.

I would like be present when one of those bales is opened in an African village market. The bales are very tightly compressed back at the warehouse because container freight is charged by volume, not weight. You pay the same for a light container as a heavy one, as I understand it, so each bale is jammed with merchandise. Merchandise just gushes out when you cut the cord. Jeff McMullin, who explained Savers operations to me, said that a good deal of care is given so that the best merchandise is right at the top when the bale is opened; that way the buyer can see that there is value and retail customers have an incentive to dive in for the choicest goods. A bale of shoes, for example, always contains at least two pairs with brand names such as Nike or Reebok, and these are packed so that they are the first thing the customer sees when the bale is opened. This isn't done to try to disguise the product mix or misrepresent the contents. It is just that every bale inevitably contains mainly a mass of items that will ultimately pay back the bale's cost, a few things that will be hard or impossible to sell, and a couple of high-demand articles that spell real profit. No one wants to have to search around hoping to find those profit-makers, so the recyclers know to put them right on top.

FREQUENTLY ASKED QUESTIONS

There are three questions that I get asked again and again when I talk to people about the recycled clothing trade. The first is, do they clean and press the clothes before they ship them to Africa? The answer is that, as I understand it, the clothes go into the containers in the same state of clean or dirty as when they were put into the donation bins. So I hope you wash those old clothes before you give them to charity. The same is true when they arrive at Africa or a similar market, except that some merchants will pick out the very best items to wash and iron and sell for a higher price, perhaps even marketing them privately to people who do not want to be seen shopping in the market for used clothes.

Does it ever happen that the person who has made a particular new shirt in a third world factory, say, ends up buying back the same item on the used clothing market? Does the global apparel trade ever circle back on itself like that? This is the second most-asked question, and my answer is that it is theoretically possible, but not very likely. One logic—the politics and economics of the Multi-Fibre Arrangement and the structures that have succeeded it—determine where clothes are made. A completely different logic of political protectionism and economic necessity determines where they go on the used clothing market. Almost none of the new clothing found in first world stores comes from sub-Saharan Africa (Malawi is one notable exception), but much of the used product ends up there. It's possible, therefore, but not likely that a shirt could come full circle.

The final question is: how do these people feel about wearing rags? And the answer is that they do not seem to view them as rags (and, objectively, most of the goods we give to charity are not really rags). Rags are what they might have to wear if they could not buy used clothes. Karen Tranberg Hansen, the anthropologist who has done the best research in this field, reports that recycled clothes in Zambia are considered "new" if they come from a newly opened bale, and so have not been picked over or worn previously by anyone in Zambia, for example. This is why the opening of a *salaula* bale of clothing is an important event—it is the opportunity to have first pick from a grab bag of "new" clothes.

MANUFACTURING GLOBALONEY

What should we think about the global trade in secondhand clothing? One thing that struck me when I first started learning about it is how important it has been, in an indirect way, in the development of globalization theory. You can hardly read a book about globalization, either pro or con, without coming across a vignette involving a T-shirt. Here's the scenario. Traveling in remote China or Africa, I unexpectedly come upon a local resident wearing a Michael Jordan T-shirt or something similar. This experience inspires a "globalization moment"; I come to understand just how deeply globalization or Americanization has penetrated the world. I suddenly realize that people in this remote locale are seeking out the same symbols of consumer society that I seek—that they are being corrupted by the same forces of media, multinationals, and overconsumption as I am. The T-shirt says it all. That's how globalization works.

Having studied the rag trade, however, we know that there is a less dramatic but much more likely explanation for that red number 23 Chicago Bulls T-shirt: it was right on top when the *salaula* bale popped open in the village market. With so many of these shirts discarded every day as American closets are cleaned out, it really isn't a miracle that people like Thomas Friedman see one or two of them in Africa or Nepal; rather, it is a wonder that they don't find them *everywhere*! Oh, I guess they do. I wonder how many globalization theories have been concocted from mistaken interpretations of America's secondhand clothing exports?

What is the *correct* interpretation? How *should* we think about the used clothing trade? It seems to me that what you think of it depends a lot on whether you look at it closely and whether you accept it for what it is. The superficial facts can very easily be molded to fit standard globalization rhetoric. The details, however, tell a story all their own. It is a classic case of details versus grand design, which is one of the hallmarks of globaloney.

Although there are people who paint too rosy a picture of how the rag trade benefits the poor who participate in it—who make more than they should of the "win-win" situation—by far the biggest offenders are those who oppose the secondhand clothing trade, seeing in it only a further manifestation of an exploitive and empty McWorld. Let me go through some of the typical charges made in the antiglobalization literature and compare them to a more detailed and nuanced view of the facts.

- The secondhand clothing trade is typical of the inequality built into the capitalist world system. Third world people wear the third-rate rags that the rich of the world cast off. The poor dress in rags so the rich can wear fine clothes.

Who says that secondhand clothes are rags? Who gives meaning to the clothes that people wear? I begin with this statement because it raises an important intellectual question: Do people have to accept the meanings that other people assign to their actions and acquisitions—or are they able to manufacture their own meanings and significance? Are the buyers sovereign, capable of forming their own opinions, or are they mere stooges assigned to play a silent part in a grand global drama? I am disappointed that some globalization critics have so little respect for the ability of people, even poor people with little education, to create meaning and significance from their own world.

One of the main conclusions of Karen Tranberg Hansen's thorough study of *salaula* in Zambia is that the people (about 80 percent of Zambia's population wear secondhand clothing) have taken full control of the meaning of these goods and have created a completely original culture from them. It isn't that they have refused to accept foreign meanings, I think, it is simply that they made their own. It probably never occurred to them that they could not do this. *Salaula*, Hansen notes, has become the opposite of rags. "Because rags are a metaphor for lack of access, salaula stands for opportunity, choice, and new chances."[10]

- It is immoral to charge third world people for these old clothes. They should be given to them for free.

I wonder how many would be given away, given the high cost of transportation and distribution, if they had to be given for free? The cost of the charity would most likely discourage the practice. Or the clothing then would get dumped in the port city and never make its way to the villages where it may be needed most. But, honestly, I think most of these clothes would go into the landfill instead of going abroad, adding to the environmental problems of the exporting countries. I also doubt that the distribution system would be as widespread and efficient if there were no money to be made.

I'm also a bit concerned about the economic and psychological effects of free goods. Economically, free clothes tend to crowd out clothes that do cost something, so there would be serious problems for the merchants who do sell clothes (unless they bribed some corrupt official to get access to the best items in each bale). Psychologically, people treat free goods differently from those things they have to pay for. This could start a cycle of waste and dependency. Maybe it is best that buyers pay for what they get and pay for the cost of getting it there, too.

- But making money is the problem, isn't it? The rag trade is just another way for the rich countries to exploit the poor.

That's not the answer I got when I did the math. Secondhand clothing is a profitable business, I am not denying that; but it seems to me that most of the profit ends up in the developing countries. Think back to the figures that George Packer cited in the *New York Times* article. The U.S. recycler received thirteen cents a pound for its bales. Out of this it had to pay shipping costs (perhaps ten thousand dollars per container), sorting costs (very labor intensive), local trucking and handling costs, and it had to make a donation to the sponsoring charity. If these firms make large profits, it must be because they move huge volumes.[11] The difference between the thirteen-cent cost and the $1.20 final selling price goes to pay expenses and provide incomes to indigenous merchants and traders.

That $1.20 price is relatively high, compared with third world income, but what do you suppose other products cost? Clothing made in inefficient local factories usually costs more. Homemade clothes are expensive, too, in the time they require, and may not have the same good quality as secondhand apparel. Actually, I think it is amazing that these goods are so cheap. The prices I read about in the African markets are about the same as I see in local thrift shops, which measure transportation costs in miles, not oceans. It is really amazing that clothing can travel so far so cheaply and get in the hands of people who want it.

But citizens of the third world aren't the only ones who wear used clothes. Plenty of first world people do, too, as indicated by the existence of thrift shops, jumble sales, and secondhand stores in Japan, Europe, and the United States. Sometimes globalization critics make it sound like everyone in rich countries wears fine new clothing and everyone in poor countries goes around in rags. In fact, however, secondhand is everywhere. Who did not receive some hand-me-down clothes while growing up? Hand-me-downs are secondhand clothes recycled within a family, and they are an accepted fact of life even in rich countries. As families have grown smaller and more fragmented, I guess, some intra-family recycling has been replaced by interfamily sales, through garage sales and so forth, and by indirect and anonymous recycling through charitable donations. Market relations have replaced family relations insofar as clothes are concerned.

Interestingly, one of the reasons that used European clothes are often preferred over American items in foreign markets may be because Americans now tend to give away clothes rather than hand them down. Clothes you hand down need to be well made and well taken care of because you personally know the recipient. Clothes you wear for a while and then give away do not—you don't feel the same connection to the new user.

- That's another problem. Doesn't this whole system just encourage global capitalism and consumerism?

I don't think having or not having a secondhand clothes market has very much to do with global capitalism. If you took away the worn clothes market, third world residents would simply have fewer options. Maybe that's the problem: I tend to think that options are a good thing—that's probably my consumerism talking—and more options are better, all else being equal. If I weren't already driven by consumerist values, I might not think this way. But there you have it; I am a victim of my culture.[12] Nonetheless, it does seem that the rag trade offers people in third world countries a good opportunity to earn an income if they sell used clothes—provided they can establish the necessary relationships and earn a good reputation—and an economic way of using their incomes to purchase what they need.

I find it interesting that the global secondhand clothing trade is seen by some as exploitive and disempowering. Microfinance, on the other hand, is viewed in just the opposite light. Micro-loans are small ten- to fifty-dollar loans made to small-scale merchants who use these funds to buy materials that they work in some way and resell. Borrowers pay back the loan, earn some income, and are able to perhaps borrow more next time. Micro-loans are seen as empowering, giving people at the grass roots income, opportunity, and independence. One of the shibboleths of the antiglobalization movement is that macrofinance (World Bank, Citicorp, etc.) is bad, but microfinance (the Grameen Bank in Bangladesh is the most famous example) is very good. But what do you think people do with their micro-loans? In Africa, at least, they sometimes use them to buy a small bale of used clothes, which they resell.[13] It seems to me that microfinance and the rag trade are not so much different, as they are two sides of the same informal economic coin.

- Huge imports of used clothes, dumped by first world economies, put indigenous textile and clothing companies out of business. This is just another example of how the neoliberal policies of the World Bank destroy third world economies and trap them in a vicious cycle of dependency by making it impossible for them to repay international loans.

These issues are raised in a documentary film called *T-Shirt Travels*, which was aired on PBS,[14] the U.S. public television network. I wasn't able to see it because my local station cancelled network programming in favor of an earnest fund-raising campaign. (They need the money, they say, so they can afford to telecast controversial and informative documentaries—like *T-Shirt Travels*.)

Although the World Bank isn't on the list of the top ten things I think of when I look at a bale of used clothes, there certainly is a connection. It is true, on one hand, that the market-oriented, open-economy policies that the World Bank, International Monetary Fund, and World Trade Organization (WTO) favor are useful to the secondhand clothing trade. But the issue isn't a simple one (globalization issues seldom are). "When it comes to salaula, the Zambian government is caught in a balancing act of mediating between its different constituencies," Hansen writes, "the overseers of the IMF/World Bank-sponsored structural adjustment program, who insist on obtaining conditions to encourage a 'free' market; local garment and textile manufacturers, who argue for import regulation to protect their ailing industry; and three-fourths of the population, who have seen both their formal job prospects and purchasing power erode over the years of the third republic. It is hardly surprising that the government's stance has been equivocal."[15] The conflict is not so much between Zambia and the World Bank as between the interests associated with the Zambia textile factories, which want to keep secondhand clothing out, and the people who buy worn clothes, who mainly want to let it in. This is a problem of intersecting domestic political interests at least as much (and probably more) than it is a story of global economic governance.

It is true that Zambia's textile industry declined (disappeared, really) at the same time that secondhand clothes imports increased, but correlation is not causation in this case. "It is easy, but too facile," Karen Tranberg Hansen writes, "to blame salaula for the dismal performance of Zambia's clothing and textile manufacturing industries."[16] She blames macroeconomic mismanagement; a combination of national economic policies that produced high inflation, making all domestic industries less competitive; and problems specific to the clothing sector: "High import dependence, high capital intensity, inappropriate technology, poor management, and lack of skilled labor, especially in textile-printing technology . . . resulted in gross underutilization of capacity."[17] It is no wonder that Zambians found imported products, even used ones, a better choice.

- Yes, but they still lost the jobs, didn't they? How will Zambians survive if they continue to lose good jobs, like those in the textile mills?

I'm surprised to find out that textile mill jobs are good ones. I usually hear textile factories described as sweatshops—the kind of jobs no one wants. I guess that when the World Bank promotes these jobs they are bad, but when its policies discourage them they are somehow transformed into good jobs.

In any case, the rag trade creates jobs, too, just like microfinance does. Think of all the people who make a living selling and sorting worn clothing. It is difficult to count up the number of jobs that the rag trade creates because they are widely dispersed; whereas factory jobs are geographically concentrated, but I know they're there. I'd like to say that these jobs are better ones and that they are free from corruption, poor working conditions, and so on, but I don't think that is always true. Textile factory jobs and market selling jobs are different. It is maybe more secure to work in the factory, but the conditions are worse. Being a merchant entrepreneur is risky but offers a better upside. Better or worse? It isn't so easy to say.

- The bottom line is that the rag trade is just another example of how McWorld works. And whom does McWorld benefit? The power elites in the infotainment telesector—the ones who create the logos that sell the products that poor African peasants line up to buy.

The bottom line is nothing like this at all. I hope it is clear that the global trade in secondhand clothes has little to do with McWorld or any of the other simplified images of globalization that you find in the press. The rag trade is what it is—it has its own unique shape, feel, and biography—and should not be treated as some pliable raw material that can be molded and pressed to fit into a standard shape or form. It is not an example of some powerful global metaphor at work but a classic case of how different institutions and practices evolve over time to try to deal with the problems of material existence in an interconnected world.

Secondhand clothes teach us that while globalization may sometimes exploit the poor of the world, at least occasionally it offers them opportunities, too. Or, more exactly, they are able to make opportunities out of it—to manufacture a piece of globalization that *benefits* them. This is a theme that I think bears closer examination, which is why we turn next to a grassroots movement that aims to use globalization to fight globalization's effects.

Chapter 7

SLOW-BALIZATION
Using Globalization to Fight Globalization

The revolution began in Rome . . . at a McDonald's. The revolutionaries came armed, appropriately, with bowls of pasta. With such small acts do empires sometimes fall.

"I remember when in 1986 Carlo Petrini organized a protest against the building of a McDonald's at the Spanish Steps in Rome," writes Alice Waters in the foreword to *Slow Food: The Case for Taste.* "The protesters, whom Carlo armed with bowls of *penne*, defiantly and deliciously stated their case against the global standardization of the world's food. With this symbolic act, Carlo inspired a following and sparked the Slow Food movement. Three years later, delegates from fifteen countries came together in Paris to pledge to preserve the diversity of the world's foods."[1]

The Slow Food movement is a global organization that aims to resist globalization and, in fact, to use the means of globalization to preserve and protect some of the very elements of local culture that global markets threaten to overwhelm. It is an ambitious movement, to say the least. There are about 100,000 Slow Food members in more than 130 countries organized into nearly 1000 local chapters or *convivia* (there is even a convivium in Turkmenistan, according to the Slow Food website). By far the highest concentration of Slow Food members is in Italy, where about a third of the convivia are located. The movement is growing rapidly, especially in the United States.

The title—Slow Food—is not a translation of an Italian phrase (I think it would be *cibo lento*). The movement is called Slow Food—English words—in all countries and all languages. (Its official logo is a drawing of a snail—*slow* food, get it?) It is impossible to misinterpret the meaning: Slow Food opposes Fast Food on its own terms (and in its own language). No one is surprised to learn, therefore, that the defining moment for the Slow Food movement was a protest at a McDonald's in Rome. It fits the picture perfectly.

But the origins of the Slow Food movement are actually much different—the image of Slow Food versus McWorld is a little bit of baloney, really, manufactured to be especially easy to digest. Slow Food is more complex than this, which is why I find it so interesting. "Many people see Slow Food as the direct antagonist of fast food, especially McDonald's," says Carlo Petrini, the movement's founder and president. "This view would be true if it were not so reductive, and if we had ever mounted a campaign against the king of hamburger chains."[2] Protests, like Bové's attack on the Golden Arches or the anti-WTO (World Trade Organization) Battle in Seattle, are not Slow Food's style. "Our choice is to focus our energies on saving things that are headed for extinction instead of hounding the new ones we dislike."[3] Like *salaula*, Slow Food is about choice.

Indeed, Slow Food is not really opposed to either McDonald's in particular or to fast food in general—there are many traditional street foods that are fast and good, Petrini says; who would want to give them up?[4] The picture of Carlo Petrini confronting Big Mac with a bowl of *penne rigate* is a false image of the Slow Food movement, really, but a very useful one because it defines the movement in a way that is obvious and familiar, especially to Americans. This is useful when your real agenda is both more subtle and more ambitious.

The Slow Food movement is rooted in the 1970s and a group of young leftist students in the Northern Italian city of Bra.[5] Petrini's account makes Bra sound like a smelly factory town in terminal decline, but one where the people had not yet completely lost their sense of connection to the earth. Petrini and his friends were members of ARCI (*Associazione Ricreativa Culturale Italiana*)—generally described as a left-wing cultural and recreation association[6]—and from this base they formed the Free and Praiseworthy Association of the Friends of Barolo. (Barolo is the great red wine produced in the Piedmont of Italy, where Bra is located.) The group's interest was food and culture and its desire was to learn more about these things and to compare their own culinary heritage with that in other regions of Italy.[7]

There is a lot to compare if you travel Italy north to south, and you are unlikely to see only the differences in pasta shape, especially if you come from the industrial north and are already a bit on the pinkish side of the political spectrum. "[I]f you paid attention to material culture and thought about people's working lives and everyday routines, and the basic enjoyment of earthly goods," Petrini writes, "you began to see the enormous potential of Italy's agricultural and regional heritage in term of both its traditions and its economic potential."[8] The group formed Arcigola: *Arci*, from ARCI, the social club (but also to suggest "arch" as in highest authority), and *gola* meaning appetite (many of the founding members worked on a culinary magazine called *La Gola)*.

MANIFESTO DELLO SLOW FOOD

Slowly, the dots were being connected, from politics to food to culture to economics and then, as we will see, back to politics again. "The first people to call themselves 'arcigolosi' or 'archeaters,'" Petrini writes, "were an offshoot of that sector of the 1970s political militancy that coalesced around the daily *il manifesto*."[9] Arcigola's first official publication, as near as I can tell, was a food and wine supplement to *il manifesto* titled *Gambero Rosso* or "red prawn." I've been told that the color of the prawn is a political rather than culinary statement and I don't doubt that it is true. The November 3, 1987, issue of *Gambero Rosso* featured the *Manifesto dello Slow Food*—the Slow Food manifesto. With publication of this statement of principles in the food section of a left-wing newspaper, the Slow Food movement was really born.

There are three things that you need to know about the Slow Food movement. First, it really is an antiglobalization movement, although it makes every effort to avoid the "G-word." The Slow Food manifesto instead refers to the "Fast Life," of which fast food is just one aspect. "We are enslaved by speed and have all succumbed to the same insidious virus: *Fast Life*, which disrupts our habits, pervades the privacy of our homes and forces us to eat *Fast Foods*," it reads in part. "In the name of productivity, *Fast Life* has changed our way of being and threatens our environment and our landscapes. So *Slow Food* is now the only truly progressive answer."[10] The movement is about food, but not *just* about food.

The Slow Food movement is true to its roots—its international organization today reflects its origins in the ARCI social club. This is to say that Slow Food is many things, not one single thing. It is, at the grassroots level, still very much a federation of social clubs. The local chapters host social events that are for the most part relevant to the organization's stated goals. But it is not a burden to attend the meetings, at least in my experience. The *gola* or appetite is well served.

If the Fast Life is about the global, then the Slow Life must celebrate the local. Slow Food events promote local foods, local cooks, local growers and makers, local ingredients, and traditional methods. To a certain extent, the Slow Food movement serves as a marketing organization for these local products and producers, adding an economic interest to the mix. Many members and convivium leaders own restaurants or specialty food shops, write newspaper columns, or are active in the food/wine/hospitality industry. Their participation in the Slow Food movement is personally rewarding, I am sure, and not entirely inconsistent with their economic interests.

Slow Food also promotes what we might call gastronomic tourism, which stems from the founders' early desire to compare their own culinary heritage with that of other regions of Italy. Slow Food has thus always encouraged members to travel, taste, and discuss—to spread the movement's message globally. The focus, of course, is on local foods, producers, ingredients, and recipes. The goal of Slow Food tourism is to have an authentic or "typical" experience.[11] The organization's grandest and most recent effort in this regard is called Slow Food Planet, an emerging world atlas of eating.[12] If you are going to Beijing, for example, and you want to know where to stay and what to eat, drink, and buy, Slow Food Planet will tell you.[13] Slow Food members have thus far posted guides for such destinations as Genoa, Turin, Budapest, Graz, London, New York, Sydney, Reykjavik, and Walla Walla, among others. Gastronomic tourism supports the movement's principles, its social mission, and the economic interests of many of its members.

The Slow Food movement is opposed to the industrialization of food, which means that it supports small farms, biodiversity, and efforts to resist mono-cropping. It opposes the introduction of genetically modified products into the food chain. This gives Slow Food a political agenda to balance or reinforce its economic and social aspects. The movement has opened an office in Brussels now, the better to lobby European Union officials on these issues.

Finally, the Slow Food movement organizes all of these elements around a program of education, not confrontation. The program is very comprehensive, beginning with the Days of Taste (Semaine du Goût) for schoolchildren and climaxing with the University of the Science of Gastronomy (Università di Scienzia di Gastronomiche) which opened in 2004. The Days of Taste are intended to introduce an element of gastronomic education into the typical school curriculum. The point is not to create pint-sized gourmets, although this may happen, but to stress the idea that we should give as much attention to what goes into our bodies as to what goes into our heads. Students are educated about food quality, with some emphasis on the classic Slow Food qualities of local, natural, and authentic.

The university is an attempt to take Slow Food education to a higher level, to facilitate research and education about food, taste, food science, and food culture at the highest level. Students take two-year and three-year degrees on two Northern Italy campuses (near Cuneo and Parma). In addition to classrooms and research facilities, the university offers a noteworthy wine library and really good restaurants.

The Ark of Taste (*Arca del Gusta*) is another aspect of Slow Food education. The Ark is a symbolic vessel meant to contain the Slow World's endangered species. Raising a product to the Ark of Taste, such as the tiny (the size of a fifty-cent piece) Olympia oysters of Puget Sound, is a way of saying that this is a food with *terroir*—a history and connection to a particular people and place. It is an excuse to publicize the product and to raise public awareness about its existence and possible extinction. It is a way of educating people about food, one product—oyster, cheese, mushroom, or berry—at a time.

The Presidia (*I Presídi*) goes one step beyond the Ark of Taste. In military terminology, the *presidia* are the defense battalion, a sort of homeland security force. Slow Food recognizes that endangered food products cannot simply be put into museums like pottery shards. They will disappear unless they have sufficient "economic impact" to be preserved in living form by the market.[14] The Presidia is the active defense against such extinction. It funds projects to help producers of Ark foods gain an economic foothold and expand local markets. A study of the Presidia's programs in Italy by economists at Bocconi University concluded that the economic impact was significant in increasing production and establishing markets for several local products. Although funding to bring together producers, establish quality standards, and so forth can be useful, the power of the Presidia is not limited to its financial impact. When a product is raised to the Presidium, all aspects of the Slow Food network are brought to bear on it. "The study showed how a Slow Food Presidium acts as a cultural matrix, bringing together territory and product, typicality and quality, in which the term 'environment' finds its clearest expression as the 'context of life in the local community'—and new recognition in the local market," according to the report.[15]

The heritage turkey project is an example of the Presidia's potential in the United States. I think everyone knows that the modern Thanksgiving turkey bears little resemblance in appearance or taste to the American wild turkey, which Benjamin Franklin famously championed as the national symbol. The big-breasted factory bird is pretty much everything that Slow Food opposes in food, but how can heritage species of turkeys be preserved in the face of market forces? The answer so far has been to use the Slow Food movement to educate members and others about heritage turkeys and to create a wider market for these products, especially at the Thanksgiving holiday. These old-fashioned turkeys can cost as much as eighty dollars each (versus ten to twelve dollars for the industrial product), and it is hard to imagine how they could generate a sustainable "economic impact" without Slow Food's help. With it, however, they just might survive.

The Presidia uses economic means to achieve political ends. The goal of these programs is not simply to keep some local cheeses in production, but to contribute ultimately to larger social and political changes. This point is clearly made in an article called "Slow Food and Lula," in the July 2003 issue of *Slow*, the magazine that Slow Food members receive. Paolo Di Croce described a visit he made to Brazil along with several other nongovernmental organization representatives, to meet with members of President Lula's then-new government. "Slow Food counts for little in Brazil," he writes. "A handful of members and a few Convivium leaders."[16] But the Brazilian officials were both knowledgeable about Slow Food and enthusiastic to gain its support for a "Zero Hunger" program.

The Lula government wanted to use Slow Food's ideas—and its global influence—to help shift Brazilian agricultural policy away from export-driven mass production toward a more diverse system that would support smaller producers and, by producing more for local markets, help eliminate hunger among the poor. Slow Food and the Brazilian government signed an agreement calling for Slow Food to use the Presidia to identify, support, and draw global attention to Brazil's program in general and to specific local products in particular. Slow Food's credibility—and its ability to focus worldwide attention and resources—made it a useful tool for Lula's government as it sought to enact radical reforms in Brazil's agricultural policy.

"This is a historical agreement for Slow Food," Di Croce writes.

> On the one hand it puts a great deal of responsibility on our shoulders, obliging us to guarantee support to a huge, complex, far-away country in the middle of a delicate political period pregnant with great expectations for the most diverse and poorest social strata. On the other hand, it reiterates our desire to share the positive experience of the Italian Presidia with the rest of the world . . . as examples of sustainable quality farming capable of responding to the demands of the most varied types of land.[17]

At the very top of the Slow Food pyramid is the Slow Food Award for Defense of Biodiversity (*I Premio*). These awards recognize individuals and small organizations for their contributions to the global mission of Slow Food. The 2003 awards ceremony in Naples recognized a number of important contributions, including that of Kuul Darjaa, a rancher who lives in the Republic of Tuva, a remote place in Southern Siberia near the border with Mongolia.[18] Kuul Darjaa's achievement was to organize a breeding program to restore and preserve native Tuva breeds of livestock and their distinctive contribution to the global gene pool. The Association Tefy Saina in Madagascar also received an award for its work with rice farmers. It developed a system of natural rice production that achieved high yields with traditional rice strains without resorting to the environmentally damaging slash-and-burn techniques traditionally used.[19]

True to its agreement with President Lula to use its influence to support and recognize Brazilian efforts, Slow Food presented a special award to the Kapéy Association—The Union of Krahô Villages.[20] The Krahô are one of 215 indigenous peoples living in Brazil. The award recognizes their efforts to recover and reintroduce a native variety of maize called *pohumpé*. The revival of this crop has helped preserve Krahô culture and practices, according to the award citation, and suggests a practical approach to preserving biodiversity.

I have not attended a Salone del Gusto (Hall of Taste) but I hope to do so eventually. The first meeting in 1996 was like a grand food and wine fair, but with a Slow Food focus on taste, *terroir*, education, and of course socializing. The meetings drew a lot of attention, which is what happens when you bring together excellent food and wine and people who want to eat and drink, talk, debate, and—oh, yes—change the world. The 2002 meeting attracted 140,000 participants and became an opportunity for what Carlo Petrini calls "cultural marketing."[21] The Salone are now a global forum for education, promotion, and political activism—an opportunity to focus worldwide attention on critical issues in a way much different than blowing up a hamburger store.

This brings me to the next important thing that you must understand about the Slow Food movement. It uses the means and media of globalization to undermine and oppose the substance, culture, and ideology of globalization, aka the Fast Life. Carlo Petrini seems to understand that a philosophy of *terroir* is more robust and sustainable if there is a market for it. The Slow Food movement builds its market in several ways, mainly at the local chapter level (I'll talk about this more in a moment). The Slow Food website (www.slowfood.com for the American movement; the global site is www.slowfood.it) certainly displays global ambitions. But it is Slow Food's command of the media that I find most impressive.

The first real publication of the Slow Food movement was a news-paper food supplement called *Il Gambero Rosso*. This modest initial effort has evolved into one of the world's great food and wine periodi-cals, and, although it is not officially part of the Slow Food movement, it certainly gives comfort to those who are. The October 2003 Italian edition of *Gambero Rosso* ran to more than 350 pages overall—a hefty size for a monthly magazine—and was heavy with advertisements. (A smaller version of *Gambero Rosso* is also published in English.) As in any food magazine there are recipes and articles about chefs and their restaurants. *Gambero Rosso*, however, pays special attention to regional foods and artisanal producers. *Terroir* has pride of place in *Gambero Rosso* just as it does at Slow Food.

The first Slow Food book was published in 1987. It was called *Vini d'Italia* and was a guide to the best wines in Italy. Now a joint publica-tion of *Gambero Rosso* and Slow Food Editore, *Vini d'Italia* is updated annually. It is the bible of Italian wines and wine tourism. My copy is a dog-eared 2004 English version.[22] It runs more than 850 pages and lists 14,208 wines from 1,937 Italian winemakers. Each producer of a quality wine receives a brief written evaluation, and the individual wines are rated, with three glasses (*tre bicchiere*) the top award. Getting *tre bicchiere* from *Vini d'Italia* is the ultimate seal of quality—only 254 wines received this rating in 2004.

My favorite Slow Food publications are the *Osterie d'Italia* guide-books.[23] These books promote gastronomic tourism in Italy by scour-ing the country, even the smallest villages, for small restaurants, ca-fes, wine bars, and restaurants that serve authentic "typical" regional dishes. In Pesaro on the Adriatic coast, for example, *Osterie d'Italia* sends you down a tiny walkway to Antica Osteria la Guercia where Roman-era frescos of winemaking (and drinking) can still be seen on the walls. This is not a Big Deal place but the home of *piatti della tradizione pesarese*—traditional dishes including a crisp and flaky griddle bread and a savory clam and bean soup.

What I like about the guidebooks and the other Slow Food publica-tions is that they make money and they sell the message. Economically, they promote the interests of the Slow Food Editore and the restau-rants, bakeries, cafes, cheese shops, wineries, and artisanal producers who get mentioned. They serve an economic function, and a social one, too, I suppose, and they serve a political function as well. They draw a world of attention and resources (both scarce in today's society) and focus them on a few matters of serious concern. Slow Food is like the rag trade in that it shows us how the grass roots do not just survive globalization, or resist it, but shape it and give it substance and meaning.

ON THE ROAD WITH SLOW FOOD

I am cautiously optimistic about the Slow Food movement's ability to reshape globalization from the ground up. My experiences in Italy, the birthplace of Slow Food, contribute to my feelings. I was in Italy to give a lecture about globaloney and I decided to use the opportunity to learn firsthand about the movement and its influence. Here's what I found.

I was fortunate to be in Bologna for the meeting of the local Slow Food chapter where a traditional local product, *mortadella classica*, was raised to the Presidia. About seventy-five of us sat at two long tables at the historic Cantina Bentivoglio on via Mascarella near the University of Bologna to do what Slow Fooders everywhere do: eat, drink, and talk. *Mortadella classica* is the real deal: it has nothing whatsoever to do with your vacuum-packed grocery store baloney. Here's how it is described in its Presidia entry:

> The Presidum's mortadella classica is made from pork from heavy-weight Italian pigs and preservatives (only a bare minimum), and flavored with salt, black pepper grains, ground white pepper, mace, coriander, and crushed garlic. It is then cooked in stone ovens at a central temperature of 75–77C. The casing is made strictly of pigs' bladders. When sliced, the meat is not red and pinkish like the industrial variety, but pale brown with much more complex aromas.[24]

Bologna is a city of great food and the everyday ordinary mortadella that you buy in the market there—at the Tamborini delicatessen, for example—is a beautiful product of great delicacy and complexity. But the *mortadella classica* we were served that night really was a thing apart, a stunning revelation not just to me but to the Bolognese there as well. I am sure that the event (along with other programs planned by the Presidia) will help create a wider market for and appreciation of the work of Salumificio Pasquini & Brusiani, the local mortadella maker.

The wines we drank with the mortadella were provided by Azienda Agricola Tizzano, a distinguished local producer. I think the Tizzano wines, including both still and *frizzante* versions of the local Pignoletto, are very good and would be well received anywhere in the world. But its market is decidedly local, and I think the Slow Food event was a good opportunity for the winery to showcase its products alongside such outstanding food. The problem with making really good wine in the Colli Bolognesi (the Bologna Hills geographic designation), one of my tablemates explained, is that Tuscany, with its global reputation for great wines, is right next door. Who is going to pay top dollar for a Bolognese wine (especially a Pignoletto variety you've never heard of) when you can buy a famous Tuscan wine that is rated in all of the magazines? So Tizzano's market must be local if they are to have a market at all. In any case, I learned, producers like Tizzano could not supply a larger demand for their wine if one were to appear. Everything that affects the quantity of production, the proprietor Gabriele Forni explained, acreage, crop yield, and so forth, is strictly regulated by the rules of the DOC. Tizzano cannot make *more* wine because of these regulations, or even very much *different* wine, so they try to make better wine and to make a better market for the wine in the local region. Slow Food, I concluded, could be very useful in this regard.

As good as the wine and mortadella were, the star of the evening was a local dentist, Dottor Romano Foschi, who had set about to make the classic Bolognese pork products using absolutely no additives or preservatives of any kind. He was willing to go far beyond tradition in search of natural flavors and processes. The results were simply magnificent—the purest expression of pork that you can imagine. But it was almost impossible to buy these meats. Production was very limited, prices correspondingly high, and distribution direct from the maker only. In a way, Dr. Foschi's incredibly delicious products were almost too pure for Slow Food, his methods too extreme and his production too tiny to be consistent with Slow Food's market methods.

The Bologna dinner was encouraging. It showed me why Slow Food could be so effective on its native soil. The event served social, economic, and educational purposes very well and the political agenda, while present, was subtly in the background.

A dinner in Norcia did less to feed my optimism. Norcia is a tiny walled city high in the mountains of southeast Umbria. It is famous for its lentils, truffles, prosciutto, and wild boar and as the birthplace of Saint Benedict. Norcia is a Slow Food city if I have ever seen one, but not a Slow City—part of the network of towns, mainly in Italy, that have made an official commitment to the Slow Food movement's principles. Indeed, Norcia did not even have a Slow Food chapter, and so none of its distinctive local products were recognized in the Ark or Presidia. Perhaps they were not as endangered as the products found just across the border in Le Marche (where the Slow Food influence is stronger). Seated at long tables with local business and political leaders, we feasted on course after course of local specialties and tried to start a conversation about Slow Food. It was a wasted effort, however. Norcia wasn't for Slow Food or against it, as near as I could tell; it was just sort of oblivious to the movement. Clearly the globalization of the Slow Food movement is as uneven as every other kind of globalization I have ever studied.

I was disappointed to discover that Slow Food was not on everyone's mind in Italy. I figured that Norcia, one of Italy's great food cities, would also be a great Slow Food city, but the movement didn't seem to have any impact there. The most common response in Norcia and elsewhere in Italy, even among "foodies," when I would bring up Slow Food was a shrug of the shoulders. Slow Food? Yes. So what about it? Maybe this is a particularly Italian response to a particularly Italian organization with particular political and geographic roots. Everything in Italy is political, I have learned, and regional, too. Slow Food sits in the left-north (left politically, north geographically) in this cultural geography and many of the people I talked to were maybe left-south or center-right-north.

I didn't find the broad grassroots support for Slow Food in Italy that I expected. But maybe a grassroots globalization movement, even one as ambitious as Slow Food, doesn't really have to infiltrate the grass roots. In fact, ironically, maybe it is most effective, from the political standpoint, when it is a grassroots movement of influential urban elites, like the people around the table in Bologna. Grassroots elites? Maybe I drank too much wine.

Another dinner in Umbria forced me to consider a dark side of the Slow Food movement that I had not previously noticed. We were staying near Deruta at an *agritourismo*, which is a sort of farmhouse bed and breakfast. The farm seemed to typify the Slow Food ideal. Not only was the prosciutto made from one of the farm pigs, for example; we even knew the pig's name, Timmy. What about the Slow Food movement, I asked? Our host shook his head. Very bad, he said. It can ruin everything. When Slow Food identifies an artisanal product, like a cheese or a salami, he explained, then suddenly everyone has to have it precisely because it has been given the Slow Food stamp. It must be the best. So they all rush in to buy this great thing, creating a new demand that the supplier, of course, cannot possibly meet. The producers try, but in doing so they cut corners or make compromises and end up destroying the very qualities that they set out to preserve. That's what my Umbrian host saw in the Slow Food movement.

This was a very different, almost cynical view of Slow Food's effects, but I knew what he was talking about. He was describing how a winner-take-all market works.

Once people or products are ranked, the way *Gambero Rosso* ranks wine and restaurants, then why settle for second best (even if it is almost as good)? The market for the finest or most authentic and wholesome products is not large in absolute terms, but it is huge compared to the ability of artisans to satisfy it once Slow Food or someone else turns on its spotlight. The flip side of the Presidia, then, is that the "economic impact" that can save a local product from extinction under one set of circumstances may instead bury it.

Another internal contradiction in the Slow Food strategy made the news as I was finishing the first draft of this chapter. Slow Food, of course, tries to think global and act local. So consumers are encouraged to purchase local products from local makers and growers. But some Slow Food projects, like the heritage turkey initiative, can only succeed if the market for critical products expands well beyond the local area. So sometimes, Slow Food says, you ought to buy products from far away, when they are "merit" goods. This contradiction—buy local except when you shouldn't—showed up on the op-ed page of *The New York Times*. "Shoppers at farmers markets in cities around the country might feel virtuous because they're filling their baskets with eggs and chard and apples offered by farmers within driving distance," wrote Patrick Martins, director of Slow Food U.S.A.

But markets and community supported agriculture programs, wonderful as they are, can't by themselves save American agriculture. To do that, we have to look beyond the "eat local" slogans at the farmers markets in New York, San Francisco, and Chicago and think of how to give American consumers across the country access to regional products that might disappear unless they are raised in much larger numbers. In some cases the answer is to think locally—but to ship nationally.

Global trade and mass communication tend to erase cultural and biological diversity, but as the writer Michael Pollan argues, we can turn them into powerful tools for rescuing this diversity.[25] Clearly, navigating this global-local geography is a tricky task.

GRASSROOTS GLOBALIZATION

The rag trade is an example of grassroots globalization, where people have been able to resist globalization or to shape it to suit their values and needs. Slow Food goes further, plotting to use global forces like the media and politics to create a different species of globalization entirely. These two examples don't prove that globalization is good for the world's grassroots cultures—it is impossible to do that with one or two or ten case studies—but they should make you doubt that globalization is *always* a menace. It ought to make you wonder if some of the arguments about a race to the bottom and scorched grass roots aren't just more globaloney.

I do believe that ordinary people have more control over their lives than is commonly acknowledged in the globalization literature. In the old days, I guess, we might have leaned upon nations and nationality to define life's parameters and establish identity. If, as I keep reading, globalization is tearing down national walls, then it might be logical to conclude that we are unprotected from global forces and can only be overwhelmed by them. But maybe, just maybe, we have the ability to manufacture our own identifies. Perhaps, as nation-states become less important as defining institutions, food and clothes (and sports teams and the like) have become more important.[26] This could account for the unexpected attention they get from globalization commentators.

The paradox is that we create globalization even as we use it to manufacture our own identities. The image that we create of globalization is thus our own image. No, that's too strong. That gives us too much responsibility for globalization (and globaloney). But it is the idea that I want you to hold in your mind as you turn the page to begin the next chapter.

The problem with globalization, I have argued, is that the way we think about it is often through stories that are mainly globaloney. We believe Financial Globaloney, that it is safe as houses; Golden Arches globaloney, that it homogenizes and Americanizes the world; and Grassroots Globaloney, that there is nothing we can do about it. We've got to cut the globaloney if we want to rebuild globalization in a useful, sustainable way.

But first we've got to get some new stories to replace the globaloney stories of the past. Why are stories so important? I'm glad you asked. Let me tell you about the French and why they hate globalization so.

CHAPTER 8

GLOBALIZATION AND THE FRENCH EXCEPTION

No book about globaloney would be complete without a chapter on the French and their attitude toward globalization, Americanization, and market forces generally. The French have a certain idea of globalization—and globaloney—that demands our attention.

Why do the French hate globalization so? What is it about globalization—or about the French—that has created and nurtured such deep and sometimes violent animosity? I have developed a theory of French antiglobalist sentiment. It is a very good theory—an excellent one by the admittedly pitiful standards of the globalization literature. It has everything a good globalization theory should have, including elephants! It is, appropriately, 100 percent globaloney. That is, it is a big theory based on vivid images, a compelling narrative, and little in the way of evidence. It is dramatic and convincing—and highly problematic. But I think it contains a good deal of truth nonetheless.

My plan in this chapter is to present my story of French globalist exceptionalism and then, as I have tried to do with the stories of others, to expose its flaws and undermine it as best I can by appealing to facts, not images, metaphors, and selective observation. Against all odds, I believe, this tortured and seemingly self-destructive process is not entirely a waste of time because it demonstrates the power of stories, when they are good and when they are bad (to paraphrase Keynes) to shape our understanding and our actions. This is an important point because in the final chapter of this book I will argue that if we want a new globalization—a feasible and sustainable globalization—we are going to need to have new stories to guide us.

AN APOLOGY TO THE PEOPLE
AND NATION OF FRANCE

This chapter is going to use the French reaction to globalization to make some broader points about how and why globaloney is produced and consumed. I will therefore necessarily and intentionally begin by distorting French attitudes and actions. I need to do this to make my point, but I acknowledge that it is unfair, so I want to apologize in advance—just as those who have similarly manipulated Michael Jordan, McDonald's, Starbucks, Coca-Cola, and Mickey Mouse probably should have apologized to their victims. Nothing personal. It's just business.

An apology to France and the French is especially appropriate, however, because in some respects they are my heroes. Although I am going to accuse them of blatant antiglobalist globaloney, I have to say that they lead the world in their resistance to globaloney of the other kind. The first edition of this book, *Globaloney*, relentlessly criticized antiglobalization rhetoric, but my earlier book, *Selling Globalization*, concentrated on the opposite side of the debate. *Selling Globalization* argued that globalization was vastly oversold. Certain political, economic, and intellectual interests promote globalization, I argued, as a way to advance their own agendas, which often as not have little connection with globalization at all. My harshest criticisms were aimed at the *hyperglobalists*—a term coined by the French—who promote globalization as an irresistible force which no state and no person can stop or control. Your only choice is to accommodate it (and accept the business-friendly policies it requires) or be left out and doomed to backwardness.

Here is where the French exception comes in. In the 1990s globalism swept the world, or nearly so. No one seemed immune to its outrageous claims—except the French. They just weren't buying it. "What is the market?" asked French prime minister Édouard Balladur.[1] "It is the law of the jungle, the law of nature. And what is civilization? It is the struggle against nature."[2] Civilization is France's mission in the world (at least according to the French). Succumbing to globalism and the law of the jungle was never an option.

French intellectuals wrote books condemning globalization, such as *Firing Back: Against the Tyranny of the Market 2* and *The Economic Horror.*[3] French farmers brought Paris to her knees by clogging the roads with agricultural equipment whenever the idea was raised that they adapt to global market forces. The Académie Française constantly monitored French language use to keep foreign words out and maintain linguistic purity and independence. The French culture ministry performed a similar function more generally, working to preserve and advance French films and music in resistance to the global assault of foreign (mainly English-language, often American) alternatives.

The defining institution for France is not the market or even the church—it is the state. Even in the heady globalization frenzy of the 1990s, the French state showed itself to be up to the task not just of resisting global forces but of advancing the interests of France and of civilization, especially through its influence on European Union policies. The single currency, the euro, is in many ways a French invention designed to allow France and Europe to resist the force of American monetary hegemony. The proposal for a European Union constitution was also a French initiative (former French president Valéry Giscard d'Estaing was the draft document's chief architect) intended to put a distinctly French stamp upon the state, globalization, and governance, at least so far as Europe is concerned. Even the European Union's famous "banana" trade war with the United States, fought over European trade preferences for Caribbean-grown bananas, was rooted in French principles—the need to resist the law of the market jungle.

The story of the unstoppable global economy is globaloney, pure and simple, and the French are to be congratulated for resisting it with such energy. But they went too far. Resisting globalist ideology is one thing (it is a French thing—*très* cool, *très* smart, *très* French). Violence directed against innocent hamburgers, and the intensity of the French reaction in general, is another. Mere resistance to globalization does not justify the actions of someone like Astérix look-alike José Bové, who became a hero for destroying a McDonald's that provoked him by its very existence.[4]

No, the French see the same images and hear the same narratives as you and I, and they seem to resist them, which is good. But it's not necessarily because they see through the rhetorical curtains that fool the rest of us. Their response is as much emotional as intellectual, and it is based upon a particularly French understanding of globalization.

AIDA VERSUS AIDA!

If you want to understand why the French react so strongly to globalization you must go to the theater—twice. First go to the opera house and see Giuseppe Verdi's great work *Aida*, which was first performed in 1871. Then go to the playhouse, or wherever touring Broadway musicals are performed in your town, and see the Walt Disney production of *Aida: The Musical* (which I'll call *Aida!* with an exclamation point to differentiate it from Verdi's *Aida*), which was first performed in 1999. Everyone thinks *Aida* is a story about elephants and pyramids (because it is set in ancient Egypt), but it is really a story about globalization and the nature of the relationships that it creates and sustains. The difference between *Aida* and *Aida!* explains why the French so emotionally oppose globalization today. *Aida* is globalization *à la français*—as the French understand it. *Aida!* is globalization as it is or seems to be—a nightmare!

Verdi's *Aida* was written during the age of Victorian globalization late in the nineteenth century. As you may know, the Victorian globalization was by some measures even more complete than globalization today. Products, people, and money moved around the world with great fluidity—less regulated, on the whole, than they are today. The political organization of globalization was much different, however. Globalization was state-based and Europe-centered. It was overtly imperialistic in form, built on explicit colonial empires (Africa and Asia) and economic dependencies (Central and South America) that amounted to the same things. Verdi's opera *Aida* was created as a commentary on imperial globalization. Here's how the story unfolds.

Aida is a story about a love triangle: an Egyptian soldier Radames is torn between his own Princess Amneris and an enslaved Ethiopian princess, Aida. Although the play is set in Egypt, complete with elephants, it is easy to see that the Egyptians are really Europeans (Romans, probably, since Verdi was Italian). That Aida is Ethiopian gives it away—Ethiopia was an Italian colony. The musical love triangle is really about the tension between imperial center (Princess Amneris) and colonial periphery (Aida), with the dual conquering/civilizing spirit of Europe (Radames) caught in the middle. Verdi's European audience was comfortable in its imperial opera society. It is no accident that so many colonial capitals featured ornate opera houses—just part of the civilizing mission. But the Europeans were also sympathetic to the demand for colonial independence that is the flip side of conquest and civilization. They could relate very well to the tensions Radames felt.

Verdi's use of symbolism in this opera is *very* powerful: noble Aida, who represents the conquered nations, is made a *slave*, not just a subject or servant. At the end of the first act priests actually consecrate the imperial sword that enslaved her. Forced to choose, Radames takes Aida the Ethiopian over Princess Amneris—a fatal mistake. The lovers are found out, captured, and sealed together in a tomb, there to die. The story ends in death and a prayer for peace. The tension between empire and colony is left unresolved, which is also a fitting commentary on Verdi's times, which left unresolved so many such themes.

Walt Disney's *Aida!* is a story about globalization today.[5] Although it is tempting to say that it is an American view of globalization, because Disney is an American company and this is an American production, the facts undermine this conclusion. *Aida the Musical* ("suggested by the opera," the program says) features music by British rocker Elton John, lyrics by Tim Rice (of *Jesus Christ Superstar*, *Evita*, and other global musicals), and book by David Henry Hwang of *M. Butterfly* and *The Golden Child* and Linda Woolverton of *Lion King* and *Beauty and the Beast*. This is a multinational, multicultural, overtly commercial operation. Maybe that *does* make it distinctly American, I suppose, but you can also argue that it is more of a global than a national product.

The Elton John musical is set in Egypt, just like Verdi's opera, but by the dress of the players we know that it is really London or New York (or perhaps even Paris). The Egyptians are waging a war of conquest against Nubia, not Ethiopia, which is a significant change. Instead of colonial revolt against the center, we have white aggression against the black periphery. North versus South, white versus black. Very clear: wealth- and power-seeking capitalists versus exploited indigenous natives. The context is thus transformed from Victorian imperial globalization to contemporary capitalist globalization. The Elton John musical makes the new context especially clear by transforming Princess Amneris, literally, into a material girl. She celebrates conspicuous consumption, even singing a song about the glory of wearing beautiful clothes (although later she shows us that she knows it is only a sad facade).

Here are three significant points to consider in comparing the *Aida/Aida!* productions. First, both involve North-South conflict. But Ethiopia initiates the violence in Verdi's version—a colonial revolt—while the capitalist center is the exploitive aggressor in the *Aida!* Disney play. The force of conquest has shifted from politics to economics, from empire to multinational corporation, from state to market, from France to the United States.

Second, both stories feature a revealing act of generosity by Radames toward his conquered foes to show us that he appreciates the moral dilemma of his (and our) position. Some of the Ethiopians get *freedom* in Verdi's opera—a significant gift in the imperial context because, of course, it stresses the power of the state and the reality of enslavement. The act is generous in the Disney musical, too, but the gift is much different: Radames gives some of the Nubians his worldly possessions (his worn or recycled material goods) rather than their freedom—a rather cynical statement about globalization today, in my opinion, and one that stresses its materialist rather than humanist values.

Finally, the endings differ in significant ways. Verdi's opera, as already noted, ends somberly with prayer and a call for peace. It is a sad ending, one dominated by the weight of fate and the hope that it can be overcome by the human heart and mind. Radames and Aida die in the Disney version, too, but I think it is actually presented as a happy ending tailored to a feel-good society. The lovers reappear post-death, apparently reborn, at a high-end exhibition of ancient Egyptian artifacts—the kind of blockbuster museum show or gallery opening you might see in London or New York (or Paris). The tension between capitalism and indigenous culture is easily reconciled by the Disney folks: capitalism triumphs, but indigenous culture lives on—in museums, movie theaters, the Broadway stage, and on pay-per-view television. We, the audience, don't need to pray that the contradictions will be reconciled—we have resolved them ourselves by the act of buying our seventy-five-dollar tickets. Redemption has a market price in *Aida!* globalization.

PROSPERO AND CALIBAN

What do *Aida* and *Aida!* have to do with the French reaction to globalization? My argument is that the French, like many people around the world, see globalization as imperialism in a new suit of clothes. This much is unexceptional. What makes France an exceptional case is the particular nature of their *own* imperial experience. French imperialism was *total* imperialism. Conquest was total: economic and political domination was not enough. French imperialism insinuated itself into every crack and crevice of colonial society: language, culture, education, food, music, literature, everything. And the relationship between imperial center and colonial satellite was not that of equals or even relative unequals. It was about civilization versus savage nature, exactly as Balladur said about globalization today. And the job of civilization does not end with money and power—it extends seamlessly to the very roots of social culture, to the seeds of savage nature. That is how France understands imperialism and therefore globalization. *Aida.*

You do not have to take my word for this. You can ask the people who were subject to French total imperialism. They have much to say, and they say it well—in the good standard French they were forced to learn as children—because their intellectuals and leaders were all educated in elite French *écoles* and came to understand their colonial condition as seen through imperial French eyes.

Total imperialism could be seen, heard, tasted, and felt in every corner of the French empire. Take clothing, for example. The citizens of France's colonies were pressured to dress like the French as well as talk and eat like them. "The way people clothe themselves," writes the Martinique-born francophone intellectual Frantz Fanon in *A Dying Colonialism*, "together with the traditions of dress and finery that custom implies, constituted the most distinctive form of a society's uniqueness, that is to say the one that is the most immediately perceptible."[6] (I am what I wear and how I dress, sings material girl Princess Amneris in Disney's *Aida!*—capturing the idea exactly.) French imperialism's single-minded drive to establish European patterns of dress and to suppress other styles, including especially the scarves worn by Muslim women in Algeria, surely had many effects on their colonial subjects. Did it civilize them? I'm not sure. But perhaps an unintended consequence was to create a market for secondhand European-style clothing in unlikely parts of the world. I wonder just how much of the global trade in worn and recycled American and European clothing owes its existence to tastes created a hundred years ago by French total imperialism.

From what I have said, French imperialism sounds rather ghastly. If antiglobalists view commercial advertisements for Nike shoes and Coca-Cola as aggressive actions of cultural oppression, I cannot imagine what they would think of French total imperialism, which explicitly sought to transform indigenous societies into caricatures of France in the name of civilization, to "transform the sociocultural complexion of the whole area by a massive indoctrination in all things French."[7]

But it was done with good intent. The special mission of France, according to French intellectual tradition, is to civilize the world, to overcome savage nature. O. Mannoni described the relationship as *Prospero and Caliban* in his book on the psychology of French colonization in Madagascar, drawing upon two famous characters from Shakespeare's play *The Tempest*.[8] Prospero is "civilized"—drawn to books, possessing mystical powers to influence people and control nature. Prospero is French, I think, although in *The Tempest* Shakespeare made him Italian. He is certainly civilized. Caliban is a brute—an ignorant *savage* (a term first used by Europeans to describe the indigenous peoples of newly discovered lands). He is a slave: he has traded his freedom for Prospero's fine language (a trade imposed by the French on their own colonial subjects). Caliban is not really civilized by this process, I suppose, as he might be in a French version of the play, but at least he is not simply exploited without a compensating benefit, as "savages" sometimes are.

These, then, are the key elements of my theory of French globalization. France's view of globalization is deeply rooted in its own imperial experience (the *Aida* experience), which continues even today in some respects through France's special relationships with many of its former colonies.[9] French leaders find it difficult even to think of globalization in other than imperial terms. In *France in an Age of Globalization*, for example, former French foreign minister Hubert Védrine says that "America today is much more than the British Empire and closer to what the Roman Empire was compared to the rest of the world in that era. . . . American globalism—the 'World Company' to use the expression of a spoof on French television—dominates everything everywhere. Not in a harsh, repressive military form, but in people's heads."[10] You can see the French attitude. Empires. Domination. Everything. Everywhere. Clearly this is hyperbole, but according to my theory it reflects the way that the French would organize globalization if they were in charge of it. It would be total globalization that seeks to alter fundamentally all aspects of politics, economy, and society, recasting them in the mold of the imperial center. That's what they expect, so that's what they see. Everything. Everywhere.

That such a globalization would be controlled (and not the result of decentralized market processes) goes without saying. The French idea of globalization is state-centered and controlled—it is *intentional* globalization, nothing accidental about it. No wonder that French-inspired antiglobalists are always looking to see who is running globalization. (Multinational corporations? Media moguls? Who?) It goes without saying that *someone* must be pulling the strings. Individualist, market-based globalization makes the French nervous. It "has its merits," Védrine writes, "but it leads to the fragmentation of collective structures. The United States is very much at home in this sort of world. I don't think France is ready to submit to this type of globalization without seriously examining it first."[11] The idea that one must *submit* to individualism says a lot in itself.

And, finally, globalization, like imperialism, is a relationship between Prospero and Caliban, between the civilized master and the savage slave. If this is true, you can see why globalization would enrage the French. You can see why a Frenchman might feel provoked, even by an innocent hamburger restaurant. The French see all around them the evidence of globalization, but not *their* globalization—not civilizing, state-centered, French globalization. Look around: foreign clothes, foreign music, foreign literature, foreign films. It must seem to the French that they are the victims of someone else's total globalization. Even their language is under constant assault, especially from the Internet, where English is the lingua franca.

And the invasion is not just on the surface; it has spread deep into the heart of France like some particularly virulent form of cancer, infecting even France's blood, its wine. The great French wines like Chateau Margaux and Chateau Latour still sit comfortably at the top of the global wine market staircase, but this may have as much to do with wine critic Robert Parker's influence (an American!) as French wine tradition. The superiority of French vine and wine is no longer unquestioned. Indeed, France's reputation in this new era of globalization has sunk so low as to permit direct insult.

The *Financial Times* reports that David Levine, a London hotelier and restaurateur, has built his own winery in the Loire Valley, importing buildings and equipment literally lock, stock, and barrel from—gasp!—Australia. "Local builders had no idea how to build a modern winery," Levin says. His white wines feature "New World winemaking techniques—modern hygiene standards, stainless-steel tanks, temperature-controlled fermentation" and so on. They reject French winemaking traditions. The new wine is intentionally sold as a simple varietal (sauvignon blanc) not under the local designation (Touraine Appellation d'Origine Controlée). The regional designation "is no longer a guarantee of quality," according to the winemaker, Thierry Merlet, a Frenchman trained in Oregon and South Australia. "What matters is the soil, the winemaking and the marketing. What drives us is what we can sell. If the customer wants to drink Sauvignon Blanc, then that's what we should put on the label."[12] Thus are a thousand years of French wine tradition replaced in one stroke by the savage law of the market jungle. You can see how insulting this would be to the French.

What is most maddening about this situation, from the French point of view, is the way that the Prospero-Caliban relationship has been reversed, as this wine example makes clear. It isn't wise, civilized Prospero, with his books and fine wine, who is directing the action of the play. No, it is a savage Caliban, who watches television situation comedies, slurps down liters of Coca-Cola, and lives by the law of supply and demand. *This* globalization is simply crazy—the culture of the *idiots* is being imposed upon the island of civilization.

And who is the Caliban? The French idea of globalization is not faceless and impersonal. (This is one reason they have succeeded in resisting the idea of pro-market globalism.) French globalization is intentional and directed; someone has to pull the strings. The French have even coined a term—*dirigiste*—to describe a directed system of central command and control. Who is in charge of globalization? It should be Prospero/France, of course, but now instead it is Caliban/America. Savage, uncultured America, the original Caliban, now plays Prospero, as Mickey Mouse did in the sorcerer's apprentice segment of *Fantasia*, and with the same disastrous result. Worse, perhaps America probably thinks that *it* is Prospero and that France and the rest of the world are uncultured Calibans. Oh my. That is more provoking still! No wonder France is upset.

Once the idea has entered your mind that the United States has assumed the imperial role and assigned to France the position of savage colonial, as I argue it has penetrated the minds of the French intellectuals, then your eyes and ears constantly seek out and find evidence that reinforces it. This is the principle behind Adam Smith's "Newtonian" rhetoric—provide an argument that lets people connect the dots for themselves and they will accept your conclusions without question. People like connecting the dots—it gives them a feeling of satisfaction to do this.

You will find plenty of evidence to support this outrageous idea, once you have it planted firmly in your mind. You will see crude American culture and products and influence everywhere and each observation will make you utter, "Caliban, Caliban"—if you are inclined to that sort of thing. McDonald's will figure prominently in your nightmares, of course. There are only a few McDonald's in France compared with the thousands of French (and Italian and Chinese) restaurants, but the Golden Arches will stand out in your mind because of their branded imagery. A similar number of unbranded souvlaki stands or sushi bars would not even be noticed both because of their unbranded visual diversity and because they represent dots that your theory cannot conveniently connect. They, and all other evidence that might contradict the theory, become invisible.

You will hear acres of English (or American) language, too, especially on television and the Internet. And each one of these un-French phrases will have the same effect, reinforcing the idea of American global imperialism. You will feel like you are submerged in American influence, drowning in it, as this exchange between Hubert Védrine and Dominique Moïse illustrates.

> Moïse: Is globalization the same thing as Americanization? Why does the United States seem to be like a fish in water in this new global world?
>
> Védrine: "Like a fish in water" is exactly the right expression. The United States is a very big fish that swims easily and rules supreme in the waters of globalization. . . . Americans get great benefits from this for a large number of reasons: because of their economic size; because globalization takes place in their language; because it is organized along neoliberal economic principles; because they impose their legal, accounting, and technical practices; and because they're advocates of individualism. They also benefit because they possess what the writer and philosopher René Girard has called the "mental power" to inspire the dreams and desires of others, thanks to their mastery of global images through film and television and because, for the same reasons, large numbers of students from other countries come to the United States to finish their studies.[13]

This exchange really captures everything that I think is true about the French attitude toward globalization and Americanization. "Rules supreme" recalls imperialism. "Mental power" reinforces the image of Prospero. And the list of items that are "imposed" rather than chosen or adopted reminds me of France's own total approach to colonial domination.

I am not the first to see a link between globalization/Americanization and French imperialism. Here is how Pierre Bourdieu, a leading French antiglobalization intellectual, diagnoses the situation in *Firing Back: Against the Tyranny of the Market 2*.

> This word [globalization] embodies the most accomplished form of the *imperialism of the universal*, which consists, in universalizing for a society, its own particularity by tacitly instituting it as a universal yardstick (as French society did for a long time when, as the supposed historical incarnation of human rights and of the legacy of the French Revolution, it was posited—especially by the Marxist tradition—as the model of all possible revolutions).[14]

Former French foreign minister Hubert Védrine also notes America's universalizing tendency. "The foremost characteristic of the United States, which explains its foreign policy, is that it has regarded itself ever since its birth as a chosen nation, charged with the task of enlightening the rest of the world."[15] "What is immediately striking about this pronouncement, the obvious fact that jumps right out," writes Jean-François Revel, "is how perfectly it applies to France herself. Even the American quotations that Védrine produces in support of his thesis nearly all have their literal equivalents in the clichés of French political and cultural narcissism."[16] France reacts so strongly to America and Americanization, these comments suggest, not because it is so foreign to the French but because its total imperialism is so familiar to them.

I understand how the French respond to globalization and why it makes them crazy, and I admire them for it, but I cannot bring myself to approve of it. This is because I am American and my sense of globalization is probably rooted in an idea of American imperialism. For Americans, globalization is about choice; it is about the French and the rest choosing to look like Americans or to use American language, if that's what they want to do. There is no central command, no *dirigiste* control. Everyone constructs an identity out of the various goods and bads that are on offer today, and globalization is the mongrel condition that results.[17] This is how we Americans rationalize our empire. We can't be blamed for it, we say; they did it to themselves the same way we have done it to ourselves. We are, at worst, only accidental imperialists.[18]

When the French backlash takes the form of ritual destruction of a hamburger store, I am dismayed, but I understand. Dismay turns to grief when a young woman is killed in the process, as happened in an antiglobalization bombing of a McDonald's store in Brittany in 2000.[19] I am more discouraged yet when antiglobalization seems to take the form of a *dirigiste* movement to resurrect total imperialism by, for example, forcing little Muslim schoolgirls to give up their modest headscarves.[20] This reminds me too much of what Frantz Fanon wrote about French policies in Algeria in *A Dying Colonialism*.[21] If anything is worse than total globalization American-style, it is total imperialism French-style.

THE STORY CRITIQUED

Having proposed a globaloney-style story of French antiglobalism, I must now subject it to critique. There is much to criticize both in style and substance. Although my story is very grand and rooted in history, it is skimpy when it comes to supporting evidence. For the most part, it relies upon metaphors (French globalization is *Aida*, the French reaction to globalization is Caliban) to advance the argument rather than cold hard facts. The rhetoric is persuasive, I think, and it contains more than a grain of truth, but let's look at it more closely to see just how convinced we should be by it.

Aida and *Aida!* (the Verdi opera and Disney musical) form the first image. The critical reader may wonder just what a nineteenth-century Italian opera and a twentieth-century Broadway musical have to do with France and its reaction to globalization. And I admit that this is somewhat problematic (translation: there is a hole in the argument big enough to ride an elephant through). It is the same problem we have with hamburgers—what do they really tell us about the globalization of anything other than hamburgers or maybe french fries? Something, but not very much. Rationalization (the key to McDonald's success) is related to globalization, but they are not the same things. The same relationship holds for *Aida* and the French view of globalization.

I asserted that Verdi's opera tells us how the French think of globalization and the Disney musical is what they see happening to the world today—and I really do think this is true. But it is incorrect to insert the French here—they are not especially relevant to this conclusion. It is natural that each musical work should reflect its own time and the particular concerns of that time. *Aida* tells us what cultural elites were worried about a hundred years ago when they thought about global problems. *Aida!* reflects contemporary concerns. Both works must make some valid connections with their audiences or they would not be performed. Taken together, they probably reveal a good deal about how popular culture and social concerns have evolved over more than a century. Inevitably, they reveal something about France, too, but not France in particular. Probably, and this is a point that I will return to later, what we see in *Aida* and *Aida!*, what we find interesting or shocking, reveals more about ourselves than about globalization.

The case is only a little better if we look closely at Prospero and Caliban. Stealing a page from Frantz Fanon's analysis of life under French rule, I used these characters from Shakespeare to suggest a particularly French attitude toward the relationship between imperial center and colonial satellite. Certainly Prospero seems to have some of the qualities some people might associate with the French—arrogance and humanism, for example. We might identify with Prospero, but not empathize with him. The portrait of Caliban is brutal and sympathetic by contrast. The image is powerful and the link to French colonialism, through Fanon's analysis, is authentic, but it would be a mistake to say, as I do, that French attitudes then or now are so stark and simple. Shakespeare's play *The Tempest* is an English work, not a French one, and the image of Caliban is probably rooted in English experience more than French.

But how do we know that Caliban symbolizes colonial domination at all? "To ask such a question may seem perversely naïve," writes literature professor Meredith Anne Skura, "but the play is notoriously slippery." She notes that

> There have been, for example, any number of interpretations of Caliban, including not only contemporary post-colonial versions in which Caliban is a Virginian Indian but also others where Caliban is played as a black slave. . . . Most recently one teacher has suggested that *The Tempest* is a good play to teach in junior colleges because students can identify with Caliban.[22]

"Interpretation is made even more problematic here," she continues, "because . . . we have no *external* evidence that seventeenth-century audiences thought the play referred to the New World."[23] As best scholars can tell, Elizabethan audiences took Caliban at face value—a universal symbol of ignorance, not a pointed and particular reference to Virginian Indians in particular or colonial peoples in general. Try as they might, scholars have been unable to make Prospero and Caliban match up to any narrative of actual colonial experience. It doesn't matter, however, for the link sticks—the power of Newtonian logic. "So long as there is a core of resemblance, the differences are irrelevant," Skura writes, stressing the irony of the situation.[24] Fuzzy logic and weak evidence may be unusual in the field of literary analysis, provoking Skura's commentary, but those of us who work with globaloney run into them all the time.

Moving beyond rhetoric, my theory is globaloney because it is so simple—it claims that a complicated condition (French attitudes toward globalization) can fully be understood in terms of a single factor (French imperial experience). Not many interesting human conditions can be traced to a single root. There are usually many factors which apply. For example, Philip H. Gordon and Sophie Meunier cite five major reasons for French antiglobalist sentiment in their excellent book *The French Challenge: Adapting to Globalization.*[25]

First, globalization challenges the central role of the state in French life "because of the degree to which it requires abandoning state control over the economy—and thereby over society."[26] By challenging the state, globalization alters the fundamental structure of French domestic relations; no wonder they are suspicious of it. Second, it threatens French culture—and not for the first time. "This is, of course, an old theme," Gordon and Meunier write, "going all the way back to the interwar period, when French writers first started to criticize U.S. mass culture, conformity, and emphasis on material wealth."[27] Third, globalization challenges the idea of France. "Whereas the French republic was based, in theory, on rationality—the enlightened state engaged in the improvement of the collective destiny of the French people," according to Gordon and Meunier, "globalization is inevitably a messy and disorderly process that interferes with the state's ability to play that role."[28]

The fourth way that globalization challenges France is by undermining its influence in international diplomatic circles. French was once considered "the language of diplomacy," and France has certainly claimed a privileged position in international relations. Globalization, Gordon and Meunier argue, shifts negotiations to a new field where the United States occupies the commanding heights. France's self-proclaimed special mission to civilize international affairs is one victim of this movement—a deeply felt loss of French influence.

Finally, say Gordon and Meunier, the French oppose globalization because they are so comfortable without it. France is a beautiful country, with rich urban cultures, strong rural traditions, good food, and good wine. What do the French (or at least the French elites) have to gain from globalization? Nothing! What do the French (or at least the French elites) have to lose? The obvious answer is everything, but that is too harsh. Globalization has its price, so something will be sacrificed, but who knows what it will be. The fact is that the French do not know what they might lose and this *uncertainty* allows them to imagine that they could lose everything. Their anxiety is understandable and not a uniquely French phenomenon.

These five factors provide a deeper explanation for French attitudes toward globalization than does my simple theory, but even they only scratch the surface. Antiglobalization reflects its *terroir* just as globalization does, in my opinion, and there are within France many social, political, and economic "microclimates" that produce distinctive attitudes and concerns. France is, after all, a nation with 246 different cheeses.[29] Why should it have fewer opinions about globalization?

In fact, the biggest problem with my theory of French antiglobalism is that it asserts that France is *against* globalization. A closer look at the facts might suggest that France is both comfortable with globalization and has successfully adapted to it.

When you ask the French if they favor globalization, they express understandable reservations and, sometimes, downright opposition, often associating it with Americanization. I think many Americans are suspicious of globalization, too, especially now that it is often associated with the "outsourcing" of jobs abroad. But if instead you present the French people with the products of globalization, they seem to take to them without much hesitation, just like people in other countries. Take McDonald's, for example. Although the McDonald's stories that get the most attention feature antiglobalization protests, perhaps the biggest story is this: McDonald's is more popular in France than in any other country in Europe.[30] The French like it in part because McDonald's has adapted its menu to French tastes (local cheeses are often featured, for example) and in part because of its American image. Don't be shocked: if Americans enjoy French wine bars and Italian coffee bars, why shouldn't a French family go to McDonald's for a simulated "American experience"? McDonald's cannot compete with France's great cuisine, but is that its purpose? "I can love good food," says Vanesse Decler, a customer at a Parisian Golden Arches store, "and I can also love McDonald's." Clearly she knows the difference.[31] *Vive la différence.*

The French intellectual Jean-François Revel questions whether anti-Americanism really exists in France (and elsewhere) in the way it is often portrayed. Anti-Americanism, he writes, "is less a popular prejudice than a *parti pris* of the political, cultural and religious elites."[32] America and globalization are useful scapegoats and straw men for elites both on the political left and on the political right. If Americanization/globalization did not exist, someone would have to invent them in order to be able to oppose them (and to sell the policies of opposition).

Are the French really "closet globalists" who outwardly oppose globalization but inwardly embrace it? Yes, I think so. France, like the United States, believes that it has a "universal message" to offer the world.[33] It is difficult to square such global ambitions with narrow, parochial attitudes and actions. France has struggled with this contradiction and chosen to embrace globalization, in my view. The die was cast more than two decades ago.

The Socialist François Mitterrand was elected president of the French Republic in 1981—at the very moment when Margaret Thatcher and Ronald Reagan were leading their countries toward free-market individualism, the ideology of globalism. Mitterrand set out to lead France in the opposite direction: nationalizing industries, not privatizing them, and reasserting the role of the state. "The Mitterrand experiment, in other words, was an early rejection of the logic that would later be called globalization," according to Gordon and Meunier.[34] The results were economically devastating, however, because France, even then, was too much tied to the world economy to pull itself back into an inward-looking *dirigiste* regime. Economic crisis came in 1983. Mitterrand installed a new policy team in 1984 and began to embrace globalization in practice while continuing to question and oppose it as a theory.

Although all of the talk is of France's resistance to globalization, the real story, according to Gordon and Meunier, is how successfully France has adapted to it. It is still taboo to talk about this, I suppose, because the myth of France's resistance to globalization is important to its national identity, but the changes are a fact of life. The mystery of France's closet globalization is partly tied up in the European Union. Europeanization (with France in the lead at least part of the time) is also globalization in many respects. Gordon and Meunier call it "globalization by stealth."[35] "While it would be an exaggeration to suggest that France has completely abandoned *dirigisme* and that the legacy of the state-led approach has disappeared . . . the country's economic landscape has changed," they write. "In a country known for its deep, ideological divisions, the differences between Left and Right on the economy since the Mitterrand U-turn (in practice if not in rhetoric) have been minimal. . . . [E]conomic management since 1983 has been driven more than anything by the need to adapt the French economy to the requirements of the European and global markets."[36]

Gordon and Meunier suggest that France in globalization is a fish in water, particularly in comparison with some other countries that have not made so determined and successful a commitment to evolve. You could say that France has embraced globalization since 1983 and, even more, it has successfully sought to shape globalization, to give it a particularly French style, through its influence upon the ever-expanding European Union. Why isn't this fact more generally appreciated? Probably because French antiglobalist rhetoric is so forceful. The rhetoric creates an image of France that is easy to understand and that emphasizes one or two memorable images and events. It is, I guess, a particular kind of globaloney: franco-baloney. The facts of French globalization are complicated and more difficult to appreciate because they require patient, detailed analysis. In a world that seems increasingly to be defined by Attention Deficit Disorder (ADD), rhetoric nearly always trumps details.

If you want to find examples of French opposition to globalization you will find them; just look for José Bové or for the latest ruling about a new word from the Académie Française. But if you want to find evidence that France is getting along swimmingly, you have only to look around. French globalization is everywhere.

French globalization is especially apparent in markets for luxury and designer products, like great champagne and couture fashions. The great names of French commercial culture dominate these markets at home and abroad. Great transnational firms have been constructed around them, extending France's global reach. This is true even in the wine business. Cloudy Bay, a prominent winery in New Zealand, for example, is owned by the French global conglomerate LVMH (Moët Hennessey Louis Vuitton). LVMH owns wineries in France, Spain, Australia, New Zealand, Argentina, Brazil, and the United States. Its other businesses (perfume, liquor, jewelry, watches, newspapers, and retail stores) are equally global in scope. If globalization did not already exist, LVMH would have had to invent it in order to spread French style and taste.

The French embrace of globalization is not limited to luxury goods; it reaches down to the grass roots. The second-largest mass-market retailer in the world (with annual sales of more than 100 billion euro) is a French firm called Carrefour.[37] Carrefour employs nearly five hundred thousand workers in its fifteen thousand stores in thirty-three countries. About half of its sales are in France, where it is the clear market leader, but its reach is nearly global: Europe (including Belgium, Romania, Spain, Greece, Italy, Poland, Portugal, Turkey, Bulgaria, Cyprus, Russia, Slovakia); the Americas (Argentina, Brazil, Columbia, Dominican Republic); Northern Africa (Egypt, Morocco, Algeria, Tunisia); and Asia (China, Indonesia, Japan, Malaysia, Singapore, Thailand, Taiwan, Bahrain, Jordan, Kuwait, Oman, Pakistan, Syria, Qatar, Saudi Arabia, the United Arab Emirates). Some of the stores are franchise operations or joint ventures. It operates 134 big-box superstores and 320 discount stores in China. The major hole in its global strategy: the United States and Mexico, Wal-Mart's home turf.

Wal-Mart, the U.S. store giant, is bigger than Carrefour, but less global. Wal-Mart employs more than two million people worldwide including 1.4 million in the United States. It operates 4,100 stores in the United States and 3,100 more in Argentina, Brazil, Canada, China, Costa Rica, El Salvador, Guatemala, Honduras, Japan, Mexico, Nicaragua, Puerto Rico and the the United Kingdom. It has entered the wholesale market in India via a joint venture with Sharti Enterprises.[38] Wal-Mart has much higher sales than Carrefour (it is the largest retailer in the world with total annual sales of nearly $400 billion and rising) because of its key position within the world's largest market, the United States. I find it interesting that each company has thus far avoided entering its global rival's home market, although this may change as Wal-Mart moves to develop a more truly global market strategy.[39] (One news report suggests that Wal-Mart will effect a global strategy in the most obvious way—buying Carrefour![40])

Wal-Mart is bigger than Carrefour in part because most of its stores are vast superstores, including especially the cavernous Sam's Club warehouse stores. Carrefour invented the superstore—it calls them *hyper-markets*—and operates more than twelve hundred of them around the world, but most of its outlets are smaller, ordinary supermarkets, discount stores, and tiny convenience stores (plus special "cash and carry" stores that provide products to restaurants and food-service operations). Carrefour's embrace of global retail markets is thus both wider than Wal-Mart's and deeper, reaching further into the villages and neighborhoods, encompassing all income classes—no wonder Wal-Mart would want to buy the company rather than compete with it. Carrefour is the world's retailer, if such a thing can be said to exist, and a particularly French expression of globalization.

Of course no argument about globalization is complete without a discussion of food. If France is such a global creature, you must be thinking, where is the French McDonald's? Why don't I see French food in every strip mall? How can you say that France has embraced globalization if it hasn't spread its cuisine to the far corners of earth?

The answer to this challenge is that France has already done so—indeed, did so decades ago—but on particularly French terms. Don't look for corporate or franchised fast-food chains, however. The French patronize these sorts of restaurants, but they are really American creations. (There is one international fast-food chain with a French name—Pret A Manger sells baguette sandwiches and some other French-style fast foods—but it is actually a British firm and most of its menu items reflect this fact.[41]) Globalization reflects its *terroir*; French globalization has to take its own distinctly French form.

French culinary globalization is less visible than the American version because it lacks a brand name and a coordinated global advertising strategy, but its influence upon global food is if anything much more total, more complete. Independent French restaurants, bistros, cafes, and bakeries cover the globe far more thoroughly than any American corporate concern could or would. One legacy of French imperialism is that good French food can be found in places, such as Central Africa, that contemporary globalization has not yet touched. You can get a good fresh croissant and decent café au lait in places around the world where the only Big Macs you will see are on satellite TV broadcasts of NBA play-off games.

There are certainly more French restaurants and food establishments outside of France than there are McDonald's, Burger King, Kentucky Fried Chicken, and Wendy's stores outside of the United States. I am tempted to declare France the true King of Culinary Globalization, but I don't think it is true. Certainly French influence is stronger than America's, but I would not be surprised to find that Italian food is almost equally ubiquitous or that Chinese food is the most global of all. American food, despite all the hype, probably rates no better than fourth or fifth (depending upon where Indian food falls in the rankings).

Here is my bottom line on France and globalization. If we judge by rhetoric, France is against globalization. If, however, we make our call based upon some of the factors that are most often cited in the globalization literature—high-end branded goods, restaurant food, and mass-market retailing—we find that France is a creature of globalization more than you might otherwise suppose.[42] Our opinion of France and globalization depends upon whether we listen to the stories or take time to consult the facts.

My theory of why France hates globalization is globaloney for several reasons, the most important of which is this: France has in fact embraced globalization, although it is a nervous embrace. I understand the feeling—it's that *Aida* embrace, isn't it? We Americans embrace globalization in the same way. The French exception to globalization is not exceptional at all.

MIRROR IMAGES

Stories about globalization are like the Mirror of Erised in J. K. Rowling's *Harry Potter and the Sorcerer's Stone*.[43] Most mirrors reflect their viewer's image, accurately for the most part, though always reversed. In Rowling's book, however, the Mirror of Erised has a special property: it reflects the viewer's deepest hopes. When you gaze into the Mirror of Erised, you see what you want to see, not what's really there.

It is easy to see why globalization should work much the same way. Globalization is devilishly complicated. It has too many data points and complicated connections for anyone's mind to process correctly. No wonder our eyes seek out familiar patterns. When we look at globalization, therefore, we tend to focus upon those parts that reflect what we want to see—or what we fear to see—and that match the stories we want to believe. Then we tend to connect these details to form grand theories or universal generalizations. We do this mostly because it is such a satisfying thing to do—Adam Smith was right about this, as about much else. The image that is reflected in the Mirror is mainly our own because each of us selects the details that are most important to us and with which we are most familiar.

This property of globalization, alas, makes it especially prone to manipulation. Hopes and fears are great motivators. Worse, we tend to accept them as valid motivators rather uncritically because they are our own.

The Crash of 2008 was caused in part by a perfect globaloney storm: Financial Globaloney (globalization is safe as houses); Golden Arches Globaloney (globalization is everywhere the same, it cannot tolerate diversity); and Grassroots Globaloney (resistance is futile: there's nothing you can do about it). If the next wave of globalization is going to avoid the old cycles of boom and bust it will need to be different—different principles, different institutions and different stories to motivate and explain, to express hopes and fears.

What would feasible and sustainable globalization look like? Turn the page.

CHAPTER 9

THE FUTURE OF GLOBALIZATION (AND GLOBALONEY)

The ideas of John Maynard Keynes were much in the news in the wake of the Crash of 2008. Economists and policy-makers found themselves looking back to Keynes's writings from the era of the Great Depression for guidance and inspiration. Keynes wouldn't be surprised at his be-lated intellectual resurrection.

"The ideas of economists and political philosophers, both when they are right and when they are wrong, are more powerful than is commonly understood," he wrote in *The General Theory of Employment, Interest, and Money*. "Indeed the world is ruled by little else. Practical men, who believe themselves to be quite exempt from any intellectual influences, are usually the slaves of some defunct economist."[1] Keynes believed in the power of ideas—good ones and bad ones—to direct our actions and to shape our world.

So do I. I've seen how flawed ideas become convincing, even compelling, when they are embedded in persuasive stories. Intelligent men and women "connect the dots" these stories create, drawing universal conclusions based on attractive images, selective evidence, and engaging metaphors. Guided by this globaloney they are led to make mistakes, disastrous mistakes, as we have all seen.

It is pretty clear that globalization is not a stable, secure economic process. Globalization is unexpectedly delicate, in fact, especially global finance. It yields many benefits—that's why we embrace it—but it creates risks and disrupts existing human arrangements—that's why the embrace is so awkward. Guided by what I call Financial Globaloney, however, individuals, businesses and governments pretended that the costs and risks just didn't exist. Their actions, as I discussed in chapters 2 and 3, made the risks even greater and the collapse even deeper.

It is clear, at least to me, that globalization is a highly diverse phenomenon. Globalization reflects its *terroir*, as the French would say—it takes different forms in different places depending upon local politics, culture, and other factors. That's why globalization is so uneven, why some people and places are so tightly connected to global networks while others are "off the grid," both literally and figuratively. The world isn't flat, even if parts of it display a sometimes uncomfortable sameness—airport hotels, for example, hamburger restaurants and shopping malls. Spend enough time in these places and you'll start to think that all the world is the same. But you have only to raise your eyes just a bit to see that Golden Arches Globaloney isn't really true.

The problem with the Golden Arches view is that it suggests that global diversity doesn't exist and the logical next step is to conclude that maybe it shouldn't exist or won't exist in the future. It denies the fact of and need for diverse political, social, and economic arrangements. By saying that everything is the same it undermines the argument for diversity.

Globalization doesn't homogenize, exactly. It is more accurate to say that globalization, because it is driven by capitalism, tends to rationalize, to encourage efficiency, as Weber and Ritzer argued. The rationalization process proceeds at many levels, not just the global one, and indeed the global element may be the least powerful and important. Efficiency is a good thing, up to a point, but it too has costs. The rationalization of finance, through financial engineering, for example, was one of the reasons huge risks could be taken as if there was no risk at all. And rationalization does lead to a certain sameness in some things in the name of efficiency.

Grassroots Globaloney tells us that these processes are total, complete, universal, and that there is nothing you can do about them. This is globaloney, too, since it is obvious that at least sometimes people are able to seize the power to shape important elements of their lives and to balance efficiency and diversity, shaping globalization to fit their needs and desires. More than this, there is the fact of "Slow-balization," where clever social entrepreneurs use globalization to resist globalization's negative effects and sometimes reverse them.

I think globalization can be a very good thing, but we've seen that it can be a very bad thing, too. Globalization collapsed in the wake of the Crash of 2008, but this didn't solve the underlying problem. The world doesn't need *less* globalization, it needs *better* globalization, globalization with fewer risks and greater diversity, globalization that people will find a bit easier to embrace because they recognize their ability to mold it into a form that suits their needs.

This chapter tries to uncover some principles on which to rebuild globalization in a form that will be both economically feasible and politically sustainable. This is not a simple task and there is no guarantee of success but it is necessary to try, if only because the consequences of failure are so high. The first step is to consult theory to help us narrow down the field of possible global arrangements. Two famous political economists will provide the framework we need for this task. Then comes the hard part—we will need to consider what is really important, what (and whom) globalization is for. Once that choice is made, the outline of feasible, sustainable globalization becomes clearer, although the difficult problem of actually constructing it remains.

FEASIBLE GLOBALIZATION: THE MUNDELL TRILEMMA

The first step to rebuilding globalization is to think seriously about its economic architecture. We can imagine all sorts of global arrangements, but many of them have hidden flaws, unseen contradictions. What are the economically feasible options?

Robert Mundell, the Columbia University professor who won the 1999 Nobel Prize in Economic Science, gives us a place to start with what is sometimes called the Mundell Trilemma or the "Unholy Trinity" of international economics.[2] Although Mundell's theory was developed fifty years ago, international economists recognize it as a powerful tool for understanding the trade-offs and tensions in globalization today.

What is a trilemma? A trilemma is a set of three mutually exclusive options. Each choice has its own logic and, while they are pairwise compatible they can't all three work at once. Choose any two and the third is impossible.[3] To take a trivial example, consider the lunchtime trilemma at a busy food court with multiple vendors or food stations. You would probably want a meal that is good, fast, and cheap, but it is hard to get all three. If it is good and cheap then there is probably a long line to get it—not fast. If it is fast and cheap then it probably isn't very good—otherwise there would be a long line. And if it is fast and good then it probably is relatively expensive. If not, what's keeping the lines of hungry diners away?[4] The trilemma doesn't hold all the time, of course—if the food court is almost empty you can probably get cheap and good without a long wait. But when things get busy the contradictions appear.[5]

Mundell's brilliant insight was to see that the lunchtime problem applies to international finance. Instead of good, fast, and cheap, a nation might want to have a stable exchange rate, international capital mobility, and domestic economic sovereignty. Each of these three economic arrangements has certain benefits. A stable exchange rate promotes international trade and investment and minimizes some of globalization's disruptive effects since unstable foreign currency prices get transmitted through the domestic economy, causing instability there as well.

International capital mobility allows for the free movement of investment flows into and out of a country. This opens a country to the risks of global finance, of course, but also to its benefits, and encourages full integration into the global economic system. International capital mobility is necessary if a nation wants to achieve "thick globalization"—economic integration through both trade and finance—as opposed to "thin globalization" through trade alone.

Finally, domestic economic sovereignty refers to a nation's ability to intervene independently in its domestic economy to deal with inflation, unemployment, or other problems as needed. There are no "golden fetters" to prevent independent action as there would be if international agreements limited domestic actions.

Although it is possible to have all three of these policy options at once when the economic system, like a near empty food court, is not under stress, tensions and trade-offs reveal a trilemma when things get hot. Suppose, for example, that inflation begins to rise. If you increase interest rates to fight it, this will bust the pledge of exchange rate stability because higher interest rates will attract foreign capital, pushing the exchange rate higher. You can raise interest rates and keep exchange rates stable, but you have to stop capital from flowing in and out (capital controls). Or you can keep capital mobility and exchange rate stability, but you won't be able to raise interest rates (the loss of domestic economic sovereignty) and so will have to let inflation run its course. It's a difficult situation . . . a trilemma. What are you willing to give up?

Since you can only have all three options so long as there are no troubles—and trouble happens in the global economy, as we have seen—it follows logically that there are three different sorts of economically feasible solutions to the trilemma problem.

- *Thick Globalization.* This is the system adopted by Japan and the United States that brings together high levels of international trade and financial flows (thick globalization by my definition), but without fixed exchange rates. Domestic economic sovereignty is retained. Capital mobility is necessary for these two countries, since Japan has a huge trade surplus that it needs to invest abroad and the U.S. has a mirror-image deficit it needs to finance. Given this first choice, the trade-off is either giving up a stable exchange rate or giving up domestic economic sovereignty. Both countries choose to retain unfettered use of their economic tools and let their currencies ride with market forces. This works for them, more or less, because exchange rate effects are small in these economies relative to domestic market forces. Better to be able to have the tools to stabilize the domestic economy rather than give them up to keep a stable exchange rate. That said, exchange rate effects can be very unsettling for trade-sensitive or dependent sectors of the economy. This is thick globalization for countries that are wary of its economic consequences.
- *Really Thick Globalization.* Really thick globalization is a strategy that takes maximum risk to try to get the maximum globalization return; it is the policy that Argentina adopted before its economic crisis a decade ago. The Argentinean government wanted to get full advantage of thick globalization so it opened its capital

markets to foreign investors and guaranteed them a fixed exchange rate (one peso per U.S. dollar). To accomplish this, however, they had to give up domestic economic sovereignty and import their economic policy moves from Washington, D.C. If U.S. interest rates went up, so did Argentinean rates, in order to keep the fixed currency pledge. The "golden fetters" of the exchange rate commitment effectively handcuffed the Argentinean economic authorities. This system worked for a while until the differences between the economic problems of the U.S. and Argentina grew too great. A single economic policy didn't fit two such different countries and economic and political collapse ultimately occurred. This is globalization for countries that are willing to take big risks to get big gains. Or don't consider the risks. Or don't think they have any choice.

• *Thin Globalization.* The final option puts stability ahead of financial globalization's potential benefits. It gives up international capital mobility (putting restrictions on cross-border investment flows) in order to have stable exchange rates and the domestic economic tools necessary to maintain a stable local economy. This is an interesting choice. China has for some years chosen thin but stable globalization. Its trade activity has been intense, of course, but international investment flows have been highly regulated, with layers of protective government controls. This allowed the Chinese government to control the exchange rate and to keep a tight lid on domestic economic problems. Thin globalization did not prevent China from experiencing contagion from the Crash of 2008, of course, since the collapsing global economy necessarily affected China's export flows and since falling global financial markets necessarily affected China's foreign investments. But the effects were less than they might have been and the choice to retain domestic economic sovereignty meant that China was free to provide massive economic stimulus to its economy.

One peculiar feature of the current system (or non-system) of economic relations is that it allows each nation to make its own Mundell Trilemma choice, so while the U.S. and Japan opt for thick globalization, other countries choose really thick globalization and some, like China, make a thin globalization selection. Thus globalization has been governed by multiple and sometimes incompatible logics. It is perhaps no surprise that attempts to piece together this policy patchwork have been problematic at times and panic-prone at others.

There is another name for thin globalization as defined here: the Bretton Woods system. Economic leaders of the Allied nations met in Bretton Woods, New Hampshire, in 1944, while the battles of World War II were still raging, to draft a plan for the postwar economy. Having watched the thick globalization of the 1920s collapse and spread across the map as contagion in the 1930s, the representatives wanted to avoid past errors, to rebuild globalization on a more stable foundation. So they opted for thin globalization—free trade, but not free investment flows. Capital controls were the order of the day and lasted until the breakdown of the system in the 1970s.

Security and stability were the highest priority at Bretton Woods, which is understandable after the global economic crisis of the 1930s and the fears of depression's return at war's end. Bretton Woods-style thin globalization was intended to be a more secure (I'm tempted to say Fail Safe) alternative. Each nation's economy was supposed to be secure because of domestic economic sovereignty, stable exchange rates, and the lack of destabilizing investment flows. The system was supposed to be secure, too, because national problems would be contained. Contagion damage was strictly limited. Thin globalization was less globalization in terms of the potential theoretical benefits, but with less risk of national or systemic financial collapse.

Mundell's Trilemma tells us which globalization options are economically feasible and which are desirable but impossible. Which ones are *sustainable*? Hmmm. That's a more complicated question, since it involves more than the technicalities of international economics.

RODRIK'S TRILEMMA: SUSTAINABLE GLOBALIZATION

The second step, once the economic alternatives are clear, is to consider how to rebuild globalization so that it will not tear itself apart. Globalization must be feasible in terms of the Mundell constraints, and also sustainable. Sustainable globalization. What an idea! Sustainable in what way? Well, the obvious reference would be ecological—environmentally sustainable globalization, but that's a big order, an important one, but something that goes well beyond the scope of this book. Environmental sustainability is a project that needs to be addressed at all levels in many ways. In the long run, little else really matters.

But in the short run we need to think about the politics and economics of globalization and find ways to prevent it from blowing up and melting down with such regularity. Rodrik's Trilemma, named for Harvard political economist Dani Rodrik, one of the most original thinkers in the globalization field, gives us a framework for analyzing globalization's *political* sustainability.[6]

Rodrik's Trilemma starts with the premise that there is a contradiction in the conventional wisdom that deep economic integration (what I have called thick or really thick globalization) is inconsistent with the existence of the nation-state as we usually think of it and democratic political accountability. Once you embrace thick globalization, Rodrik says, you have to choose—the nation-state or democracy? You can't have both. Here is the reasoning behind this unexpected conclusion.

Thick globalization, as I have defined it, means that international economic relations involve both relatively free trade and high levels of capital mobility. Once the domestic economy is deeply integrated into the global economy the space available for independent economic policy is limited. The interests of foreign investors in particular must be taken seriously at some point, creating explicit or implicit "golden fetters" that limit domestic policy actions. Even the United States, which has theoretical domestic economic sovereignty in the Mundell framework, cannot afford to ignore the interests of foreign investors completely, especially in the post-Crash world where they finance trillions of dollars of U.S. government debt. At some point the logic of investment dollars trumps the logic of citizen votes. Democratic accountability is sacrificed to the expediencies of global finance.

Rodrik calls this option the "Golden Straightjacket" after a phrase coined by Thomas Friedman in *The Lexus and the Olive Tree*. To get the global gold, states restrain themselves from taking independent economic action. In Rodrik's terms, this is equivalent to sacrificing democratic accountability, since the state is no longer able to respond to voters' demands regarding economic policy. You will recognize this as the option that Argentina adopted in the 1990s.

Rodrik calls the second option "Global Federalism" and it is a vision of the world where governance structures expand to embrace the global markets' domain. The nation-state, too small to regulate global flows and too weak to resist their interests, recedes into the background, assuming a more modest economic role in a multilevel global governance framework.

If you want democratic accountability and thick globalization, then the powerless nation-state just gets in the way. Some system of global governance is needed to assure that citizen concerns are addressed. Global Federalism? This sounds very utopian, but maybe it isn't. "Global federalism would align jurisdictions with markets and remove the 'border effects,'" Rodrik says. "Politics need not, and would not, shrink: it would relocate on the global level. This is the United States model expanded on a global scale."[7]

One way to think about the differences between Rodrik's Global Federalism and Golden Straightjacket versions of thick globalization is to consider the case of the European Union and the single currency, the euro, which most of its members have adopted. The EU has long been committed to thick economic relations among its member states. The single-market program of the 1990s called for member states to adopt four economic freedoms: free trade of goods, free trade in services, free movement of labor, and free movement of capital. And now, for most of the states, one currency and therefore one basic macroeconomic policy, too. If you think of the EU economy as a sort of globalization test project, then this is about as thick as globalization can get. And it has caused many tensions because the EU-wide democratic system is very weak (there is a "democracy deficit"). Voters hold their national governments accountable on economic issues, but those governments have relatively little power to deal with these issues, having ceded this authority to the EU central bank.

The current EU setup is problematic—politically unsustainable in my terminology—because it seeks to have it all: thick globalization, sovereign nation-states, and democratic accountability. Something will have to give. If the EU remains a "Europe of States" the democratic deficit—responsibility without accountability and accountability without power—will remain. It is hard to imagine that this will be tolerated forever. If it becomes "a United States of Europe," with stronger central government and pan-Europe democratic accountability, the nation-state will wither away or, in the spirit of Global Federalism—evolve to play a more minor, if still very important, role. That's how Rodrik's Trilemma works.

There is, of course, a third option, since everything about a trilemma comes in threes. Thick globalization dictates that either the nation-state (and the diversity of policies and programs that come with it) or democracy must be sacrificed—you must choose! But what if national sovereignty and democratic accountability are privileged above thick globalization? Then a third option appears: thin globalization (free trade, more or less, but regulated international investment flows), with democratic accountability achieved through a system of diverse nation-states. Trading thick globalization for thin restores a measure of political accountability to the nation-state at the sacrifice of deep economic integration.

REVALUING GLOBALIZATION

I am drawn to the puzzle trilemmas pose and the fact that they resist the tendency to boil down complicated questions to simple answers. Trilemmas can be deceptive, however, because they make it seem like the three points of the policy triangle are equally important. Choose any two and you are good to go.

But some things are always more important than other things—values really do matter—and, once you've rotated one choice to the top priority, then a more manageable dilemma appears. The first choice is the key. For some time now the first priority has been given to thick globalization—it has seemed to "trump" everything else. It doesn't seem to have mattered that thick globalization, with its sometimes unstable capital movements, has a poorer risk-return profile than thin globalization's more secure focus on international trade flows.

The most obvious instance of this choice, as I have said, is the European Union where the choice was made early on to have thick internal economic relations, and the struggle ever since has been to make this work politically within a union of weak nation-states and weaker central institutions—an arrangement that is economically feasible but politically unsustainable in its present form.

Things change, however, if you rotate Rodrik's Trilemma to put democratic accountability at the top. This, in my view, is that key to political sustainability, but I'm not the only person who thinks so (or the first one to point this out). Barry Eichengreen made the case better than I ever could in his book *Globalizing Capital*. Once upon a time, Eichengreen argues, it was possible to put globalization first, but not today. Monarchs and autocratic rulers could sacrifice domestic interests on the altar of globalization because they were insulated by power and position from popular opinion. Even democratically elected governments could put globalization first in the days before Keynes invented his macroeconomic theory, which established government's role in stabilizing the economy. After Keynes, however, it is impossible to put the genie back in the bottle—to tell voters that the government cannot or should not take action to address domestic economic concerns. The government *will be* held accountable now, one way or another.

If you put democracy first, which I argue is the only politically sustainable option, then the choices are nation-state (and the Bretton Woods system) or thick globalization (and Rodrik's global federalism). Hmm. Global federalism is a very attractive idea, but it seems problematic for now because of the lack of both the necessary governance infrastructure and the apparent political will to create it. The European Union is the most advanced example of an attempt to develop the institutions of transnational democracy, and even after more than fifty years of broadening and deepening, it is difficult to declare it a real political success.

Global federalism is unrealistic for now, but the alternative—the contemporary nation-state—is also problematic. Nation-states and economic nationalism go hand in hand; protectionism rooted in shortsighted visions of national interest has always been a stronger barrier to globalization than any theoretical trilemma constraint. And it is pretty clear that nation-states can have their own "democracy deficits." The nation-state is an imperfect way to organize government (and we should try to improve it) in a global age, but it is ours, at least for now.

TWO CHEERS FOR THIN GLOBALIZATION

Connecting the dots, it looks like this argument is leading to thin globalization—more secure globalization based on trade more than finance, in a diverse and accountable nation-state system. I would like to say "Three Cheers for Thin Globalization," but the case isn't that strong. In a world of trilemmas, three cheers may be too much to ask. Two cheers will have to do.

The Mundell and Rodrik trilemmas outline the constraints for economically feasible and politically sustainable globalizations. As I rotate the trilemma triangles and view the results I am struck by the fact that thick globalization seems incompatible with political and economic stability. Economic instability goes back to my arguments about the nature of global finance and why money isn't really "safe as houses." Political instability comes from the trilemmas themselves, where really thick globalization seems to require the sacrifice of domestic economic sovereignty (Mundell) and democratic accountability (Rodrik). That's a big loss of local control. Absent a realistic "global federalist" solution or effective regulation to tame global financial excess, thick globalization carries a very high price. Too high, as we have seen.

What should we think of this result? If you believe that globalization is an end in itself, as hyper-globalizers and market fundamentalists seem to think, then thin globalization is a terrible thing to suggest. If more globalization is better than less and thick is better than thin, then settling for something akin to the old Bretton Woods system of strong states, capital market restrictions, and free trade seems like a step in the wrong direction, a sort of evolutionary retreat.

But globalization is a means, not an end. People don't trade, invest, or migrate to create a global economy; they do it to take advantage of opportunities they see abroad. These opportunities exist because of global diversity—because everyplace isn't the same as everyplace else. But opportunity is generally accompanied by risk, that's fundamental. Diversity, opportunity, risk, return, globalization—they all come packaged together and the extent of globalization—how thick or thin it is—depends upon how the other factors balance out.

SECURITY AND DIVERSITY

Thin globalization has two big advantages over its thicker alternatives: security and diversity. Thick globalization is high-risk globalization. Driven by sometimes chaotic capital flows and lacking a democratic global governance structure to oversee it and hold it accountable to the citizens, it is the globalization of boom and bust, crash and burn. Thin globalization dials down the risk, giving away some of the potential upside gain to get a more stable and therefore more governable system of economic relations.

Maybe that's why Keynes and his colleagues at Bretton Woods opted for a thin globalization plan for the postwar era. Global Federalism would have been out of the question then, of course, just as it seems to be a bit unrealistic or premature just now. Thin globalization is sustainable globalization, or potentially sustainable globalization anyway. (The collapse of the Bretton Woods system in the 1970s reveals a gap between theory and practice when it comes to political sustainability.)

Thin globalization, as defined here, is also diverse globalization, the opposite of the Golden Arches, since authority is intentionally located at the national level, encouraging a diverse range of solutions to the problems of managing a thin, but still dynamic, global economy. Dani Rodrik's 2007 book *One Economics, Many Recipes* makes the case for a system that encourages diverse solutions to global economic problems. Using a method he calls "growth diagnostics," Rodrik drills down into the details of local problems, resources, and institutional arrangements, arguing that differences in local conditions require custom-tailored policies. Policies that make sense in advanced industrial countries can have very different—and often negative—effects when applied in different environments.

This obviously contradicts everything that market fundamentalism holds true and I think it is not too strong to view Rodrik's book as an indictment of market fundamentalist policies. Although the principles of economics may be universal—opportunity costs, the power of incentives, and so on—it is important to remember that economics is not a surface phenomenon, like a coat of paint. Economics is embedded deeply in society and shapes itself around the resources and constraints, political and social values, of different nations and cultures. You ignore these differences at your peril.

I learned this lesson from one of my grad students a few years ago when I was teaching in Bologna at the Johns Hopkins School of Advanced International Studies Center there. I was reviewing basic supply-demand analysis with a student from Spain who was struggling with the basics. I drew out a labor market graph and put a minimum wage above the market equilibrium price. With wages "too high"—higher than market wages—an unemployment gap appeared.[8] How to you get rid of unemployment, I asked the student. The correct answer, as anyone who has read an economics textbook knows, is to cut wages. Lower wages give employers an incentive to hire more workers. That's the answer I was expecting.

"Raise wages," he said. Ouch! Wrong! Wrong according to *my* logic, but possibly right according to his.[9] His logic, the logic of someone who understood pretty well the reality of the labor market condition on the ground in Spain at that time, is that a lot of unemployment existed because of government benefits that gave some people little incentive to work. The problem wasn't a lack of open positions, in my student's view; it was lack of incentive to seek them out. Higher wages would solve this particular kind of unemployment, he told me; lower wages would just make it worse. Economic incentives mattered in both of our analyses (Rodrik's "One Economics"), they just worked in different ways depending upon the characteristics of the social system ("Many Recipes").

Another vision of diverse globalization comes from an unlikely source. Columbia economics professor Frederic Mishkin is a leading authority on finance. Many (most?) of the people who built today's complex system of global finance got their start reading Mishkin's money, banking, and financial markets textbook. At first glance his 2006 book *The Next Great Globalization* looks like his Last Great Mistake, but it is not. Mishkin's argument is that financial globalization has many benefits, especially to less developed countries. Plugging into global capital markets—moving from thin globalization to thick globalization—is, to quote the book's subtitle, "How disadvantaged nations can harness their financial systems to get rich." Looking back from today's perspective, Mishkin's premise—that being part of the global financial system is the key to prosperity—seems wrong-headed. A closer look at his reasoning, however, reveals a different story.

Much of Mishkin's book is devoted to financial crises, their causes and effects. He makes it pretty clear, as I have in this book, that financial markets are not "safe as houses." He puts the benefits of financial markets—and there are many benefits—into the context of the costs and risks. Risk and return—exactly right. One reason less developed countries have failed in the past to profit from global finance, Mishkin argues, is that they have adopted what I might call "Golden Arches Globaloney" policies. They have implemented the same policies as the developed countries, when their financial markets and financial institutions are much different. One result is that when crises strike the remedies applied, based upon first world orthodoxy, cause third world havoc.

A simple example will help make this clear. Many loans in developed countries are long term with fixed or occasionally adjustable interest rates. An emergency interest rate increase (to attract foreign capital inflows) in this environment has a big effect on incremental loans but a smaller effect on existing loans. Borrowers have locked in their interest costs and are less affected or more slowly affected by changing conditions.

Lending in less developed countries is frequently a different matter. Loans are generally much more short term (loan terms may be months instead of years) and interest rates therefore more sensitive to changing conditions. Loan agents may visit clients each week, collecting payments and rolling over loans as needed. A sharp increase in interest rates in this environment has a much larger impact. New loans become more expensive, but so do existing loans (or existing short-term loans that must be renewed). Result: many more borrowers are hit harder and more quickly by financial changes in less developed countries. The same monetary medicine, to use a medical analogy, is quicker and stronger in LDCs. Sometimes it can even be fatal.

I find a lot to agree with in the details of Mishkin's book. I think his concern over financial crises is wise and his argument that financial policies in different countries need to be tailored to actual local conditions is sound. Solid financial institutions are very valuable and less developed countries would gain if stable banks, insurance companies, and credit agencies were developed to meet local needs while reflecting local conditions. The local institutions are very useful, as the rise of microfinance, micro-banking and micro-insurance surely proves. Connecting these institutions to uncertain global markets is less important overall, especially if instability is imported along with foreign funds.[10]

Mishkin is an optimist—or at least he was in 2006—taking the view that better global financial governance and wise local implementation can make thick globalization work. I'm a pessimist, at least when it comes to the possibility of global financial crises. I'm willing to sacrifice some of the potential benefits of thick globalization to get a more stable foundation for global economic relations. Give me thin globalization any day.

SEMI-GLOBALIZATION

Thin globalization instead of thick—is this a radical proposal? A crazy idea? No . . . and yes. In terms of economic history, thick globalization has always been the exception, not the rule. The grand rhetoric of globalization disguises in some respects how very limited it has been in both time and place. I argued that globalization was oversold in a previous book, *Selling Globalization*, and think it is still true today.

Pankaj Ghemawat, Professor of Global Strategy at the IESE Business School in Barcelona, examined globalization's actual viscosity in his 2007 book, *Redefining Global Strategy*. Ghemawat's basic argument is that most measurable economic activities that can be pursued either globally or locally still show a very strong local bias. Differences between and among countries matter very much, creating both opportunities and constraints. Ghemawat's book is an attempt to convince corporate strategists to "resist a variety of delusions derived from visions of globalization apocalypse: growth fever, the norm of enormity, statelessness, ubiquity and one-size-fits-all."[11] He calls the actual state of the world *semi-globalization*.

What prevents globalization from achieving its presumed universal destiny? In theory, world borders of all sorts melt away in the face of the logic of market integration. In the real world, however, layer upon layer of differences persist, creating a pattern of diversity that is a barrier to global strategies and a world of opportunity to those who appreciate the differences and take advantage of them. Ghemawat breaks down the cross-border differences into four categories: cultural differences, administrative differences, geographic differences, and economic differences.[12] Together they create a kaleidoscope of colors, shapes, and patterns that vary according to country and industry and over time. Leveraging some of these differences, overcoming others, and accepting the rest—these are the keys to success in a semi-global business world. Semi-globalization is a useful concept because it forces us to think about how globalization actually works and it suggests that thin globalization might not be such a foreign concept.

So my proposal for feasible, sustainable globalization via thinner global flows is not radical in one sense. Economic flows are only semi-global now and recognition of the risks inherent in uncontrolled international capital movements is unlikely to alter this fact substantially. In any case, the instability of capital movements would prevent globalization from becoming very much thicker. But I am a radical in a different way because I want to change the way that people think about globalization. Because ideas are what matter in the long run.

TELLING STORIES

Economists tell stories—that's what we do. And for better or for worse, the stories seem to matter. Unfortunately, many of the stories we have been telling about globalization for the past few years have been globaloney.

- Because the textbook models of markets are stable and secure—stable as an apple in a bowl, according to Alfred Marshall—we told stories that convinced ourselves that financial markets must be stable, too. Safe as houses.
- Because you find McDonald's restaurants and other symbols of American consumer culture lots of places we convinced ourselves that globalization is everywhere the same, undercutting the very idea of global diversity and missing the point that McDonald's doesn't create sameness as much as it promotes efficiency.
- Because our stories of globalization are dominated by images of faceless markets and powerful global corporations we convinced ourselves that grassroots movements are a waste of time, that people have no ability to define and shape globalization to suit their needs and desires.

These stories opened the door to the grand experiment in high-risk, finance-driven thick globalization that crashed in 2008. When globalization returns—and it will—it will need a new configuration: thin, secure, diverse globalization, which, I have argued, is both economically feasible and politically sustainable; new regulations and regulators (beyond the scope of this book) and, of course, new stories. Stories about real globalization, not the same old globaloney.

Where will the stories come from? I suggest they will come from people like you who look around and report what they actually see, not what globaloney has conditioned them to see. There will be stories about the risks of global arrangements, not just their benefits. Stories about the diversity of globalization, not just its semi-global sameness. And stories about empowerment—how people can sometimes seize the power to shape globalization to meet their needs or even use globalization's tools to undermine globalization's negative effects.

This book is a start. The stories I've told here—about fast food, Slow Food, soccer, secondhand clothes, and of course the Crash of 2008— don't *prove* anything about globalization. They are just a few data points in a complex web of human arrangements. But, like Adam Smith with his Newtonian rhetoric, I encourage you to "connect the dots" of your own experience in a different way so that we begin to think differently about what globalization is and what it should be. That would be a start—a good start—to a new kind of globalization, one that achieves a better balance of local and global, risk and return.

So when someone tells you about the benefits of globalization, especially global finance, ask about the risks and tell the story of the Crash of 2008. When someone tells you that globalization is a one-size-fits-all phenomenon, and that size is American XXL, ask them if everything is *really* the same and tell them about David Beckham, the American soccer exception, and the French exception generally. And when someone hints that "there is no alternative" and that globalization imposes its will on people at the grass roots, ask them if nations, groups, and individual are really so powerless and tell them about *salaula* and Slow Food.

I used to think that you could fight stories with facts, but I've wised up. Facts are still important, but they didn't prevent an unsustainable global bubble and the Crash of 2008. Stories are more persuasive than spreadsheets. Learn the facts, then tell the stories that make the facts convincing.

To close this book I want to return to Keynes's famous essay, "The Economic Possibilities of our Grandchildren," which opened chapter 1. Writing in 1930, as the world economy was imploding around him, Keynes talked about the future. In the short run, he said, we face the Economic Problem, the crisis we now call the Great Depression.[13] The Economic Problem will eventually disappear, Keynes wrote. Our grandchildren—by which I suppose he meant the grandchildren of people in advanced industrial countries—will be wealthy, far wealthier than we are today. Their real needs will be rather easily satisfied, not for all of them or all at once, but eventually. The Economic Problem will disappear, leaving them with a rather more serious concern, which he called the Permanent Problem. The Permanent Problem is how to live a worthwhile, satisfying life. How to create a just and cultured world. In my terms, how to create a feasible and sustainable globalization.

We are the grandchildren Keynes had such high hopes for and we seem to have made rather a mess of things. We are wealthy—much wealthier in fact, those of us in the developed world, than even Keynes imagined. But we can't seem to get past the Economic Problem so that we can begin to address more permanent solutions. I don't know how we will do it, or if we ever will, but rethinking globalization must be part of the process. Globalization that takes better account of financial risks, encourages global diversity and accommodates change from the grass roots up—that would be a move in the right direction.

And that's not globaloney.

Notes

INTRODUCTION

1. Now Russell Investments.

2. Michael Veseth, *Globaloney: Unraveling the Myths of Globalization* (Lanham, MD: Rowman & Littlefield, 2005), 4.

CHAPTER 1   GLOBALIZATION? OR *GLOBALONEY?*

1. John Maynard Keynes, "Economic Possibilities for our Grandchildren," in *Essays in Persuasion* (New York: W. W. Norton, 1963), 358.

2. Keynes, "Economic Possibilities," 359.

3. John Maynard Keynes, *The General Theory of Employment, Interest, and Money* (New York: Harcourt Brace Jovanovich, 1964), 383.

4. William Greider, *One World, Ready or Not: The Manic Logic of Global Capitalism* (New York: Simon & Schuster, 1997).

5. This quote and the next one are my own fabrications, of course, meant to capture a particular style of rhetoric. I don't mean to suggest that Greider or Wolf actually wrote these *particular* phrases or that they would go so completely over the top.

6. Kenichi Ohmae, *The Borderless World: Power and Strategy in the Interlinked Economy* (New York: Harper Business, 1990).

7. Adam Smith, *An Inquiry into the Nature and Causes of the Wealth of Nations* (New York: Modern Library, 1937), 3. Original publication year: 1776.

8. Smith, *Wealth of Nations*, 4.

9. Smith, *Wealth of Nations*, 4–5.

10. Smith, *Wealth of Nations*, 5.

11. Smith, *Wealth of Nations*, 5.

12. Smith, *Wealth of Nations*, 5.

13. Smith, *Wealth of Nations*, 11.

14. Smith, *Wealth of Nations*, 17.

15. Ian Simpson Ross, *The Life of Adam Smith* (New York: Oxford University Press, 1995), 88–94. Interestingly, Ross is a professor of English (not economics) at the University of British Columbia.

16. Wodrow's notes quoted in Ross, *Life of Adam Smith*, 91.

17. Vivienne Brown, *Adam Smith's Discourse* (London: Routledge, 1994), 10–18.

18. Wodrow's notes on Smith's lectures, quoted in Ross, *Life of Adam Smith*, 93.

19. Friedrich List, *The National System of Political Economy*, trans. Sampson S. Lloyd (London: Longmans, Green and Co., 1904). Original publication year: 1841.

20. List's Commercial Union was an idea whose time had not yet come.

21. List's biography is found in "A Brief Memoir of the Author" in *National System*, xxix–xxxvi.

22. List, *National System*, 102.

23. List, *National System*, 102.

24. List, *National System*, 103.

25. List, *National System*, 103.

26. "Mr Wallace's article in the American magazine is on a very high plane indeed," said the new Republican congressman from Connecticut. "In it he does a great deal of global thinking. But much of what Mr Wallace calls his global thinking is, no matter how you slice it, globaloney." *Congressional Record* 89:1, 761.

27. See chapter 1 of the first edition of *Globaloney* for a more detailed discussion of the Luce-Wallace debate and the origins of the term globaloney.

28. Greider, *One World, Ready or Not.*

29. Greider, *One World, Ready or Not*, 12.

30. Greider, *One World, Ready or Not*, 12.

31. If you want to follow up on this idea, I recommend that you begin by reading Oz Shy, *The Economics of Network Industries* (Cambridge: Cambridge University Press, 2001).

32. Thomas Frank, *One Market under God: Extreme Capitalism, Market Populism, and the End of Economic Democracy* (New York: Doubleday, 2000).

33. William Greider, *The Soul of Capitalism: Opening Paths to a Moral Economy* (New York: Simon & Schuster, 2003).

34. Greider, *Soul of Capitalism*, 7.

35. Greider, *Soul of Capitalism*, 7.

36. Motherhood is the unused symbol.

37. Greider, *Soul of Capitalism*, 300.

38. Paul Krugman, *The Great Unraveling: Losing Our Way in the New Century* (New York: Norton, 2003).

CHAPTER 2 FINANCIAL GLOBALONEY: SAFE AS HOUSES

1. Charles P. Kindleberger, *Manias, Panics, and Crashes: A History of Financial Crises* (New York: Basic Books, 1978).

2. See details in Kindleberger's appendix, 253–59.

3. Kindleberger, *Manias, Panics and Crashes*, 216.

4. Carmen M. Reinhart and Kenneth S. Rogoff, "This Time is Different: A Panoramic View of Eight Centuries of Financial Crises," National Bureau of Economic Research (Working Paper 13882, March 2008).

5. Reinhart and Rogoff, "This Time is Different," 3.

6. Reinhart and Rogoff, "This Time is Different," 5.

7. Harold James, *The End of Globalization: Lessons from the Great Depression* (Cambridge: Harvard University Press, 2001).

8. This section builds upon research I did for my 1998 book *Selling Globalization: The Myth of the Global Economy.*

9. I've used this image before to describe financial markets. See my *Selling Globalization*, 15.

10. John Kenneth Galbraith is another economist whose status outside the profession was much higher than within it due to his unorthodox views.

11. See chapter 2 of Kindleberger, *Manias, Panics, and Crashes*.

12. Walter Bagehot coined the term "blind capital" to refer to uninformed but enthusiastic amateur investors who are drawn into speculative bubbles.

13. For a more complete treatment of this topic see my *Selling Globalization*, especially chapter 5, "Turbulence and Chaos."

14. Reprinted in Edward Lorenz, *The Essence of Chaos* (Seattle: University of Washington Press, 1993), 181–184.

15. From Walter Bagehot's "Essay on Edward Gibbon," as quoted in the epigraph to Kindleberger, *Manias, Panics, and Crashes*.

16. Paul Krugman's *The Return of Depression Economics* is the standard reference regarding the unlearned lessons of past financial crises.

17. "A Place for Capital Controls," *Economist*, May 1, 2003.

18. I suppose Friedrich List would call it a cosmopological theory.

19. Thomas Friedman, *The World is Flat: A Brief History of the 21st Century* (New York: Farrar, Straus and Giroux, 2006).

CHAPTER 3 THE CRASH OF 2008 AND THE GLOBAL MARKET MYTH

1. The arguments presented here were developed during the 2008–2009 academic year in my classes and in a series of public seminars. Thanks to my students and faculty colleagues for creative suggestions and constructive criticism as the arguments were developed and tested.

2. For an excellent analysis of the housing bubble and financial crisis see chapter 2, "Housing and Financial Markets" in the President's Council of Economic Advisors' *Economic Report of the President 2009*. It is available as a free download at www.gpoaccess.gov/eop/.

3. For an excellent discussion of the transformation of financial arrangements see the *Economist*, "Briefing: A Short History of Modern Finance," October 18, 2008.

4. For a good discussion of the limits of financial engineering see the *Economist*, "Greed and Fear: A Special Report on the Future of Finance," January 24, 2009.

5. See George Soros, "My Three Steps to Financial Reform," *Financial Times*, June 17, 2009. This is an application of the well-known Principal-Agent problem.

6. *Fail Safe* is a 1964 Stanley Lumet film that effectively exploited Cold War fears of nuclear annihilation. The title refers to nuclear weapons systems with multiple safeguards to prevent an accidental detonation. The safeguards fail in the film and New York and Moscow are destroyed.

7. See Krugman, *The Return of Depression Economics* for a longer discussion of non-bank banks, especially chapter 8, "Banking in the Shadows."

8. "When Fortune Frowned: A Special Report on the World Economy" (*Economist*, October 18, 2008) includes a good account of the role of central banks in the crisis.

9. A full account of the Crash of 2008 and its aftermath is beyond the scope of this book, so a brief outline will have to do. Whole books are being written now about the crash, and its causes, effects, and lessons will likely be debated for years to come.

10. For a good discussion of deglobalization and economic nationalism see the *Economist*, "Briefing: Globalization under Strain," February 7, 2009.

CHAPTER 4   GOLDEN ARCHES GLOBALONEY

1. Karl Marx and Friedrich Engels, *The Communist Manifesto: A Modern Edition* (London: Verso, 1998), 39.

2. Marx and Engels, *Communist Manifesto*, 39.

3. Marx and Engels, *Communist Manifesto*, 40.

4. Taken from Vernon's obituary in the the *New York Times* (August 28, 1999), reprinted in Michael Veseth, *New York Times Twentieth Century in Review: The Rise of the Global Economy* (Chicago: Fitzroy Dearborn, 2002), 15–16.

5. Facts about the first McDonald's restaurants are taken from John F. Love, *McDonald's: Behind the Arches* (New York: Bantam, 1995), 9–29.

6. Love, *McDonald's*, 15.

7. Love, *McDonald's*, 19.

8. This is the Big Mac Index of purchasing power parity. See www.economist.com/markets/Bigmac/Index.cfm.

9. Thomas L. Friedman, *The Lexus and the Olive Tree: Understanding Globalization* (New York: Anchor Books, 2000), 486.

10. McDonald's online shareholder information at www.shareholder.com/mcd/Charts.cfm [accessed February 10, 2004]. The current investor website does not provide a breakdown of the McDonald's international store count.

11. Stefano Polacchi, "Ristoranti d'Italia Unitevi!" *Gambero Rosso* 135 (April 2003): 48–51. You need to do more than just sell pizza to make this list of Italian restaurants abroad.

12. If you want to know what Tomaso's book might say about globalization and Americanization, read Beppe Severgnini, *Ciao America! An Italian Discovers the U.S.*, translated by Giles Watson (New York: Broadway Books, 2002).

13. Lizzie Collingham has written a wonderful book that explains the ebb and flow of Indian food around the world in her *Curry: A Tale of Cooks and Conquerors* (New York: Oxford University Press, 2006).

14. I have discovered Tao Friedman. Like Thomas Friedman, she works for the *New York Times*. Her real name is Jennifer 8. Lee (yes, 8 is her middle name—a lucky number in China, the booknotes explain). Her book is called *The Fortune Cooking Chronicles: Adventures in the World of Chinese Food* (New York: Twelve Publishers, 2008).

15. David Y. H. Wu and Sidney C. H. Cheung, eds., *The Globalization of Chinese Food* (Honolulu: University of Hawaii Press, 2002).

16. The other Friedmans know better—they are more likely to assume that their native cuisines can only be prepared properly at home.

17. Saritha Rai, "Tastes of India in U.S. Wrappers," *New York Times*, April 29, 2003, W1, 7. The menu in Muslim regions of India includes chicken but not, obviously, pork.

18. Rai, "Tastes of India," W7.

19. Tyler Cowen, *Creative Destruction: How Globalization Is Changing the World's Cultures* (Princeton, NJ: Princeton University Press, 2002).

20. Available online at www.theatlantic.com/politics/foreign/barberf.htm.

21. Benjamin R. Barber, *Jihad vs. McWorld: Terrorism's Challenge to Democracy* (New York: Ballantine, 2002).

22. Regardless, anyone seeking specific insights into the Islamic response to globalization will find few insights here. That's not what Barber wants to talk about.

23. The index listing for McDonald's reads like this: McDonald's, 7, 23, 78, 99, 128, 132, 297, in France, 12; in Japan, 18; and local culture, 12, 155, 182; in Russia, 198, 249.

24. Barber, *Jihad vs. McWorld*, 23.

25. Barber, *Jihad vs. McWorld*, 129.

26. Barber, *Jihad vs. McWorld*, 12.

27. Barber, *Jihad vs. McWorld*, 155.

28. Barber, *Jihad vs. McWorld*, 78.

29. Barber, *Jihad vs. McWorld*, 7. Barber uses a quote from George Steiner to complete his thought here.

30. Barber, *Jihad vs. McWorld*, 99.

31. OK, so maybe Barber has a point.

32. I make an exception to this generalization, however, for the first McDonald's in Russia. Launched as a partnership between McDonald's of Canada and the Moscow government, it was a creature of the Cold War—more about politics, at least initially, than economics. The Moscow McDonald's *was* a Trojan horse.

33. Sidney W. Mintz, "Swallowing Modernity," in *Golden Arches East: McDonald's in East Asia*, edited by James L. Watson (Stanford, CA: Stanford University Press, 1997), 189.

34. "Management Brief: Johannesburgers and Fries," *Economist* (September 27, 1999), 75–76.

35. For example, Matt Haig, *Brand Failures* (London: Kogan Page, Ltd., 2003). There are many others of this genre.

36. James L. Watson, ed., *Golden Arches East: McDonald's in East Asia* (Stanford, CA: Stanford University Press, 1997).

37. James L. Watson, "Transnationalism, Localization, and Fast Foods in East Asia," in *Golden Arches East*, 6.

38. Watson, "Transnationalism," 7.

39. Watson, "Transnationalism," 7.

40. Watson, "Transnationalism," 9.

41. David M. Cuttler, Edward L. Glaeser, and Jesse M. Shapiro, "Why Have Americans Become More Obese?" *NBER Working Paper* w9446 (Cambridge, MA: National Bureau of Economic Research, January 2003).

42. The study also suggests that obesity is due less to increased amounts consumed at each meal (the "super size" effect) and more to an increased number of meals consumed, which may be related to convenient access. The study's findings may be especially applicable to fast foods, but they apply to foods generally.

43. George Ritzer, *The McDonaldization of Society* (Thousand Oaks, CA: Pine Forge Press, 1993, 2000).

44. Ritzer, *The McDonaldization of Society*, 23.

45. Just as *Jihad vs. McWorld* is not, Barber says, about Islam.

46. Ritzer, *The McDonaldization of Society*, 15–16.

47. This upside of dehumanization was the subject of a cartoon, which featured two dogs seated at a computer. "On the Internet," one dog tells the other, "no one knows you're a dog."

48. Joseph A. Schumpeter, *Capitalism, Socialism, and Democracy*, 2nd ed. (New York: Harper and Brothers, 1942, 1947).

CHAPTER 5   THE ONLY GAME IN TOWN

1. I will use the terms *soccer* and *football* interchangeably, with a preference for *soccer* to avoid confusion, since I do also talk about American football in this chapter. Both terms refer to the game known as "association football" ("soccer" it is said, has its roots in the term "association").

2. The film's website is www2.foxsearchlight.com/benditlikebeckham/ [accessed June 8, 2004].

3. *Metrosexual* was one of the buzzwords of 2003. To be metrosexual means to be a heterosexual male who is interested in fashion, design, jewelry, cosmetics, and so forth. David Beckham's name is often used in the explanation of *metrosexual*.

4. "Top 100 Movers & Shakers," *World Soccer* (May 2008), 30–39.

5. "The Football Rich List 2009," *FourFourTwo* (February 2009), 48–73.

6. Sid Lowe, "The Circus Starts Here," *World Soccer* (August 2003), 5.

7. American readers of this book, who have an obvious interest in globalization, are probably disproportionately likely to be able to identify David Beckman.

8. There is much to say about how the business of soccer evolved in the second half of the twentieth century, but I don't have room to do the story justice. So I am leaving out many dots here and not connecting all of the rest. For a complete analysis see Stephen Dobson and John Goddard, *The Economics of Football* (Cambridge: Cambridge University Press, 2001).

9. See Immanuel Wallerstein, *The Capitalist World Economy* (Cambridge: Cambridge University Press, 1979).

10. The Confederations Cup is a competition among teams that were champions of their regional groups. It was played in South Africa as a prelude to and warm-up for that nation's World Cup in 2010.

11. Alex Bellos, *Futbol: Soccer the Brazilian Way* (New York: Bloomsburg, 2002), 10.

12. Eric Weil, "Carry On Selling," *World Soccer* (September 2003), 26.

13. For a deeper study I recommend Richard Giulianotti, *Football: A Sociology of the Global Game* (Cambridge: Polity Press, 2000).

14. Quoted in Rachman, "Passion, Pride and Profit," *Economist* (June 1, 2002), 6. Significantly, Valdano does not characterize the Argentine style.

15. Giulianotti makes this point.

16. This account is based on Bill Murray, *Football: A History of the World Game* (Aldershot, UK: Scolar Press, 1994), 134–37.

17. Murray, *Football*, 136.

18. See Giulianotti, *Football* for a very readable introduction to this literature.

19. Tim Parks, *A Season with Verona* (New York: Arcade, 2002).

20. One of the racist issues involves "monkey grunts" that the fans use to insult opposing players, particularly black players. This practice certainly seems racist to me, but my impression from reading Parks's book is that his fellow *ultras* simply tried to pick the most insulting possible response to each opposing player—and "monkey grunts" seemed to work against black players. When they were accused of racism, one reaction was to chant "monkey

grunts" against opposing white players, too. They saw themselves as harsh and aggressive fans, extremists, but not racists.

21. Derek Hammond, "Class War!" *FourFourTwo* (January 2004), 83–86.

22. Which, I think, makes this a globalization effect.

23. Giulianotti, *Football*, 18.

24. Giulianotti, *Football*, 19.

25. See the film's website at www.finelinefeatures.com/sites/cup/ [accessed June 8, 2004].

26. David White, "Choice between Demands of Club and Country Puts Africa's Soccer Stars in a Dilemma," *Financial Times*, January 24/25, 2004, 3.

27. Eric Weil, "Buenos Aires: Busyness as Usual," *World Soccer* (June 2003), 22.

28. Franklin Foer has recently argued that the American exception goes beyond indifference to resentment of soccer. Foer, a political journalist, claims that the American reaction to soccer mirrors the social divisions created by globalization. I don't agree with this conclusion, but I still find Foer's book very interesting in other respects. See Franklin Foer, *How Soccer Explains the World: An (Unlikely) Theory of Globalization* (New York: HarperCollins, 2004).

29. Markovits and Hellerman, *Offside: Soccer & American Exceptionalism* (Princeton, NJ: Princeton University Press, 2001). Answers three, four, and five in this section are based upon the analysis presented in this book.

30. Joe McGinnis, *The Miracle of Castel di Sangro: A Tale of Passion and Folly in the Heart of Italy* (New York: Little, Brown, 1999).

CHAPTER 6   GRASSROOTS GLOBALONEY

1. Karen Tranberg Hansen, "Transnational Biographies and Local Meanings: Used Clothing Practices in Lusaka," *Journal of Southern African Studies* 21:1 (March 1995): 131–46.

2. Now that agriculture and textiles are back on the negotiating table, you can expect trade agreements to be harder to reach.

3. Pietra Rivoli, *The Travels of a T-Shirt in the Global Economy: An Economist Examines the Markets, Power and Politics of World Trade* (New York: Wiley, 2005).

4. I believe this figure includes shipping, which may be as much as a third of the cost.

5. tse.export.gov/MapFrameset.aspx?MapPage=NTDMapDisplay .aspx&Unique-URL=4iibom2gi4e50ijbqd0kux45-2009-6-29-13-9-55 [accessed June 29, 2009].

6. Karen Tranberg Hansen, *Salaula: The World of Secondhand Clothing and Zambia* (Chicago: University of Chicago Press, 2000), 248. Hansen's excellent

book is the source of much of what I know about the used clothing trade and the inspiration for this chapter.

7. Michael Durham, "Clothes Line," *The Guardian*, February 25, 2004, www.guardian.co.uk/g2/story/0,3604,1155254,00.html [accessed April 21, 2004].

8. You can learn about this family-owned company at www.savers.com/.

9. George Packer, "How Susie Bayer's T-shirt Ended Up on Yusuf Mama's Back," *New York Times Magazine* (March 31, 2002), 54.

10. Hansen, *Salaula*, 229.

11. This same principle—small margins, huge volume—is what makes hedge funds profitable.

12. Scott Bailey's comments on an earlier draft "provoked" these remarks.

13. Thanks to Phil McMullin of Savers, who suggested this point.

14. Here is the website for the program: www.pbs.org/independentlens/tshirttravels/.

15. Hansen, *Salaula*, 229.

16. Hansen, *Salaula*, 233.

17. Hansen, *Salaula*, 233.

CHAPTER 7   SLOW-BALIZATION: USING GLOBALIZATION TO FIGHT GLOBALIZATION

1. Carlo Petrini, *Slow Food: The Case for Taste*, trans. William McCuaig (New York: Columbia University Press, 2001), ix.

2. Petrini, *Slow Food*, 26.

3. Petrini, *Slow Food*, 26.

4. Petrini, *Slow Food*, 32.

5. The details for this section are drawn from chapter 1 of Petrini, *Slow Food*.

6. ARCI today has over a million members in six hundred clubs in Italy. It remains a social club with political leanings and interests. It fights, as its webpage says, to eliminate social and political exclusions and to promote solidarity. It supports, among other things, activities for children and social and cultural tourism. See www.arci.it/present-ing.htm.

7. There is no such thing as Italian cuisine, according to Mario Batali, only the regional cuisines of Italy.

8. Petrini, *Slow Food*, 5.

9. Petrini, *Slow Food*, 10.

10. The current version of the manifesto can be found on the SlowFood.com website: www.slowfood.com/eng/sf--cose/sf--cose--statuto.lasso [accessed April 20, 2004].

11. I find it interesting that "typical" in the United States generally means "unexceptional," whereas within the Slow Food movement it means "authentic."

12. Slow Food Planet currently exists as a frequently expanded web offering. See www.slowfood.com/eng/sf--sloweb/sf--arch--planet.lasso [accessed April 20, 2004].

13. www.slowfood.com/eng/sf--sloweb/sf--arch--planet.lasso?-database-sfesloweb&-layout-tutti&-response-sf--sloweb--dettaglio.lasso&-recordID-35125&-search.

14. See the complete description at www.slowfoodfoundation.com/eng/presidi/lista.lasso [accessed April 20, 2004].

15. www.slowfoodfoundation.com/inc--sito/eng/bocconi--short.pdf [accessed April 20, 2004].

16. Paolo Di Croce, "Slow Food and Lula," *Slow: The International Herald of Taste* (July 2003): 4–5.

17. Di Croce, "Slow Food and Lula," 5.

18. The Republic of Tuva was an independent republic until it was absorbed by the Soviet Union in 1944. It is now a member state of the Russian Confederation.

19. Information about the 2003 winners is found at www.slowfood.com/eng/sf--premio/sf--premio--vincitori.lasso.

20. www.slowfood.com/img--sito/PREMIO/vincitori2003/pagine--en/Brasile--03.html [accessed April 21, 2003].

21. Petrini, *Slow Food*, p. 63.

22. Slow Food Editore, *Italian Wines 2004* (New York: Gambero Rosso, 2004).

23. Slow Food Editore, *Osterie d'Italia 2002* (Bra, Italy: Slow Food Editore, 2001). Not available in English at this time.

24. www.slowfoodfoundation.com/eng/presidi/lista.lasso?lista-si&id--nazione-1 07&id--tipologia-&id--regione-5 [accessed April 21, 2004].

25. Patrick Martins, "Set That Apricot Free," *New York Times*, April 24, 2004, A-17.

26. The source of this insight is Alexander Stille, "Slow Food: An Italian Answer to Globalization," *Nation* 273 (August 20, 2001): 6. www.thenation.com/doc.mhtml%3Fi-20010820&s-stille [accessed June 28, 2004].

CHAPTER 8 GLOBALIZATION AND THE FRENCH EXCEPTION

1. Balladur was prime minister of France from 1993 to 1995.

2. "Thatcherites in Brussels (Really)," *Economist* (March 15, 1997), 23.

3. Pierre Bourdieu, *Firing Back: Against the Tyranny of the Market 2*, trans. Loïc Wacquant (New York: The New Press, 2001); Viviane Forrester, *The Economic Horror* (Oxford: Blackwell, 1999).

4. He has written a book about this: José Bové and François Dufour (interviewed by Gilles Luneau), *The World Is Not for Sale: Farmers against Junk Food*, trans. Anna de Casparis (New York: Verso, 2001).

5. The lyrics have many references that suggest contemporary globalization besides those that are cited here. There is even one reference to a borderless world that eerily recalls the Henry A. Wallace versus Clare Boothe Luce debate that was detailed in the first edition of this book. You should listen to the original cast recording.

6. Frantz Fanon, *A Dying Colonialism*, trans. Haakon Chevalier (New York: Grove Press, 1965), 35.

7. Edward M. Corbett, *The French Presence in Black Africa* (Washington, D.C.: Black Orpheus Press, 1972), 1.

8. O. Mannoni, *Prospero and Caliban: The Psychology of Colonization*, trans. Pamela Powesland (New York: Praeger, 1950).

9. Many former French African colonies used the French franc as domestic currency until the euro was introduced a few years ago, for example.

10. Hubert Védrine with Dominique Moïse, *France in an Age of Globalization*, trans. Philip H. Gordon (Washington, D.C.: Brookings Institution Press, 2001), 44.

11. Védrine, *France in an Age of Globalization*, 43–44.

12. All quotes in this paragraph as from Sheryle Bagwell, "A New World Sauvignon Blanc Built on French Soil," *Financial Times*, April 16, 2004, 10.

13. Védrine, *France in an Age of Globalization*, 3.

14. Bourdieu, *Firing Back*, 85–86.

15. Quoted in Jean-François Revel, *Anti-Americanism*, trans. Diarmid Cammell (San Francisco: Encounter Books, 2003), 44.

16. Revel, *Anti-Americanism*, 44.

17. G. Pascal Zachary has written about how people use globalization to construct distinct personal identities. See his *The Diversity Advantage: Multicultural Identity in the New World Economy* (Boulder, CO: Westview, 2003). Tyler Cowen discusses the result in his *Creative Destruction: How Globalization Is Changing the World's Cultures* (Princeton, NJ: Princeton University Press, 2002). Cowen argues that the world seems more homogeneous to global travelers because each individual place is in fact more diverse and multicultural. In the final chapter, Cowen asks, "Should National Culture Matter?" You can see how that would infuriate a French imperialist, especially coming from an American.

18. I present this as the "conventional wisdom" even though I find the argument that America has always had a strong imperialist streak to be very

persuasive. See, for example, Niall Ferguson, *Colossus: The Price of America's Empire* (New York: Penguin, 2004).

19. Revel, *Anti-Americanism*, 37.

20. Elaine Sciolino, "France Has a State Religion: Secularism," *New York Times*, February 8, 2004, WK4.

21. Fanon, *A Dying Colonialism*. See chapter 1, "Algeria Unveiled."

22. Meredith Anne Skura, "The Case of Colonialism in *The Tempest*," in *Caliban*, ed. Harold Bloom (New York: Chelsea House, 1992), 225.

23. Skura, "The Case of Colonialism," 225.

24. Skura, "The Case of Colonialism," 226.

25. Philip H. Gordon and Sophie Meunier, *The French Challenge: Adapting to Globalization* (Washington, D.C.: Brookings Institution Press, 2001).

26. Gordon and Meunier, *The French Challenge*, 8.

27. Gordon and Meunier, *The French Challenge*, 9.

28. Gordon and Meunier, *The French Challenge*, 9.

29. The link between cheese and public opinion comes from Charles De-Gaulle, who is said to have complained, "How can anyone govern a country with 246 cheeses?"

30. Todd Richissin, "The French Love Fine Food but also Have a Taste for Les Big Macs," *Seattle Times*, March 31, 2004, 1.

31. Richissin, *Seattle Times*, 1.

32. Revel, *Anti-Americanism*, 143.

33. Védrine, *France in an Age of Globalization*, 28.

34. Gordon and Meunier, *The French Challenge*, 18.

35. Gordon and Meunier, *The French Challenge*, 14.

36. Gordon and Meunier, *The French Challenge*, 21.

37. Carrefour translates as "crossroads" in English.

38. Wal-Mart corporate fact sheet walmartstores.com/FactsNews/Fact Sheets/ [accessed June 30, 2009].

39. See "Wal-Mart Aims to Set Up Shop across Europe" by Susanna Voyle and Daniel Dombey, *Financial Times*, May 25, 2004, 1. Wal-Mart's current position in Europe is due largely to its acquisition in 1999 of the British retailer Asada. According to this article Wal-Mart is considering several options for European expansion, including opening its own stores, opening Asada stores, and acquiring local retail chains.

40. Ann Zimmerman, "Ultimatum at France's Wal-Mart," *Wall Street Journal*, July 9, 2004, C1.

41. www.pret.com/philosophy/ [accessed May 24, 2004].

42. I'm not saying that these are the right factors to consider, only that they are popular indicators in the globalization literature.

43. J. K. Rowling, *Harry Potter and the Sorcerer's Stone* (New York: Scholastic, 1997).

CHAPTER 9   THE FUTURE OF
GLOBALIZATION (AND GLOBALONEY)

1. John Maynard Keynes, *The General Theory of Employment, Interest, and Money* (New York: Harcourt Brace Jovanovich, 1964), 383.

2. For a good discussion of the Mundell Trilemma in a contemporary context, see Frieden, *Global Capitalism: Its Rise and Fall in the Twentieth Century* (New York: W. W. Norton, 2006), 459–64. Benjamin J. Cohen coined the term "Unholy Trinity" to describe Mundell's Trilemma.

3. Hence the term Mundell Impossibility Theorem that is sometimes applied to this result.

4. The easiest way to think of a trilemma is to draw a triangle with one option at each corner. The sides of the triangle represent the three available options. Once you've connected two points the third option vanishes.

5. Some of my students tell me that McDonald's is the solution to the lunchtime trilemma—good, fast, *and* cheap. This suggests that tastes and preferences are a factor in trilemma problems.

6. See Rodrik, "Feasible Globalizations" (Cambridge, MA: Harvard University, 2002). Obviously Rodrik and I use the terms feasible versus sustainable differently, but I think we are talking about the same things.

7. Rodrik, "Feasible Globalizations," 16.

8. This is a "classic" supply-demand problem that is found in probably every introductory economics textbook.

9. The problem of Spanish unemployment in the 1990s (or unemployment anywhere at any time) was more complicated than just higher or lower wages, of course.

10. This argument is made by Justin Lin, chief economist at the World Bank in his "Walk Don't Run," in "Economic Focus," *Economist* (July 11, 2009), 76.

11. Ghemawat, *Redefining Global Strategy: Crossing Borders in a World Where Differences Still Matter* (Cambridge, MA: Harvard Business School Press, 2007), 31.

12. Ghemawat, *Redefining Global Strategy*, 110.

13. It is ironic that the term "depression" was originally used in an attempt to play down the severity of the economic crisis of the 1930s. It's not a recession—a pulling back—just a depression, a bump in the road. Even then stories and rhetoric were used to try to shape public perception. Now depression suggests something entirely different.

BIBLIOGRAPHY

Alfino, Mark, John S. Caupto, and Robin Wynyard, eds. *McDonaldization Revisited: Critical Essays on Consumer Culture*. Westport, CT: Praeger, 1998.

"A Place for Capital Controls." *Economist* (May 1, 2003).

Bagwell, Sheryle. "A New World Sauvignon Blanc Built on French Soil." *Financial Times*, April 16, 2004, 10.

Barber, Benjamin R. *Jihad vs. McWorld: Terrorism's Challenge to Democracy*. New York: Ballantine, 2001.

Bellos, Alex. *Futbol: Soccer, the Brazilian Way*. New York: Bloomsbury, 2002.

Bhagwati, Jagdish. *In Defense of Globalization*. New York: Oxford University Press, 2004.

Bourdieu, Pierre. *Firing Back: Against the Tyranny of the Market 2*. Trans. Loïc Wacquant. New York: The New Press, 2001.

Bové, José, and François Dufour (interviewed by Gilles Luneau). *The World Is Not for Sale: Farmers against Junk Food*. Trans. Anna de Casparis. New York: Verso, 2001.

"Briefing: A Short History of Modern Finance." *Economist*, October 18, 2008, 79–81.

"Briefing: Globalization under Strain." *Economist*, February 7, 2009, 69–71.

Brown, Vivienne. *Adam Smith's Discourse*. London: Routledge, 1994.

Carr, Edward. "Greed—and Fear: A Special Report on the Future of Finance." *Economist*, January 24, 2009, 1–22.

Collingham, Lizzie. *Curry: A Tale of Cooks and Conquerors*. New York: Oxford University Press, 2006.

Corbett, Edward M. *The French Presence in Black Africa*. Washington, D.C.: Black Orpheus Press, 1972.

Cowen, Tyler. *Creative Destruction: How Globalization Is Changing the World's Cultures*. Princeton, NJ: Princeton University Press, 2002.

Cuttler, David M., Edward L. Glaeser, and Jesse M. Shapiro. "Why Have Americans Become More Obese?" *NBER Working Paper* w9446. Cambridge, MA: National Bureau of Economic Research, January 2003.

Deloitte & Touche. *Deloitte & Touche Annual Review of Football Finance*. www .footballfinance.co.uk/publications/arff2003release.pdf [accessed June 8, 2004].

Di Croce, Paolo. "Slow Food and Lula." *Slow: The International Herald of Taste* (July 2003): 4–5.

Dobson, Stephen, and John Goddard. *The Economics of Football*. Cambridge: Cambridge University Press, 2001.

Durham, Michael. "Clothes Line." *The Guardian*, February 25, 2004. www.guard ian.co.uk/g2/story/0,3604,1155254,00.html [accessed April 21, 2004].

Eichengreen, Barry. *Globalizing Capital: A History of the International System*. 2nd ed. Princeton, NJ: Princeton University Press, 2009.

Fanon, Frantz. *A Dying Colonialism*. Trans. Haakon Chevalier. New York: Grove Press, 1965.

Ferguson, Niall. *Colossus: The Price of America's Empire*. New York: Penguin, 2004.

Foer, Franklin. *How Soccer Explains the World: An (Unlikely) Theory of Globalization*. New York: HarperCollins, 2004.

Forrester, Viviane. *The Economic Horror*. Oxford: Blackwell, 1999.

Frank, Robert H., and Philip J. Cook. *The Winner-Take-All Society*. New York: Free Press, 1995.

Frank, Thomas. *One Market under God: Extreme Capitalism, Market Populism, and the End of Economic Democracy*. New York: Doubleday, 2000.

Frieden, Jeffrey A. *Global Capitalism: Its Fall and Rise in the Twentieth Century*. New York: W.W. Norton, 2006.

Friedman, Thomas L. *The Lexus and the Olive Tree: Understanding Globalization*. New York: Anchor Books, 2000.

———. *The World is Flat: A Brief History of the 21st Century*. New York: Farrar, Straus and Giroux, 2006.

Galeano, Eduardo. *Football in Sun and Shadow*. Trans. Mark Fried. London: Fourth Estate, 1997.

Ghemawat, Pankaj. *Redefining Global Strategy: Crossing Borders in a World Where Differences Still Matter*. Cambridge: Harvard Business School Press, 2007.

Giulianotti, Richard. *Football: A Sociology of the Global Game*. Cambridge: Polity Press, 2000.

Gordon, Phillip H., and Sophie Meunier. *The French Challenge: Adapting to Globalization*. Washington, D.C.: Brookings Institution Press, 2001.

Greider, William. *One World, Ready or Not: The Manic Logic of Global Capitalism*. New York: Simon & Schuster, 1997.

———. *The Soul of Capitalism: Opening Paths to a Moral Economy*. New York: Simon & Schuster, 2003.

Haig, Matt. *Brand Failures*. London: Kogan Page, Ltd., 2003.

Hammond, Derek. "Class War!" *FourFourTwo* (January 2004): 83–86.

Hansen, Karen Tranberg. "Transnational Biographies and Local Meanings: Used Clothing Practices in Lusaka." *Journal of Southern African Studies* 21:1 (March 1995): 131–46.

———. *Salaula: The World of Secondhand Clothing and Zambia*. Chicago: University of Chicago Press, 2000.

James, Harold. *The End of Globalization: Lessons from the Great Depression*. Cambridge, MA: Harvard University Press, 2001.

Kay, John. *Culture and Prosperity: The Truth About Markets—Why Some Nations are Rich but Most Remain Poor*. New York: HarperBusiness, 2004.

Keynes, John Maynard. "Economic Possibilities for our Grandchildren." In *Essays in Persuasion*. New York: W.W. Norton, 1963, 358–73.

———. *The General Theory of Employment, Interest, and Money*. New York: Harcourt Brace Jovanovich, 1964.

Kindleberger, Charles P. *Manias, Panics, and Crashes: A History of Financial Crises*. New York: Basic Books, 1978.

Krugman, Paul. *The Great Unraveling: Losing Our Way in the New Century*. New York: Norton, 2003.

———. *The Return of Depression Economics and the Crisis of 2008*. New York: W.W. Norton, 2009.

Lee, Jennifer 8. *The Fortune Cooking Chronicles: Adventures in the World of Chinese Food*. New York: Twelve Publishers, 2008.

Lenin, V. I. *Imperialism: The Highest Stage of Capitalism*. New York: International Publishers, 1939.

Lin, Justin. "Economic Focus: Walk, Don't Run." *Economist* (July 11, 2009): 76.

List, Friedrich. *The National System of Political Economy*. Trans. Sampson S. Lloyd. London: Longmans, Green and Co., 1904.

Lorenz, Edward. *The Essence of Chaos*. Seattle: University of Washington Press, 1993.

Love, John F. *McDonald's: Behind the Arches.* New York: Bantam, 1995.

Lowe, Sid. "The Circus Starts Here." *World Soccer* (August 2003): 5–6.

McGinnis, Joe. *The Miracle of Castel di Sangro: A Tale of Passion and Folly in the Heart of Italy.* New York: Little, Brown, 1999.

"Management Brief: Johannesburgers and Fries." *Economist* (September 27, 1999): 75–76.

Mannoni, O. *Prospero and Caliban: The Psychology of Colonization.* Trans. Pamela Powesland. New York: Praeger, 1950.

Markovits, Andrei S., and Steven L. Hellerman. *Offside: Soccer & American Exceptionalism.* Princeton, NJ: Princeton University Press, 2001.

Martins, Patrick. "Set That Apricot Free." *New York Times,* April 24, 2004, A17.

Marx, Karl, and Friedrich Engels. *The Communist Manifesto: A Modern Edition.* London: Verso, 1998.

Miller, Karen Lowry. "Globaloney: The New Buzzword." *Newsweek Issues 2003* (Winter 2002/2003): 52–58.

Minton, Zanny. "When Fortune Frowned: A Special Report on the World Economy." *Economist,* October 11, 2008, 1–34.

Mintz, Sidney W. "Swallowing Modernity." In *Golden Arches East: McDonald's in East Asia,* ed. James L. Watson. Stanford, CA: Stanford University Press, 1997.

Mishkin, Frederic S. *The Next Great Globalization: How Disadvantaged Nations Can Harness their Financial Systems to Get Rich.* Princeton: Princeton University Press, 2006.

Murray, Bill. *Football: A History of the World Game.* Aldershot, UK: Scolar Press, 1994.

Packer, George. "How Susie Bayer's T-shirt Ended Up on Yusuf Mama's Back." *New York Times Magazine,* March 31, 2002, 54.

Parks, Tim. *A Season with Verona.* New York: Arcade, 2002.

Petrini, Carlo. *Slow Food: The Case for Taste.* Trans. William McCuaig. New York: Columbia University Press, 2001.

Polacchi, Stefano. "Ristoranti d'Italia Unitevi!" *Gambero Rosso* 135 (April 2003): 48–51.

President's Council of Economic Advisors, *Economic Report of the President 2009.* Washington DC: Government Printing Office, 2009.

Rachman, Gideon. "The Globe in a Glass." *Economist* survey, December 16, 1999.

———. "Passion, Pride and Profit." *Economist* special section, June 1, 2002.

Rai, Saritha. "Tastes of India in U.S. Wrappers." *New York Times,* April 29, 2003, W1, 7.

Reinhart, Carmen M. and Kenneth S. Rogoff, "This Time Is Different: A Panoramic View of Eight Centuries of Financial Crises." National Bureau of Economic Research. Working Paper 13882, March 2008.

Revel, Jean-François. *Anti-Americanism.* Trans. Diarmid Cammell. San Francisco: Encounter Books, 2003.

Richissin, Todd. "The French Love Fine Food but also Have a Taste for Les Big Macs." *Seattle Times*, March 31, 2004, 1.

Ritzer, George. *The McDonaldization of Society*. Thousand Oaks, CA: Pine Forge Press, 1993, 2000.

———. *The McDonaldization Thesis: Explorations and Extensions*. Thousand Oaks, CA: Sage, 1998.

Rivoli, Pietra. *The Travels of a T-Shirt in the Global Economy: An Economist Examines the Markets, Power and Politics of World Trade*. New York: Wiley, 2005.

Rodrik, Dani. "Feasible Globalizations." Cambridge: Harvard University, 2002. ksghome.harvard.edu/~drodrik/Feasglob.pdf [accessed July 2, 2009].

———. *One Economics, Many Recipes: Globalization, Institutions and Economic Growth*. Princeton: Princeton University Press, 2007.

Ross, Ian Simpson. *The Life of Adam Smith*. New York: Oxford University Press, 1995.

Rowling, J. K. *Harry Potter and the Sorcerer's Stone*. New York: Scholastic, 1997.

Schumpeter, Joseph A. *Capitalism, Socialism, and Democracy*. 2nd ed. New York: Harper and Brothers, 1942, 1947.

Sciolino, Elaine. "France Has a State Religion: Secularism." *New York Times*, February 8, 2004, WK4.

Severgnini, Beppe. *Ciao America! An Italian Discovers the U.S.* Trans. Giles Watson. New York: Broadway Books, 2002.

Shy, Oz. *The Economics of Network Industries*. Cambridge: Cambridge University Press, 2001.

Skura, Meredith Anne. "The Case of Colonialism in *The Tempest*." In *Caliban*, ed. Harold Bloom. New York: Chelsea House, 1992.

Slow Food Editore. *Italian Wines 2004*. New York: Gambero Rosso, 2004.

———. *Osterie d'Italia 2002*. Bra, Italy: Slow Food Editore, 2001.

Smith, Adam. *An Inquiry into the Nature and Causes of The Wealth of Nations*. New York: Modern Library, 1937.

Soros, George. "My Three Steps to Financial Reform." *Financial Times*, June 17, 2009, 9.

Stille, Alexander. "Slow Food: An Italian Answer to Globalization." *Nation* 273 (August 20, 2001): 6. www.thenation.com/doc.mhtml%3Fi-20010820&s-stille [accessed June 28, 2004].

"The Football Rich List 2009." *FourFourTwo* (February 2009), 48–73.

"Top 100 Movers & Shakers." *World Soccer* (May 2008), 30–39.

Védrine, Hubert, with Dominique Moïse. *France in an Age of Globalization*. Trans. Philip H. Gordon. Washington, D.C.: Brookings Institution Press, 2001.

Veseth, Michael. *Globaloney: Unraveling the Myths of Globalization*. Lanham, MD: Rowman & Littlefield, 2005.

———. *Selling Globalization: The Myth of the Global Economy*. Boulder, CO: Rienner, 1998.

———. *Mountains of Debt: Crisis and Change in Renaissance Florence, Victorian Britain and Postwar America.* New York: Oxford University Press, 1990.

———, ed. *The New York Times Twentieth Century in Review: The Rise of the Global Economy.* Chicago: Fitzroy Dearborn, 2002.

Voyle, Susanna, and Daniel Dombey. "Wal-Mart Aims to Set Up Shop across Europe." *Financial Times*, May 25, 2004, 1.

Wallerstein, Immanuel. *The Capitalist World Economy.* Cambridge: Cambridge University Press, 1979.

Watson, James L. "Transnationalism, Localization, and Fast Foods in East Asia." In *Golden Arches East: McDonald's in East Asia*, ed. James L. Watson. Stanford, CA: Stanford University Press, 1997.

———, ed. *Golden Arches East: McDonald's in East Asia.* Stanford, CA: Stanford University Press, 1997.

Weil, Eric. "Buenos Aires: Busyness as Usual." *World Soccer* (June 2003), 22.

———. "Carry On Selling." *World Soccer* (September 2003), 26.

White, David. "Choice between Demands of Club and Country Puts Africa's Soccer Stars in a Dilemma." *Financial Times*, January 24/25, 2004, 3.

Wolf, Martin. *Why Globalization Works.* New Haven: Yale University Press, 2004.

Wu, David Y. H., and Sidney C. H. Cheung, ed. *The Globalization of Chinese Food.* Honolulu: University of Hawaii Press, 2002.

Zachary, G. Pascal. *The Diversity Advantage: Multicultural Identity in the New World Economy.* Boulder, CO: Westview, 2003.

Zimmerman, Ann. "Ultimatum at France's Wal-Mart." *Wall Street Journal*, July 9, 2004, C1.

ABOUT THE AUTHOR

Michael Veseth is the Robert G. Albertson Professor of International Political Economy at the University of Puget Sound. Veseth's publications include *Mountains of Debt: Crisis and Change in Renaissance Florence, Victorian Britain and Postwar America* (1990), *Selling Globalization: The Myth of the Global Economy* (1998), the *New York Times Review of the 20th Century: The Rise of the Global Economy* (2002), and the first edition of *Globaloney* (2005). Veseth has taught at the Bologna Center of the Johns Hopkins University School for Advanced International Studies and at the American Institute on Political and Economic Systems in Prague. He served as academic advisor to the interactive education website for the PBS/WGBH series *Commanding Heights: The Battle for the World Economy*. Veseth is an authority on global wine markets and writes frequently for *The Wine Economist* (WineEconomist.com). He is currently writing a book titled *Great Expectations: Globalization, Two Buck Chuck and the Future of Wine*. Veseth has received a number of teaching awards and academic honors. The first edition of *Globaloney* was named a Best Business Book of 2005 by *Library Journal*. He lives in Tacoma, Washington, with his wife Sue Trbovich Veseth.